# Mantan the Funnyman:

# The Life & Times of Mantan Moreland

# Mantan the Funnyman:

# The Life & Times of Mantan Moreland

### Michael H. Price

Midnight Marquee Press, Inc.
Baltimore, Maryland

## Also by Michael H. Price

Daynce of the Peckerwoods:
The Badlands of Texas Music
The Ancient Southwest
& Other Dispatches from a Cruel Frontier
(with Geo. E. Turner)
The Cruel Plains
(with Geo. E. Turner)
What You See May Shock You
(with Mark Evan Walker)
The Big Book of Biker Flicks
(with John Wooley)
The Forgotten Horrors Series
(with Geo. E. Turner & John Wooley)
Spawn of Skull Island:
The Making of King Kong
(with Geo. E. Turner)
The Southern-Fried Homicide Series
Human Monsters: The Definitive Edition
(with George E. Turner)
V.T. Hamlin's Collected Alley Oop,
Vols. No. 2 & 3
(with Frank Stack & Geo. E. Turner)
The Cinema of Adventure,
Romance & Terror
(with George E. Turner et al.)
MHP's Hollywood Horrors

The Spider
(with Timothy Truman et al.)
Roy Crane's Collected Wash Tubbs &
Captain Easy, Vol. No. 10
Al Capp's Collected Li'l Abner,
Vol. No. 6
Midnight Marquee Actors Series
(Contributing Author)
It's Christmas Time at the Movies
(Contributing Author)
Lex Eicon and the Numerologist
(With Jerome McDonough)
The A-to-Z Encyclopedia
of Serial Killers
(Contributing Illustrator)
Krime Duzzin't Pay!
The Guitar in Jazz
(Contributing Author)
R. Crumb: The Musical
(With Robert Crumb
& Johnny Simons)
The 50 Greatest Cartoons
(Contributing Author)
Michael H. Price's Hollywood Horrors
Electrified!
(With Timothy Truman)
Bloody Visions, Vols. I-III

---

Cover and interior Design: Susan Svehla
Copy editor: Linda J. Walter
Copyright © and ™ 2006 A.D., Michael H. Price

Portions of this book have appeared, in markedly different form, in M.H.P.'s *Daynce of the Peckerwoods: The Badlands of Texas Music*, from Music Mentor Books of Great Britain, and in the Forgotten Horrors series of movie-history books, from Midnight Marquee Press; and in the periodicals *Mad about Movies* and *The Business Press* of Fort Worth.

Without limiting the rights reserved under the copyright above, no part of this publication may be reproduced, stored in or introduced into a retrieval system, or transmitted, in any form, or by any means (electronic, mechanical, photocopying, recording, or otherwise), without the prior written permission of the copyright owner or the publisher of this book.
ISBN: 978-1-887664-70-X
Library of Congress Catalogue Card Number: 2006937717
Manufactured in the United States of America

First Printing by Midnight Marquee Press, December 2006

Dedication

In Memory of
T-Bone Walker
R. Bob Cooper
Grady L. Wilson


What you gonna do—
What you gonna say—
Without your funnyman
To pick on night and day?
—Johnny McCrae
"You're Just About To Lose Your Clown"
(E.B. Marks, BMI; 1966)

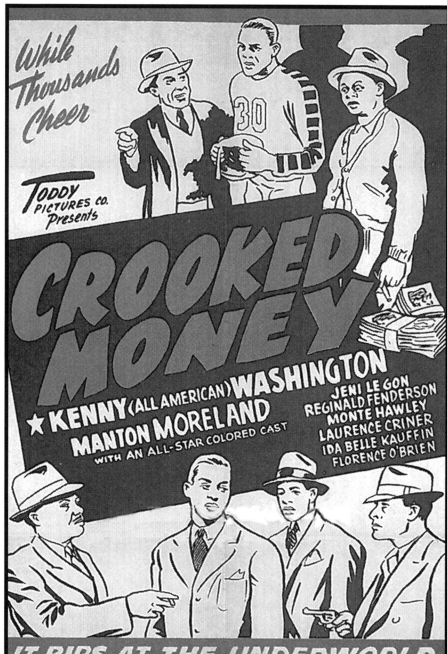

# Table of Contents

| | |
|---|---|
| 8 | Preface by Gregory Kane |
| 10 | Introduction by Josh Alan Friedman |
| 13 | Preamble: Love Will Abide—Take Things in Stride |
| 16 | Prelude: In Search of Historic Mantan |
| 23 | Chapter 1: Don't Let 'Em See You Sweat |
| 24 | Chapter 2: Can't Keep from Cryin', Sometimes |
| 28 | Chapter 3: Stifle That Grin, or Else What? |
| 32 | Chapter 4: Move Over, Boys—I'm One of the Gang, Now |
| 35 | Chapter 5: Multiculturalism before There Was a Word for It |
| 38 | Chapter 6: In Which a Crucial Connection Gets Made |
| 41 | Chapter 7: Beating the Blues, Eight- and/or Four-to-the-Bar |
| 46 | Chapter 8: So Who's Bamboozling Whom, and to What Purpose? |
| 52 | Chapter 9: An Intolerance of Tolerance |
| 54 | Chapter 10: Work Is Work, and the More, the Better |
| 56 | Chapter 11: A Collision Between Good Fortune and Bad |
| 59 | Chapter 12: Everything To Gain and Nothing To Lose |
| 62 | Chapter 13: A Mantan for All Seasons, So Long as the Seasons Keep Coming |
| 77 | Chapter 14: Like Father, like Daughter |
| 90 | Chapter 15: Down at Duffy's Tavern—Puerto Rican Branch |
| 103 | Chapter 16: Moe on Moreland—and Hoodooing the Hoodoo Man |
| 114 | Chapter 17: Indefinite, Most Definitely |
| 135 | Chapter 18: Mingled, if Not Mangled, Ancestry |
| 148 | Mantan and Chan |
| 163 | Appendix: Mantan Moreland: A Representative Stage- and-Screenography |
| 260 | Recommended Video Sources—and a Bit of Context |
| 263 | Acknowledgments |
| 265 | Index |

# Preface
by Gregory Kane

Where in the world is Mantan Moreland's apology?

Those buying this book know that America in the first decade of the 21st century is in the age of apology. Everybody's apologizing to somebody for sins committed centuries ago.

Americans of all races had to apologize—through official government edict — to those Japanese-Americans who were sent to relocation centers during World War II. (Those addicted to political correctness prefer the more drastic terms "detention centers" and "concentration camps" to describe those relocation centers.) We even had to apologize to the ones who were allowed to leave the centers to attend American colleges and those who remained loyal to Japan and asked to return there when the war ended.

Advocates of reparations for black Americans whose ancestors were slaves demand an apology from the U.S. government, the same one that actually outlawed chattel slavery with the 13th Amendment.

Whenever slights real or perceived are hurled at a racial, religious, ethnic or sexual orientation group, you can rest assured an apology will be demanded. So where's the one for Mantan?

Moreland has been maligned, forgotten, shunted aside and, to coin a phrase in Afro-American vernacular, 'buked 'n scorned by those who've appointed themselves the protectors of the image of black folks. His crime?

Being funny. Or being funny in what are considered stereotypical, buffoonish roles that "degrade" and "demean" black folks. Moreland had his heyday in the 1930s and 1940s, playing the comic relief in a number of films. He was at his comic best in the film *Lucky Ghost*. Watching it, I understood perfectly why Moe Howard of the Three Stooges wanted Moreland to join the act after Shemp Howard died.

If Moreland's humor was "degrading" and "demeaning," what are we to make of the movie *Soul Plane*? Made in 2004—decades after the last of Moreland's films—this trash was the worst display of degrading, demeaning and stereotypical "humor" about black folks ever to grace the silver screen. It left me actually pining away for Moreland's films.

The self-appointed guardians of the racial image of black folks abhor "demeaning" and "degrading"? How's this for "demeaning" and "degrading":

1. A "jail issue" of *XXL* magazine, which targets a black audience, features rapper 50 Cent and some character named Tony Yayo in an orange prison jump suit.
2. A journalism colleague of mine, a black man in his late 50s or early 60s, tells me his son visited Mexico and nearly everyone he met thought he was a drug dealer or a rapper. Or both.
3. Black journalist Juan Williams says the racial stereotypes of black people in rap videos—stereotyping done by black rappers—is perhaps the worst that has been done to black Americans in the history of the country. That would include the time of Moreland's films.
4. The wealth of rap videos that feature the n-word as a running theme.

Not once in a Moreland film will you hear that word. You won't even hear a hint of it. See why I'm feeling the guy? See why I'm feeling Moreland's films? See why I enjoyed this book?

And that's why I'm recommending it too. Moreland may not get his apology. But maybe it's time he got some long overdue appreciation. This book is it.
—Gregory Kane
October 2006

*Gregory Kane is an award-winning columnist for the* Baltimore Sun. *In 1997 he was a finalist for the Pulitzer Prize for his reporting on slavery in the Sudan. That work won him the 1997* Overseas Press Club *Award.*

# Introduction
by Josh Alan Friedman

This land be my land
This land be your land
From the Lena Horne lands
To the Mantan Morelands
From the old slave quarters
To the Muddy Waters
This land be made for you and me
—After Woody Guthrie

It has been shown that somewhere around the world, there's a new book on Shakespeare released every day. I've heard there have been upwards of 14,000 books published on Lincoln. (The latest revisionist tome ponders whether the Great Emancipator was gay.) So why would anyone want to write the 14,001st biography of Lincoln—when they could cover some of the same terrain by writing the first biography of Mantan Moreland? Moreland was funnier than Lincoln—or Elvis Presley, for that matter (3,000 books).

This is where my favorite scholar, Michael H. Price, comes in. He is the first to shine light on stubborn pockets of our big, disenfranchised culture that demand attention, but don't otherwise receive it. He rights wrongs when he writes. Price is Right. Just take a glance at his "Also By" credits at the front of this book. He is a credit to his race.

Today's hip-hoppers hark back and hover so close to the minstrel show that you anticipate their eyes to bug out and their hair to frazzle at sight of a ghost. Mantan Moreland was never considered "a credit to his race," like Joe Louis or Jackie Robinson. But Moreland seems not to have lost sleep over it. Whether he ever ate ribs, *Nêgro à Nêgro*, with Paul Robeson, Dr. Ralph Bunche, or W.E.B. DuBois, I don't know (although Price probably does). Pigmeat Markham, Moreland knew, along with the utterly fascinating and forgotten world of Negro Vaudeville—a criminally overlooked subject.

How might race relations be different if Mantan Moreland had not been born? I'll tell you. The answer is this: *Why can't a great performer just be a great performer, without having to inspire his whole goddamn race?* Mantan was as true to lowbrow comedy as Marian Anderson was to opera, even though Mantan didn't cross the color line for *commedia dell'arte*.

Can't a career in Low Comedy be more honorable than, say, Urology? It takes more training and heartbreaking dedication, and the dues that a comedian pays surpass any urologist's, or proctologist's, med-school tuition.

Mantan be made for you and me.

—Josh Alan Friedman
Stovall Plantation, 2006

*Journalist-satirist-composer Josh Alan Friedman is the author of such cross-cultural memoirs as* Tales of Times Square *and* When Sex Was Dirty; *co-editor of* Now Dig This: The Unspeakable Writings of Terry Southern, 1950-1995; *and the central figure in Kevin Page's documentary film* Blacks and Jews: Josh Alan Friedman—A Life Obsessed with Negroes *(2004).*

# Preamble: Love Will Abide —Take Things in Stride

> Dr. Jones did all that he could—
> Only your love did me some good—
> You're good for me...
> Like the honey is good for the bee,
> You're good for me.
> —Johnnie Taylor: "You're Good for Me"
> (David & Collins; Unart Music, BMI; 1969)

Mantan Moreland was in no position by now to instruct anybody to step aside. A line from one of his movies, "Move over, boys—I'm one of the gang, now," had served him well as an ad-libbed throwaway—and then, the declaration had caught on sufficiently well to find its own life outside the motion picture that had spawned it.

But now, the only gang in which Moreland could claim immediate membership was that of Those Not Long for This World. He had a bed to himself, and that was all the space he needed to be occupying for the moment.

Once having reigned over a narrow cultural landscape of Old Hollywood and its Sepia Town suburbs, Moreland had fought long and hard to retain a bit of that higher ground for himself and his daughter Marcella, who had stayed the course through the trying times. Which is more than can be said for her mother, who had jumped ship at the first sign of trouble but still hovered about, looking for a way back in on her terms.

Hazel Moreland could not live with Mantan Moreland—not with his having so much affection reserved for their daughter, and so much generosity toward the rest of the civilized world. But then, Hazel could not very well live without him, either.

"She had never understood how my Daddy could love me and love her, too." Marcella Moreland Young recalled in 2005. "With Mom, it was always a case of 'I–me–mine,' and then some more of 'What's in it for *me*?'"

Marcella's words contain nothing of rancor—just the sad understanding that one of the richer love stories of Old Hollywood was destined to meet an ending more complicated than the storybook type: "He understood her more profoundly than she understood him."

But then, there was a great deal to understand about Mantan Moreland, whose gifts were as manifold as his personal needs were few: "Give Daddy his cigar money and a little spending-change, and he was fine."

Mantan Moreland and daughter Marcella Moreland Young, in a candid snapshot from the early 1970s.

By the close of the 1960s, Mantan Moreland had arrived at an uneasy truce with the prospect of death, his life expectancy having dwindled to an any-day-now proposition as a consequence of a long-controlled but persistent diabetic condition and rampant, surge-and-ebb blood pressure to match. Now hospitalized in A.D. 1973 at a moment when he should have been making good on the renewed promise of a home-stretch show-business comeback, he wanted nothing so much as to pass along peaceably. Either that, or else to whip the odds one last time and resume his business of making people laugh.

Hazel Moreland wanted a way back into the circle—especially so, now that an ending seemed near. A last reconciliation could only prove to exert a healing effect.

"Mom called to ask about her chances of coming up to see Daddy." Marcella went on. "I hadn't encouraged any of that because I wanted to keep things calm and restful for Daddy. Mom and I had been feuding for years, in any case, and it seemed more important to me that I should attend to Daddy's comforts.

"But she was insistent. So I asked Daddy if he wanted to see her.

"Well, he was dying, and he knew that. Of *course* he wanted to see her, even if he did kind of roll his eyes at the prospect of her barging in on him. The doctors and the nurses were worrying at the time about an accumulation of fluid in Daddy's lungs, but we figured that a reunion might lift his spirits, at this stage. Not the best of odds, considering their emotionally combative history—but a chance, all the same.

"Well, okay, and so here she comes, in all her haughty grandeur," said Marcella. "My mother was not a *big* woman, now, but she *carried* herself big. Always put on a show of her being *Mrs. Moreland*, their long-ago divorce notwithstanding, and she made certain that everybody knew her as such. 'Mrs. Moreland is here—make way for Mrs. Moreland!'—just like that.

"So here she comes, shooing the nurses out of her way, and then she announces: 'Pops, I'm *here*! Let's get you *comfortable*!' Just takes over, as the one-and-only Mrs. Moreland asserts herself as being in charge of things. She's going to administer a back-rub to Daddy and give him some soothing sweet-talk while she's at it.

"I'd explained it to her about that build-up of fluid in his lungs, and she's here to attend to that, whether or not the hospital staff wants her to do so.

"'You get away from me!' she says to one of the nurses who's trying to keep an eye on things. So Mom goes to rubbin' on Daddy's back, talking sweet to him—he starts to coughin' up a storm—and sure enough, he seems to experience some relief. Just like that.

"And then, she looks up at this nurse and says, like this: 'I *know* what I'm doing for my *husband*.'

"I left the room right about then," said Marcella. "Thought it best to give them some solitude, a last tender encounter. And after a while, Daddy passed on. The date was the 28th day of September, 1973."

Marcella pondered the memory for a moment. Then she continued:

"I start to weep when I remember how much they truly loved one another, all their disagreements and estrangements aside. Daddy had married Mom when she was in her teens and already an utterly spoiled Daddy's Girl, within her own household. And my Daddy and my Mom had fought with one another for most of their life together.

"I don't mean any physical kind of fighting, *you* know. I mean that kind of *emotional* struggle, the kind that occurs when a generous soul loves and understands a *needy* soul who loves being the center of attention.

"But they truly cherished one another. Daddy *never* loved another woman but my mother. And Mom reserved all her deeper affections for Daddy.

"And it was that love that saw him on through, there, right at the end. He was able to die in the knowledge of how much she had loved him. And that one, solitary deed on her part helped Mom and me—eventually, I mean—to come back onto good terms with one another."

# Prelude
# In Search of Historic Mantan

"How 'bout bitin' 'im?"
"Yeah! Go on ahead an' bite 'im!"
—Andrew H. Brown and Amos Jones
contemplate a strategy for survival amidst combat
in "The Rasslin' Match," 1934

One afternoon during the waning 1990s, some 10 years-and-change after I had taken part in the discovery, salvaging and preservation of a historic archive known as the Tyler, Texas, Black Film Collection, I traveled with two friends to Southern Methodist University in Dallas to spend a few hours in communion with those lost-and-found movies.

Now, T. Sumter Bruton, III and Josh Alan Friedman and I are booshwah white boys, at least by natural origins, who owe our souls and our sanity to Negritudinous music. Which was the point of this junket—a big-screen showing that I had arranged of the only 35-millimeter safety-stock print extant of a movie called *Juke Joint*, which owes its insane soul to the blues of the black Southland.

Thus having acknowledged the film's wild streak, I should add that *Juke Joint* also is an utterly middle-class affirmation of such eternal values as family ties, grace-before-dinner and Don't Sass Your Elders, or Else. A little something for everybody, in sensible proportions.

*Juke Joint* is a centerpiece of the collection at SMU and perhaps the most accomplished of nine pictures that Spencer Williams, Jr. had directed for an off-Hollywood production company of Jewish white-folks proprietorship, based in Dallas. His six-year span of productivity in Texas had prefaced Williams' cracking of the big leagues as a network-television star, thanks to a track record of resourceful inventiveness and the benevolent influence of a fellow black actor-turned-casting director named Flournoy E. (a.k.a. F.E.) Miller. Williams' vehicle to that greater prominence was a prime-time situation comedy of the early 1950s, called *Amos 'n' Andy*.

And *Amos 'n' Andy* (if you'll indulge a digression) was a watershed for black America, in many respects. But the program also had touched off within America's piebald excuse for a culture a provocative surge of newfound prominence that struck many forward-thinking black citizens as a throwback to Uncle Tom, at the best, and to Jim Crow at the worst. And whether *Amos 'n' Andy* would prove a lasting or influential phenomenon or sink under the weight of

massed protest, it had locked Williams—the most ambitious and all-'round gifted member of that ensemble cast—into a dead-end career.

For Williams' part, there was no turning back to those happier days of shirt-tail provincial moviemaking, of which *Juke Joint* had been a crucial part. *Amos 'n' Andy* had triggered an upheaval of broadened opportunities for black talent, exposing that historically repressed subdivision of the entertainment business to a mainstream audience of all ethnic varieties—any household, that is, within reach of one of those newfangled teevee sets.

And in its burgeoning popularity, the program helped to put an end to the separate-but-unequal filmmaking industry in which Williams had become a prolific and bankable artist and businessman. Though hardly the only outcropping of featured black talent on early-day network television, *Amos 'n' Andy* was the first such series to boast a thoroughly black ensemble cast of leading players. And it would be the last, for another generation's span.

But neither could Williams have moved forward from *Amos 'n' Andy*. The organized controversy, driven largely by the National Association for the Advancement of Colored People, grew practically as intense as the popular acclaim (along with sequestered objections) that since 1928 had attended the program's radio-network version, which had been enacted primarily by its white-guy creators with the help of black supporting talents. The generalized acceptance of *Amos 'n' Andy* was such that—as the screen director Robert Altman insisted in 1996 while contemplating the prospect of a big-screen adaptation of the property—"that program pretty well defined the American perception of black folks, for nearly half a century."

Had *Amos 'n' Andy* lasted beyond 1953, the burly Williams would have found himself stereotyped (in terms of personality, more so than of ethnicity) without regard to the greater versatility that he had shown as a big-screen artist. His movie work had found Williams writing and directing, delivering box-office moneymakers on skimpy budgets of less than $25,000 per picture, impersonating the law and the lawless, presences sacred and profane, fringe-dwellers and credentialed citizens. But then, *Amos 'n' Andy* had redefined him indelibly as Andrew H. Brown, a sure-fire funnyman with dead-accurate dramatic timing but suicidally repercussive social-agenda timing.

And so CBS Television quit producing *Amos 'n' Andy* after a final season of new episodes, these for syndication only as opposed to regimented mass-audience exposure via broadcasting over a centralized network. The series' 78 episodes nonetheless would remain in play into the 1960s, in the ghostly afterlife of local-market distribution.

Spencer Williams quit making pictures, living on in deepening obscurity and failing health until his death in 1969 from a chronic ailment of the kidneys. Williams' breakthrough with *Amos 'n' Andy* would avail him no greater recognition over the long term than the sad extremes of popular nostalgia and popular disdain. He had claimed no residual royalty-payment stake in the lucrative potential of the rerun market, which the networks strategically had kept a secret from most of their star players. The purported boon of recycling, whether of junk or of art, pays off only for those who own a piece of a corrupt and wasteful packaging-and-repackaging industry.

Meanwhile, the Poverty Row sector of the movie industry quit making pictures expressly for black-neighborhood theaters, on the fair and eventually accurate assumption that the approach of integration, or at least of desegregation, would seal shut a lucrative pocket of niche-market showplaces. But half a century and more down the pike, mainstream Hollywood is still playing catch-up at the sluggish start of a supposedly Bold New Millennium—which still feels a great deal like the Old Worn-Out Millennium.

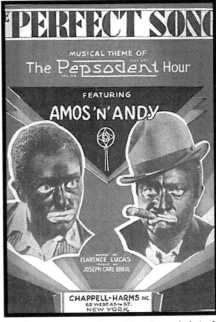

1929 sheet music from the *Amos 'n' Andy* radio show

The industry talks a good game, but oftener than not its pronouncements are mere lip-service to the fashionable concept of Cultural Diversity. Television and the movies overcompensate, then, with crass and superficial, easy-gratification pandering in shallow appeasement of ethnic-group sensibilities. And how else to explain the Dubya-Bee TV Network and its merger-driven descendants? To say nothing of Halle Berry's overwrought Oscar-night speech, touting a starring role (in 2001's *Monster's Ball*) whose generalized acclaim had been more a response to epidermis than to artistry.

Nowadays, maybe 10 people out of 1,000 will recognize the name of Spencer Williams, Jr., who in his sheer ebullient friendliness had done more than Martin Luther King, Jr., and Malcolm X, together or separately, to endear the black community to a massed populace.

But I was talking about that jaunt over to Dallas' SMU campus in 1996. Sumter Bruton and Josh Alan Friedman and I scarcely could prevent a load of *Amos 'n' Andy* baggage from accompanying us into the screening room. We had known the teleseries as youngsters, of course, and we had lamented its demise even as we understood the factions that had found its more facile stereotypes and dialectical excesses objectionable. (A recurring, if futile, question: Yes, and where *was* the Ebonics movement when these artists could have exploited it to their greater advantage?) But Sumter and Josh Alan and I set aside as much of that foreknowledge as we could and settled in to watch Spencer Williams' *Juke Joint* in a form very close to that which its original audiences had experienced.

The picture dates from 1946—a fertile period for black musical artistry in Texas. Williams, as the writer–director–star, portrays Bad News Johnson, a genial confidence man who finagles his way into a house-guest situation under the guise of a show-business promoter.

A juke joint—hence the title, and hence the root of the more widely familiar term *jukebox*—was a black-community nightclub. Such locales (not sound-stage sets, but authentic jukes in Dallas and San Antonio, Texas) were focal to Sumter Bruton's interest in viewing the film. As one of Texas' preeminent third-generation blues guitarists and a partner with me in a band dedicated to preserving the post-WWII styles, Sumter also has become an ethno-musicologist of formidable knowledge. He was particularly keen on observing the roles in *Juke Joint* of a bandleader named Red Calhoun and his sidemen. Sumter spent the screening taking notes and relishing the music and the rough-hewn genuineness of the play-acting.

My interest on this occasion was more generalized, though focused on the technical quality of the print and its curatorial presentation. I had been on the scene in 1983 at Tyler, at the edge of East Texas' Piney Woods region, when *Juke Joint* and a bunch of other kindred pictures had been unearthed where abandoned, having piled up unclaimed since the 1950s, in a decrepit warehouse. And I had helped Southern Methodist University's film-archive founder, the since-deceased G. William Jones, to identify and inventory this batch of movies and to get them removed to a secure place and prepared for a systematic transfer from volatile nitrocellulose film stock onto chemically stable footage. Even so, I had seen most of the transfers only in the virtual-cinema form of videocassette copies, and now I was backtracking gradually to watch the entire collection unspooling from actual reels of real film, borne to a 20-by-40-foot reflective screen upon an actual lamp-light beam from a high-wattage projector. Better than this, moviegoing don't hardly get.

Josh Alan Friedman's interest was of a third kind. He had not been introduced as yet to this particular sphere of moviemaking, although his own career(s) as a blues guitarist and a working journalist in New York and Dallas had steered him long since toward the cultural blackness that pervades and nourishes the entertainment racket, whether one-sidedly or reciprocally. Among our party, Josh's absorption in the showing was probably the most thorough, and as we were leaving SMU's Greer Garson Theatre—so named in honor of a star of Old Hollywood who had married into Texas oil money, light-years removed from the scrappy domain of Spencer Williams—Josh Alan told me this: "That movie has changed my life."

And sure enough, within a matter of weeks Josh began proving that assertion with a new outpouring of original storytelling and songwriting. You could look it up, because much of that fresh inspiration has made it into print and onto Josh's commercial recordings as both soloist and bandleader, notably in such compact-disc albums as *Blacks 'n' Jews* and *Strike a Match*.

I can relate, okay. I had made such an altering discovery a good many years earlier, when I had first caught the rambunctious act of Mantan Moreland on late-night television, in a resurrected movie from the early 1940s called *King of the Zombies*. Not even the friendly black-self authenticity underlying *Amos 'n' Andy* had impressed me as profoundly as this Moreland guy did in just one chump-change motion picture, and I had determined right then and there, more or less, to find out as much about him as there was to be found out. (It came scarcely as a surprise to learn that Moreland was a colleague of Spencer Williams and Flournoy E. Miller—and might have been a candidate for

an *Amos 'n' Andy* role, if only Mantan had been working in the United States when that television program had begun taking shape.)

The task of learning Moreland's larger story has taken a while, he said understatedly. The process of discovery has yielded results all along, but the suppression and frustration of Moreland's career—by those same well-intentioned killjoys who had squelched *Amos 'n' Andy*—has resonated into times very recent. I have managed over the long haul to catch up with the greater extent of Moreland's movies, and I have studied his occasional phonograph records (from the sacred to the scrofulous, to the deliriously silly) and a generous sampling of his radio work. And I have compared impressions with people who had socialized with him, worked with him and learned from him. I have observed how Moreland's spontaneity and generosity influenced the beginnings of rock 'n' roll music—so where do *you* think Joe Tex got his trademark of a soaring chuckle, or the Coasters their prevailing attitude of droll insubordination?—and how those qualities helped to shape the beginnings of a new wave of Afrocentric filmmaking, for good or ill, late along into the 20th century.

And as a consequence of a fortunate connection with Moreland's daughter and her daughter, I have managed to bolster and sometimes challenge my perceptions with biographical facts and one outlandish family-tradition legend, dating from the first decade of the 20th century and reaching into times very recent.

In my collaborative *Forgotten Horrors* books and in various articles elsewhere, I often have declared Mantan Moreland to have been Old Hollywood's most energetic comedian—all due respect to the enshrined houses of Marx, Fields, Keaton, and Chaplin. And Moreland's story, related in the most direct terms short of his own account, shows him to have been the most resilient, defiant and resurgent of that lot, as well. That is, within the limits imposed by the spirit of the times, a forgetful mass audience, and the disloyal marketplace itself.

Spencer Williams survived the collapse of his TV show, but he might as well not have done so. The most flamboyant member of *Amos 'n' Andy*'s ensemble cast, Tim "Kingfish" Moore, retrenched within the nightclub arena whence he had come, retaining the "Kingfish" moniker for use as needed and when appropriate.

Eddie "Rochester" Anderson weathered such controversies with a strategic attachment to Jack Benny's prominence within the Dominant Culture, often playing more boss than butler to Mistah Benny.

Willie Best, who had subbed on occasion for Mantan Moreland in the postwar *Charlie Chan* pictures, once might have retained a similarly strategic attachment to Bob Hope's lasting stardom. Hope, after all, had prized Best as a co-star (in *The Ghost Breakers* and *Nothing but the Truth*, from 1940-1941), in a class with Bing Crosby and Dorothy Lamour. "Willie was the best actor I ever worked with," Hope told me in 1979, "and I'm not just making a pun on his name." Willie Best wound up owning a liquor store in Los Angeles, forsaking second-class stardom in favor of a tiny empire all his own, and more power to him.

On the ofay side of the equation, Old Hollywood could claim a good many name-brand comedians who wore out their welcomes with the major studios and never quite managed to find a way back in through the front gates. W.C. Fields and Buster Keaton boozed themselves into oblivion, Fields sloshing his way into an early grave and Keaton reanimating himself at undignified intervals (though with his artistry and adventurous nature intact, no matter how shabby the circumstances) over a lengthier span by far. Sir Charles Chaplin, knighthood notwithstanding, politicized and womanized his uneasy way out of popular favor. Groucho Marx survived the inexorable erosion of his brotherly team of funnymen to become one of the first prematurely Grey Eminences in the realm of television, placing his audacious wit at the service of a Mass Culture that once he had found a ready target for ridicule.

Mantan Moreland kept working at whatever diminishing opportunity.

A central revelation to be deployed here is that the artist's christened name was not Mantan, or Moreland, or any combination thereof. Not, at any rate, until he took a rechristening into his own hands, in search of an identity more meaningful than that into which he had been born.

But more about all that presently.

# 1
# Don't Let 'Em See You Sweat

> My memory is like a sundial—it only records the sunny hours.
> —Ronnie Barker, *It's Hello from Him*; 1989

Somewhere between the surge-and-ebb of the Harlem Renaissance and the grudge-match battle of Dr. King vs. the Kingfish, that epic and inescapable Rumble in the Jungle of the Soul, there arrived an entertainer who called himself Mantan Moreland and invited everybody else within earshot to do likewise.

This Mantan Moreland (1903–1973) would become Louisiana's richest gift to the funnyman traditions of Old Hollywood, whether or not he sensed any such importance in his rudimentary career-building strategy of doing what came naturally and hoping that somebody might notice. Moreland found his place in the spotlight, if not quite the sun, during the waxed-and-waning years of the Great God A'mighty Depression as These United States lurched back toward prosperity via warfare.

Thus situated, Moreland stood his ground for more than a decade before he found himself maneuvered toward a lower station in an upheaval of Cultural Correction.

That this act of concerted marginalization and repression came from within the very populace that had championed Moreland as One of Its Own, Made Good, lends a current of ironic tragedy.

That Moreland summoned the gumption to keep laughing—his birthright, and the persuasive dowry with which he had wedded himself to Show Business—argues against a case of outright martyrdom. *Don't let 'em see you sweat.*

The Civil Rights movement that found its traction in the wake of World War II was as much an internalized struggle as it was a struggle against entrenched external forces. A great deal of indigenous black artistry found itself torn between the extremes, within a campaign of presumed solidarity. And so who gets to call it art, anyhow?

Thus did Mantan Moreland prove too funny for some factions—the altercators of a mighty altercation, as it were—to tolerate. Moreland's forced exclusion stood as an example of a Righteous Cleansing upon the land, and of course this process became an instance of throwing out some perfectly healthy and happy babies right along with the stale bathwater.

The movement was no laughing matter, of course. So stifle that grin, already. But how much more effectively might the cause have progressed if it had retained an extroverted sense of humor?

# 2
# Can't Keep from Cryin', Sometimes

> Mama, she's dead and gone
> And I know I am all alone
> I can't keep from cryin', in my soul
> —Traditional Southern spiritual

Black American culture, which like America herself contains many cultures,[1] has a great deal to do with the folksy-sounding philosophical notion of "laughin' to keep from cryin'." This tactical attitude is a linchpin of a musical idiom known as *the blues*—the term is singular or plural, as suits the occasion—which itself had started out as an attitude, a frame of worried mind and insolent spirit, before it could evolve into a musical form. Most people who attempt to Moan Those Weary Blues in the here-and-now haven't the foggiest notion of how the blues might feel, like a fire settled deep in one's bones, or of why one might feel compelled to laugh in order to keep from crying.

The historian Paul Oliver has traced the blues as a state of mind—the term is more evocative by far than the present day's fashionable notion of Clinical Depression—to the late-middle years of the 19th century.

Oliver cites a day-book entry from 1862. The authorship is attributed to a freeborn and educated black Northerner named Charlotte Forten, who had journeyed South to become a teacher to the slaves lodged off coastal North Carolina.

She had written of being awakened one Saturday night by "terrible screams coming from the [slaves'] Quarters." Charlotte Forten then told of how she had attended church services the next day, struggling to shake the impression left by whatever ordeal it was that she had overheard.

The diary continues: "Nearly everyone was looking gay and happy," she wrote, "and yet I came home with the blues…and for the first time since I have been here, felt very lonesome and pitied myself. But I have reasoned myself into a more sensible mood and am better now." The context and usage suggest that *the blues* might have become, by Forten's time, a phrase of self-evident meaning.

The diary neglects to record whether the suffering heard from the Quarters proved recurrent, or how any such personally felt miseries might have been reasoned away. If its author "had been writing her entry shortly before she died, 50 years later," wrote Oliver in a book called *The Story of the Blues* (1969), "she would doubtless have rationalized her worried state in much the same way. But the slave's successor might well have sung away his unhappiness with a blues song."

*Laughin' to keep from cryin'*. Plantation Pagliacci. The tracks of the tears of a clown, as Smokey Robinson would invert and re-phrase the notion a century after Charlotte Forten's day. Variations upon that phrase occur in innumerable blues songs and jazz compositions, both homespun and pop-commercialized. And who, short of Pete Seeger or Alan Lomax, can say with any certainty where folk music leaves off and popular music begins? Whether folkloric or work-for-hire, though, the defiant tonic of a horselaugh in the ugly face of misery rings true enough to have lasted.

"You can't jus' *sing* the blues," the Texas pianist and singer Robert "Fud" Shaw (1908–1985) told me during the middle 1970s. "You gots to *live* the blues and learn to laugh at 'em before you can *sing* any blues and make it stick. Otherwise, you [are] jus' goin' through the *motions*." Wise counsel from a master, there, and I sure-enough learned more and better piano-pounding skills from just spending time in Shaw's company than I had picked up in an entire childhood of academic conservatory training.

All the same, I couldn't exactly see myself "living the blues," per Shaw's *caveat*, when it was just as easy to appropriate and adapt the techniques and approximate the feeling. The blues as *lieder* makes for an intriguing pose, though ridiculous if sustained for any length of time. This commercial heritage of art-song posturing has produced, nonetheless, such capable players as Emmett Miller and Gene Austin during the 1920s, Dave "Snaker" Ray and "Spider" John Koerner during the 1950s and '60s, and Eric Clapton and Bonnie Raitt over an unexpectedly long haul into the present day. But technical proficiency and a knack for inventive mimicry are hardly the basis of the blues.

An immense sense of ironic humor courses through Robert Shaw's huge catalogue of songs and comparatively small body of recorded work. This batch includes a 1963 session issued in part on the record labels of Almanac and Arhoolie; plus private-stock recordings captured by the Austin, Texas guitarist Kurt Van Sickle and the second-generation boogie pianist Ben Conroy, in addition to a lengthy interview-with-music that my pal and fellow journalist Larry D. Springer and I conducted at Shaw's house in 1974. One such line of Shaw's is a stern warning from a worried mother and father to their skirt-chasing son: "Don't let these Cadillac womens make no flat tire out of you."

Shaw's humor in waking life cut deeper yet: While working as an academic bureaucrat toward the close of the 1970s, I arranged for Shaw to visit the campus of Amarillo [Texas] Junior College as a main attraction at the affiliated Amarillo Art Center. The Powers That Did Be seemed eager to welcome "an authentic Negro folk musician," as one of the deans put it. (In fact, Shaw had spent most of his life as a commercial entertainer, and he had a formal background in classical piano.) The college's administration was just as eager, or as anxious, to see how

Shaw's act might fit into a concert hall that had been designed to accommodate chamber-music quartets and pretenders to the throne of Van Cliburn.

Shortly after his arrival from Austin one chilly morning in March of 1978, Shaw and I reconnoitered the concert hall to scope out the piano, an Olympian Steinway Grand. This instrument was a far cry from the battered but sturdy Schaeffer upright that occupied Shaw's household, but he found it suitable: "Pianos is pianos, all right."

Shaw was testing the keys with a strenuous ragtime-meets-boogie instrumental piece that he called "The Ma Grinder," remarking a few out-of-tune strings as he warmed up, when suddenly we were interrupted by one of my more apprehensive colleagues, Dr. Dale Roller, who managed the Art Center.

"I demand to know," demanded Dr. Roller, "what this [*a studied pause, here*] person is doing with *my* piano!" I made with the appropriate explanations, then, while Shaw kept playing, undistracted, but Roller was adamant: "Well, we must follow some formalities, here," and "Why was I not contacted beforehand?"—the usual indignant posturings of I'm in Charge Here, and Don't You Forget It.

Finally, Shaw stopped playing in order to impose some meaning upon an otherwise pointless commotion.

"You the boss-man around here?" he asked Roller.

"I'll have you know that I'm the Director of this Art Center." This, without so much as an introduction-by-name or a proffered handshake.

"Well, I'm Robert Shaw from Austin, Texas, and I'm gonna sell out your little chicken-shack, here, tonight, just like I've packed 'em into the whorehouses and juke joints from Ga'veston to El Paso ever since back in the day before *you* even knew what a piano was *meant* for," said Shaw, exhaling the friendly invective without pausing to catch a breath. He neglected to mention that he also had toured Europe on behalf of the U.S. State Department.

Then, Shaw got down to business: "And I'm here to tell you: This inst'ument is *not* in A-440 pitch, and you'd best get you a piano-tuner in here befo' tonight, 'less you want us to *all* wind up lookin' bad."

A tuner was duly summoned from the Tolzein Music Company.

Shaw received a warmer greeting, if no less arrogant, on our way back across the windswept campus. H.D. Yarbrough, vice president of the college, spotted us from a distance and came rushing over. Dr. Yarbrough had sat in on the planning sessions for this event, in which he sensed what he called "an opportunity for this institution to reach out decisively to the Negro community." (The full-house audience proved entirely of the Caucasian persuasion, though not for want of citywide publicity.)

So Dr. Yarbrough, a snappy dresser whose wardrobe that day had patently anticipated warmer weather, came marching up to Shaw with a well-intentioned welcome: "I hear you play those good old down-home blues," Yarbrough said.

Shaw gave his greeter the once-over and replied, laughing: "You'd best not stay out here too long in that li'l ol' candy-ass suit. You [are] li'ble to *freeze!*"

Dr. Yarbrough went huffing back toward the Administration Building. I couldn't have stifled a guffaw much longer. Finally, I asked Shaw, "Did you ever hear of a guy named Mantan Moreland?"

"You mean the ol'-timey Chitlin' Circuit comic?" Shaw asked in reply. "I knew a feller by that name—and how many fellers can there be named Mantan? We used to play some of the same joints, around South Texas, before he went big-time and I stayed put."

"Well, you kind of remind me of him."

"He wasn't a piano player, was he? Oh—you mean 'cause I don't take no guff off of nobody?"

"Well, yes, that—and because you seem to find the humor in just about everything."

"A man's got to laugh, boy."

[1] And so what else is new?

# 3
# Stifle That Grin, or Else What?

> Stop—stop! Baby, stop ticklin' me!
> —Mantan Moreland, 1947

A great deal of purposefully applied laughter had yielded to anger and sorrow during the immediate postwar 1950s as black America began to cast itself in a grimmer light of social upheaval. Even the blues became an endangered idiom for a long while, there, falsely stigmatized by its perception as a throwback to primitivism and the plantation mentality of subservience. And Mantan Moreland, whose career hinged upon both comedy and music with no overtly political bearings, found himself thwarted at precisely the time that his star should have been gaining further momentum.

Thus sidelined as the 1940s gave way to the '50s, Moreland found the first seven years post-Hollywood to be the most difficult. Or so his daughter, Marcella Moreland Young, recalled in 2004, adding: "Economically, and on the domestic household scene and in terms of Daddy's own health, that period was bad enough. But the [social and professional] rejection came near breaking Daddy spiritually, too. Fortunately for all of us, he was a determined man who didn't want to be anybody but who he already was." (Marcella's story bears telling in her own words, so stay tuned and stay attuned.)

Perhaps Tim Moore, a.k.a. *Amos 'n' Andy*'s George "Kingfish" Stevens, experienced a more noticeable rejection, given his immense if brief popularity as a network-television star. But then, Moore never had pursued much in the way of a movie career.

Primarily a Vaudeville-and-nightclub entertainer, Moore had appeared sporadically on Jazz Age Broadway and in black-ensemble cinema before finding massed recognition in 1951 as the Kingfish, the most vividly realized of the characters featured on the *Amos 'n' Andy* television series. When the CBS Television Network agreed to drop *Amos 'n' Andy* in 1953 in response to mounting protests, Moore was still well connected with the stage community and, in any event, past the traditional age of retirement. Moore also held fast and unapologetically to the Kingfish identity, appearing in that guise as late as 1957-1958 on localized radio broadcasts in Southern California. Moore died late in 1958, four days after his 71st birthday.

Edna Turner, longtime publisher of the Fort Worth, Texas–based *Sepia* group of magazines, once showed to me a cartoon from her inventory of memorabilia. The ink drawing—unsigned, in the generic big-foot gag-caricature style favored by *Hep* and *Jive* magazines, companion titles of *Sepia*—depicted the Rev. Dr. Martin Luther King, Jr. administering a swift kick to the backside of

**Mantan Moreland's google-eyes gimmick—sheer wordless eloquence.**

the Kingfish. The scenario was not unlike Chic Young's famous recurring image of J.C. Dithers giving the boot to Dagwood Bumstead in the syndicated comic strip *Blondie*.

"Wow!" I said, with all due understatement. "When'd *this* piece run?"

"Never ran at all," replied Mrs. Turner. "Too inflammatory. 'Specially so, for those dodgy times."

"Okay, then—but wouldn't that have been the *point*?"

"Well, yes, and there might've been a good case for our running it, back when *Amos 'n' Andy* was still a hot-button issue," said Mrs. Turner. "But nobody amongst us could ever quite figure it out what side the cartoon was trying to assume—whether it was supposed to depict the Rev. Dr. King as a hero, or the Kingfish as a victim. We were all pretty mixed on the topic."

Mantan Moreland, unlike Tim Moore in his breakout to a short-lived mainstream stardom, had been a movie star with both a tenured contract and credentials at practically all the old-line major studios and many of the minor-leaguers. Moreland had the ambition and the determination with which to combat the bewilderment of a stalled career.

But even with a measure of regained momentum, Moreland would spend another two decades-and-then-some scuffling to recapture the dignity of steady and fulfilling work, much as he had gone striving and scuffling through his earlier days of breaking into the Southland's Chitlin' Circuit (and from there, onto Broadway and toward the movies). Then, finally, age and infirmity caught up with him. He passed away in 1973—leaving an obscured legacy of hundreds of hours of moving-picture film, radio appearances and phonograph records—at precisely the moment when a briefly insurgent black-cinema movement was beginning to rediscover his worth. This value was that of a force of social benevolence and downright rib-tickling good humor that could transcend the facile gratification of Entertainment Value.

For a solid generation, there raged a humorless scattergun campaign to purge the culture of stereotypes. Many popular impressions of the black citizenry ranged, sure enough, from the shallow and condescending to the hateful and dehumanizing. But just as many popular impressions, such as those left by Moreland, yielded the balm of humor without self-ridicule. If a medicinal metaphor bears hammering, here, then the commonest effect of a purgative is to flush out the good right along with the bad, and the devil take the hindmost. Or consider the more scientifically grounded remedy of an antibiotic (literally spoken, a destroyer of life), which tends to kill off the benevolent organisms in its path while its truer targets mutate their way around its effects.

One precise effect of this purportedly healing crusade was that of preventing Moreland from reaching the very audiences that would have benefited most from his convulsively self-amused and blessedly apolitical (however playfully subversive) approach to slapstick comedy and bizarre wordplay. To discourage stereotypes as a class is one thing; to thwart careers in the name of a cleansing veers perilously close to genocide. Or at least to a book burning rally.

This push was not entirely successful, of course, for it failed to suppress such star-vehicles-by-default as *King of the Zombies* and a companion-piece, *Revenge of the Zombies* (1941–1943), along with *The Strange Case of Dr. Rx* and *Phantom Killer* (both from 1942). Being conventional Hollywood horror pictures, more or less, this handful bobbed back to the surface as convenient fodder for local night-owl television toward the close of the 1950s, reaching an audience of mostly white, mostly adolescent male enthusiasts.

And this audience, adventurous and receptive, was bound to find in Moreland a worth greater than the assorted fiends and monsters on parade—even though it was the hair-raising element that had drawn the youngsters to those movies in the first place. The accidental discovery, that revelation dispensed during one's search for something else entirely, often packs the more lasting charge of worth.

# 4
# Move Over, Boys—I'm One of the Gang, Now

*If there's anything I wouldn't want to be twice,
zombies is both of 'em!*—Mantan Moreland, 1941

His horror movies, loosely defined as such, provided my first encounters with the artistry of Mantan Moreland, during my schoolboy days in Northwest Texas: The bait would be some movie that my neighborhood of fellow creep-show fans had found touted in one or another of a then-epidemic onslaught of newsstand magazines. These mass-market publications sported such mastheads as *Famous Monsters* and *Fantastic Monsters* and *Horror Monsters* and—but you get the idea; not to impose too fine a point upon their shared agenda. The imperative common to such titles was less journalism than hype, payola-in-print for the postwar horror-movie factories, with a liberal seasoning of plain old reactionary nostalgia on the part of their editors.

The payoff of sitting through any or all of these resurrected wartime movies was hardly the zombie-raising and brain-swapping renegade surgeons, nor the serial murderers or hair-suit gorillas and not even the ambulatory cadavers that lurched through the proceedings.

The greater reward, rather, was this one actor, an antically funny black man, plump and balding, apparently of middle age but possessed of a childlike ebullience and a philosophical sense of wordplay to rival Charlie Chan in his epigrammatic prime or Bud Abbott & Lou Costello at their pinnacle of say-*what*? punsterism. This comedian not only stole the show(s) away from the ostensibly heroic white players; he also provided an identifiable dramatic scale by which to size up the terrors thus deployed. And he demonstrated to us white kids in a conspicuously segregated community how much better a place this old world might be if only we had some chums as quick of wit and generous of spirit as Mantan Moreland.

We eventually would match the name with the personality, only to search mostly in vain for more of Moreland's pictures in those days when one's home-viewing choices were at the mercy of the programming syndicates and the wobbly accuracy of the newspapers' broadcast logs.[1] For the time being, any passing mention of "that funny colored guy" (much as the cowboy movies' George "Gabby" Hayes, Andy Clyde, former blackface entertainer Lee "Lasses" White, and Al "Fuzzy" St. John were "those funny ol' geezers") would provoke fond chuckling among our ranks—along with awkward white-boy attempts to mimic the actor's choicer lines.

*Revenge of the Zombies*—less a sequel to than an elaboration upon *King of the Zombies*.

Case-in-point: "*Move* over, boys—I'm one of the gang, now," as spoken by Moreland to a raggedy platoon of Central Casting zombies, became a done-to-death byword. Taken out of context and applied wherever it might seem appropriate, the declaration took on a ritualistic socializing context all its own, in a language unknown to teachers, school principals, coaches, parents, and other such figures of stern authority. To discover Mantan Moreland within the narrow context of 1950s television, whose tailored-to-the-tube comedy stars tended to follow the insipid examples of Milton Berle, of the Borscht Belt gone mainstream, and Ozzie Nelson, of the mainstream gone ever further mainstream. Such discovery was akin to a rock 'n' roll neophyte's discovery of Bo Diddley as an antidote to Pat Boone.

I had no idea that Mantan Moreland had by now become a cultural taboo—more a pariah than *one of the gang, now*—any more than I understood how come the lovable *Amos 'n' Andy* series, a pointer toward integration if ever there were one, had vanished from family-night television, or why there should exist a World Apart in my own native borough of Amarillo, Texas. The more polite souls in my orbit referred to this visible-but-untouchable community as Colored Town. And denizens of Colored Town who ventured into what the Chamber of Commerce called Greater (than what?) Amarillo would find innumerable backhanded amenities to remind them: Don't Forget Your Place.

The most blatant of these totems was the tradition of the Colored Only drinking fountain, so labeled at the Woolworth and Kress companies' nickel-and-dime stores, among other cash-on-the-barrelhead outposts of less strictly segregated commerce. I found early on that these restricted faucets provided a caliber and quality of hydration identical to that spouting forth from any other such fixture. And so what's with the division? And of what are the Dividers of Humankind so blasted afraid, that they would quarantine a public spigot-rhymes-with-bigot? For my part, I just kept wishing that some of that enticing counter-cultural mojo might rub off on me. And one never knows—*do one?*—whether to take such a remark literally or figuratively.

---

[1] Hometown newspapers as a class seem to have played things fast and loose all along with their television-show listings, especially in terms of syndicated programming subject to the whims of local-station operators. Showtimes and program titles appeared with a reliably consistent inaccuracy in my city's daily paper of the 1950s and '60s, with some occasionally hilarious typographical glitches: *The Black Sheep* (for 1956's *The Black Sleep*), *Where Has Louie Gone?* (for 1964's *Where Love Has Gone*), *The Leotard Man* (for 1943's *The Leopard Man*), and a back-to-back situation-comedy listing for *Leave It to Lucy* and *I Love Beaver*. I kept a late-movie vigil one night in 1962 for a TV-encore of *King of the Zombies*, only to find it replaced, with no apologies whatsoever, by 1945's *Zombies on Broadway*—and no, not all zombie pictures are created equal. When queried about this or that mis-statement in print, city editor Don Williams of Amarillo, Texas' *Globe-News* papers would deadpan this reply: "Yeah, our proofreader's seeing-eye dog must've been out sick that day."

# 5
# Multiculturalism before There Was a Word for It

A wop bop a loo bop a lop bam boom!
—Little Richard Penniman, 1955

It was around this time, during the lapse of the 1950s into the '60s, that I learned to value a cultural trump card that had been dealt me from within my own family: My maternal-side uncle, a picture-show operator named Grady L. Wilson,[1] made no secret of his integrationalist politics—he would be the only one among my blood-kin elders to vote the Kennedy ticket, and he entrusted his dental care to one Dr. Richard W. Jones, a fellow combat veteran of World War II who also held forth for many years as president of Amarillo, Texas' branch of the National Association for the Advancement of Colored People. No Café Society pretensions of fashionably liberal superciliousness for this uncle of mine; he merely made the choices that suited him and stuck nonchalantly by them.

As early as 1956, when I was eight years old, Grady had taken me to see a show at Amarillo's Nat Ballroom, a cavernous, balconied dancehall of customarily white-folks patronage, with a general procession of big-band, rockabilly, and country-Western entertainment.[2] Little Richard Penniman, a profoundly black rock 'n' roll star born of amen-corner gospel and barrelhouse R&B, was the headliner on this occasion. The crowd was salt-and-pepper, and the promoters had made none of the standard provisions for segregated seating. The program, frantic and thrilling, ended prematurely in a strategically timed police raid that resulted in several arrests on formal charges of miscegenation—a misdemeanor complaint, calculated to divide and conquer by sheer dehumanizing force of humiliation—for a number of mixed-color couples on the dance floor, along with a disturbing-the-peace bust for Little Richard. The law made its Grand Entrance just as Penniman, in the midst of a frenzied number, had run screaming from his station at the piano, climbed the stage's curtain to the top, and dropped to pounce nimbly back to ground-level, landing on spring-heeled feet—and never missing a beat.

The entertainer's face, framed by the bars of the Potter County Jail but still beaming with jolly defiance, adorned the next morning's *Daily News*, front page above-the-fold.

Now, the Globe-News Company's resident publisher, S.B. Whittenburg, had imposed a standing policy that no Negro individual's face should appear upon Page One of any given day's editions. But Whittenburg also knew better than to enforce that rule when its exception might help to sell a few thousand additional copies.[3] As my father ranted over breakfast about the disgrace thus visited upon our town and the pernicious influence of rock 'n' roll none-dare-call-it-music, I kept mum. The official account, from where I sat, allowed as how Uncle Grady and I had attended a movie at one of his theaters; I had accordingly studied up on the synopsis from the film's publicity kit, just in case. And yes, it certainly had been one hum-dinger of a movie, whatever its name was.

More sedate, though also more enlightening, were those somewhat later occasions on which Grady and I would head out to our town's black-nightclub district to hear the likes of an up-and-coming Ray Charles, and the established artists Big Joe Turner (1911–1985) and T-Bone Walker (1910–1975). Turner and Walker remained loyal to the Southland's Chitlin' Circuit despite Big Joe's newfound acceptance among the rock 'n' roll crowd (the blues, camouflaged) and T-Bone's inroads into white Country Club society (the blues, bleached and mollified). Both had long since struck up friendships with my uncle, who supplemented his picture-show salary and nourished his Blues Jones by booking talent for these clubs along the north-by-northwestern fringes of downtown Amarillo, just off Route 66. Of these dozen-or-so establishments, the Tip Top Club (which lasted into the 1980s) was the most thoroughly devoted to music of provincial origin. The Atmosphere, which sat very close to a boulevard lined with Negro church-houses of various denominations, had more of a reputation as the place to visit if one was looking for a fight. The nearby Green Gables Motor Lodge provided housing for traveling black musicians—whether they might be playing in a darktown venue, or entertaining for some special occasion staged by the white folks at some big downtown hotel, the *goyishe* Amarillo Country Club, or the Jewish Tascosa Country Club.

The elite establishment among the black-district clubs was the La Joya Hotel, which showcased most of Amarillo's name-brand touring acts in the realms of jazz and the blues. The La Joya also thrived as a brothel and as a gambling house for high-rolling blacks and wealthy whites alike, with all due nods and winks and under-the-table payoffs to the authorities. The since-famous poker-playing champion, Amarillo Slim Preston, got his start at the La Joya, overseeing a numbers-racket lottery. The resident bandleader at the La Joya, from around 1955 until the 1970s, was Wilmot Lott, who had been a percussionist with Cab Calloway's orchestra. Lott also ran a smokehouse

and barbecue restaurant several blocks across the way, drawing a mixed clientele of black-neighborhood residents and big-shot white businessmen from the downtown office district.

It was aboard Big Joe Turner's tour bus, parked outside the Green Gables Motor Lodge, that I first visited at any length with the great singer. Sensing right off my affinity for the blues, Turner undertook to teach me the means by which he summoned and projected the mighty voice that he had developed as a singing bartender in Depression-era Kansas City.

"Everybody's got 'em a big voice," Turner would explain, "but don't near enough singers know where to find it or what to *do* with it when they find it. But if you train this big muscle, here, right on top of your belly"—this, underscored with a gentle gut-punch from a fist the size of a rib-roast—"why, it'll throw your voice clean out the door and into next week."[4]

As the upshot of this money-couldn't-buy-it tutelage, I was managing a middling okay imitation of Big Joe Turner before my voice had begun to deepen. I asked one of my Euro-classical tutors at the Musical Arts Conservatory for additional enlightenment as to this discovery and was informed that I was too young even to contemplate such pretensions to serious vocalizing. All thanks to Big Joe Turner and none at all to the Musical Arts Conservatory, I can still crank those pipes today as a middle-aged blues shouter. Which is a story for another day.

---

[1] My uncle's christened name was Grady Levi Wilson, but he had modified the middle moniker to Lee.

[2] Featured acts at the Nat Ballroom during the 1950s included Tex Beneke, leading the Glenn Miller Orchestra (with Henry Mancini on piano, prior to his *Peter Gunn* breakthrough); Bob Wills & His Texas Playboys (during Wills' span of residency in Amarillo); and first-generation rockers Roy Orbison, Jimmy Bowen, Buddy Knox, Gene Vincent, and so forth. (Elvis Presley had too big a following for the Nat; he played Amarillo's Municipal Auditorium.) My own rock 'n' roll band played the Nat during the middle '60s.

[3] S.B. Whittenburg became my boss in 1968, when I broke out of college journalism into a sure-enough newspaper career, and remained so until his oil-and-cattle family sold its mass-media subsidiaries in 1972.

[4] I followed Big Joe Turner's career avidly over the long haul, and I came within an ace of working with him in a commercial-recording situation. This was a might-have-been project that Otis Redding had proposed in 1967 for development at Stax Records in Memphis; Otis' unexpected death that same year left a great deal of unfinishable business. My last reunions with the Boss of the Blues occurred during Turner's final touring engagements of 1984.

6

# In Which a Crucial Connection Gets Made

No Blacks—No Whites—Just Blues.
—Tee-shirt slogan, 1995

Aaron Thibeaux "T-Bone" Walker was something of an intimidating figure in my view, if only because he was my Uncle Grady Wilson's favorite guitarist and Grady recently had given me a guitar with one daunting catch: "I want you should learn to play this like T-Bone." Walker was plenty approachable, however, and an obliging conversationalist-storyteller, to boot. He picked right up on an offhanded admiring reference that I made to Mantan Moreland.

"Mantan Moreland!" said Walker. "Now, where'd a little boy like you ever run across Mantan Moreland?" What he meant, I suspect, was "a little *white* boy like you."

"On teevee," I answered. "He's the star of my favorite monster movie—*King of the Zombies*."

"Oh, yeah. *King of the Zombies*. Isn't that the one where he says, 'Move over, boys—I's joined the club,' somethin' like that?" (And here, Walker affected a Deep Southern dialect quite unlike his usually mannered and genteel speech.)

"Well, actually, Mr. Walker, he says, 'Move over, boys—I'm one of the gang, now.'"

"Yeah. 'One of the gang, now.' What a great guy, that Mantan—good blues singer, too, when he lets it out."

"You *know* him?"

"Why, he's just my best friend, that's all."

My favorite comedian—even taking into account Abbott & Costello, Stan Laurel & Oliver Hardy and W.C. Fields and the Three Stooges, all of whose pictures had become staples of local television—and T-Bone Walker's best friend. All of a sudden and straight out of left field, two of my more persistent passions, blues and comedy, had fused into an imperative greater than either by itself.

I learned from Walker about the bitter developments that had seen Moreland branded an unacceptable combination of Jim Crow and Uncle Tom—pronounced ill-suited, by that influential bloc within his own restless society, to ply his trade before a massed audience. Walker understood the situation, though with a certain bewilderment and anxiety: His own style of blues, despite the jazz-tinged

Mantan Moreland, left, holds court amid revelries at the Los Angeles nightclub of Elihu "Black Dot" McGee, ca. middle nineteen-forties. Standing is Moreland's blues-guitarist pal Aaron "T-Bone" Walker. Seated rightward from Moreland are club-boss McGee, who also ran a thriving underground lottery known as a numbers racket; Mantan's high-strung wife, Hazel; Inez and R. Bob Cooper; and an otherwise unidentified couple noted in a Cooper family scrapbook as "some guests of Mantan's."

sophistication that Walker had developed during the 1940s, was in eclipse just then, having been absorbed into rock-and-roll only to be assigned a Jim Crow stigma in its more nearly pure forms.

Walker learned during the 1950s to shape his music according to the nature of any given audience. A set of privately held tape recordings from this period, cut during a party in Dallas' swanky Highland Park neighborhood, finds Walker minimizing the blue notes from his Gibson hollow-body electric guitar and singing more in the manner of some ofay crooner. The wealthy white folks might have imported Walker here in much the same manner that their Manhattan counterparts of times earlier had employed Bessie Smith, Josh White, or Huddie "Leadbelly" Ledbetter to enliven various ruling-class soirées. But the instructions now were different. Instead of bringing a taste of the juke joint to Silk Stocking Row, Walker found himself better advised to assimilate, at least as a vendor of entertainment.

"If folks want Perry Como, then we can Perry Como it up with the best of 'em," Walker averred. "In South Central [Los Angeles], somebody came up with a term for it: *sepia Sinatra*. It's not the blues, but it sells where it sells."

But we, and T-Bone Walker, were talking about Mantan Moreland.

"Mantan's not working too awful much these days," Walker told me during the early 1960s. "Not like in the days before your time. Got him some stage gigs—Hollywood's been scared off of him by pressure from our own blessed N.A.A.C.P.—and some record-and-radio gigs, reciting Bible stories and doing the littler Negro nightclubs where people remember him more fond-like. Same reason I enjoy playing these little ol' Colored Town clubs, nowadays. Not as *highfalutin'* and dicey. Mantan deserves better."[1]

The repressive attitude of which T-Bone Walker spoke so long ago had made it unsafe, or *incorrect*, to admire Moreland's pioneering work. This condition is particularly so in the case of his signature horror-and-whodunit movies, which pivot on a black comedian's indignant and laugh-inspiring responses to extravagant menaces.

In *Dracula* and its kindred films, Edward Van Sloan and Lionel Barrymore, *et al.*, have their sanctified icons and their suffocating garlands of garlic and bat-thorn with which to subdue Bela Lugosi and his living-dead offspring. Confront Boris Karloff, or any of the heirs to his life-stolen-from-God role of the Frankenstein Monster, with a controlled burst of flame, and any threat of rampage is dispensed with: Promethean fire, fought with Promethean fire. Mantan Moreland had his laughter—that, and the good sense to scram or to stand and fight, as suited the occasion—with which to assail the Dead Who Walk, the Demon Blues made rancid flesh.

---

[1] Walker pronounced the name, by the way, as *MAN-TAN*, stressing each syllable with equal weight. Some other acquaintances would put more of a *MAN-tuhn* spin on it, as if attempting a British accent. Closer collaborators, from Flournoy E. Miller in the early days to Janet Taylor in later times, would address Moreland simply as "'Tan."

# 7
# Beating the Blues, Eight- and/or Four-to-the-Bar

> I keeps laughin' instead of cryin'—
> I must keep fightin' until I'm dyin'.
> —Paul Robeson's 1952 revision
> of Oscar Hammerstein's lyric for "Old Man River"

"It makes no diff'rence if I win or lose—I got a system to beat the blues," sang Ella Logan, recording in Hollywood with the Spirits of Rhythm on September 4, 1941.[1] The song, "From Monday On," was almost a generation old by that time, and the "system to beat the blues" thus suggested by its white but black-inspired composers, Harry Barris and Bing Crosby, is nothing more nor less than the blues' own sure-fire formula of "laughin' to keep from cryin'," recast in terms more baroque but no more eloquent.

Mantan Moreland had coincidentally re-codified that same attitude earlier in 1941 with his scene-stealing and show-stopping portrayal of a wool-dyed denizen of Harlem, transplanted by virtue of an airplane crash to some Third World Hoodoo Hades, in Jean Yarbrough's *King of the Zombies*. Here, Moreland defies any and all attempts to transform him into a mo-

bilized stiff, finally out-lasting a conspiracy to cultivate a corps of living-dead cannon fodder for deployment by the Third Reich. Moreland declares the case closed with one of the strangest punch-lines ever uttered: "If there's *any*thing I wouldn't want to be *twice*, zombies is *both* of 'em!"[2]

The heroism is undeniable. The illusion of genial buffoonery complicates its perception as anything greater than extroverted comic relief, but heroism it is. This argument rings especially true in *King of the Zombies*' scenario involving a stand-off against Voodoo, or *Vodun*, an African-Caribbean system of ancient faith, as simplified for popular consumption in American fiction. This Hollywood Voodoo serves to confront Moreland with a menace more ethnically appropriate than, say, Middle European vampirism or the *Frankenstein* yarns' neo-Greco-Roman conceit of power wrested from the heavens.

A Voodoo curse, in conceptual essence, relies upon the power of suggestion in order to transform its victim into his-or-her own worst enemy. Such a hoodoo can't harm you, but it might make you hurt yourself. By this principle, an *ouanga*, an object symbolic of a curse, can serve to leave its recipient agonizing his way into an early grave. A *papaloi*, a priest of Voodoo, might steal an article of clothing from a funeralized corpse and bestow that shirt or pair of trousers upon a fellow human being. The garment *per se* packs no particularly harmful charge—but inform its new wearer that he is swathed in a Dead Man's Shirt, and watch the power of morbid suggestion kick in to transform a fashion statement into a shroud-in-waiting. Every culture has its equivalent of a Pygmalion myth, the self-fulfilling prophecy, but this version in particular prizes the summoning of death over the activation of life.

Such psychology-as-supernaturalism served during the middle 1930s to jinx an entire moving-picture project, George Terwilliger's *Ouanga* (1936; a.k.a. *Love Wanga* and *Crime of Voodoo*), in its attempts to shoot authentic ceremonial footage in Haiti. A curse bestowed upon the crew at Port-au-Prince *apparently* forced Terwilliger's company to retrench in Jamaica, where the presumed curse *appeared* to follow along and jinx the venture further. Terwilliger nonetheless managed to complete his movie despite a treadmill path of hardships, injuries, and two deaths within the troupe.[3]

The more ambitious practitioners of Voodoo might (claim to) raise legions of the dead to perform menial, industrial or agrarian chores. Zombiism, they call it. This is hardly the theft of the life-bestowing fire of Prometheus and/or Mrs. Shelley's Dr. Frankenstein, but rather the suggestibility that causes a victim of zombiism to believe himself dead to the world but unable to roll over and croak. A form of enslavement and zero-budget forced labor results, perhaps caused and bolstered by hypnotism and controlled dosages of narcotics. This, at least, is the situation laid forth in the pop-anthropological literature of William B. Seabrook (whose credulous book of 1929, *The Magic Island*, introduced the term *zombie* to polite civilization) and fostered all along, with gradual infusions of *Frankenstein*-styled science fiction, by the movies, the pulp-fiction magazines and the comic books.

No telling whether *King of the Zombies* intends that its title creatures be taken literally as dead men, resurrected. But the attempted transformation of Mantan Moreland into one of their kind leans decisively toward the side of hypnotic control, more so than supernatural necromancy. Dour Henry Victor, playing the purported ruler mentioned in the title, commands Moreland's fixed attention and begins feeding him the repeated assurance that he has, indeed, become a zombie.[4] Moreland commences to mouth this assertion, as if mesmerized—and then snaps out of the apparent trance, only to resume the zombie-fied act while laboring to keep a straight face. He is stringing Victor along by playing the goof, hoodooing the hoodoo man, and the subterfuge will help to bring about a decisive undermining of this tropical outpost of Hitlerism.

But the act of playing the goof also served as something of a red flag, earning conspiratorial laughter from the paying customers and indignation from the sober-sided Afrocentric observers, while leaving it to the more sharply attuned viewers, of no particular color or class, to pick up on the artist's subversive sensibilities.

Subversive attitudes crop up now and again in black Hollywood before Moreland's heyday. Perhaps the most noticeable example is a throwaway line from Lincoln "Stepin Fetchit" Perry, in *Charlie Chan in Egypt* (1935): While attempting to woo a Nubian beauty (played by Anita Brown) while in the service of

Stepin Fetchin, at right—thoroughly out of his element in *Charlie Chan in Egypt*.

a desert expedition, Stepin Fetchit suggests that she might accompany him home to the American Southland, where he knows some folks who will provide her with "a *good* job." The sarcastic emphasis is unambiguous as to the notion of servitude, though occluded by the actor's contrived, keening drawl and his shuck-and-shuffle carriage.

Lincoln Perry (1902–1985) more commonly lent his patented play-acting character a figurative impotence, in the court-jester tradition, and he seldom dealt in nuance or subtext. Likely as not, the actor improvised that bit of business for *Charlie Chan in Egypt*, and the line either clicked with the cast and crew or went whizzing unnoticed into one ear and out the other. Stepin Fetchit's star was in gradual eclipse by the time of Mantan Moreland's decisive ascent, although the men were friends and occasional co-workers, and quite nearly the same age. But like Moreland, Perry was to experience a postwar scourging from the N.A.A.C.P. and allied interests. There is a gap of almost 20 years, from 1953 until a hit-and-miss attempt at a comeback of 1972–1976, in Perry's movie-town résumé, although he would capture the attention of the Associated Press and other news-syndicate services during the 1960s and '70s with a recurring plea that he might be forgiven for his long-ago successes as a living, breathing, ticket-selling caricature.

Moreland practiced a greater skill at the task of testing the resilience of the color bar. One knowledgeable enthusiast has replied to my earlier published accounts of Moreland's career with these observations:

"I've always felt that Mantan made many coded statements and actions that flew over the heads of the whites in the gallery and into the ears and eyes of blacks sitting in the balconies of those segregated theaters...," wrote Chris Chatfield of Cleveland, in December of 2002. The correspondence pertained to my collaborative book *Forgotten Horrors 2*, whose title-by-title movie commentaries cover a good deal of Moreland's work.

Chatfield's note adds this: "I think *King of the Zombies* is a good example: Mantan defies orders, is the first to spot the problem, and even (almost) implies [that he might be] a descendant of Andrew Jackson—'I'm Jefferson Jackson, named after my great-grandfather, who was President of the... [*a pause, here*] Knights of the Pink Garter!'" (The Knights of the Pink Garter would be a lodge-hall of the sort crucial to the civic life of black gentlemen, not unlike *Amos 'n' Andy*'s Mystic Knights of the Sea.)

"In another...," Chatfield's memo continues, "I believe [1940's] *Chasing Trouble*, [Moreland] gives his name as Thomas Jefferson, not long after the first modern-times book about Sally Hemming was published."⁵

**Marguerite Whitten and a ravenous Mantan Moreland in *King of the Zombies*.**

Yes, well, and those very lines of Moreland's—or their interpretations, as suggested here—had gone sailing clean over my white-guy-in-the-gallery head, despite repeated viewings and a clear-cut recognition of the defiant attitude that distinguishes Moreland as anything but the "Yowzah, Boss" type.

---

¹ That date, if anyone is keeping track of such things, fell a day after Mantan Moreland's 38th birthday.
² The lyrical texture of Moreland's delivery is largely a matter of *italicizing* the spoken word at the right moments, a deep-rooted Southern custom not unlike that of worrying or drawing out certain notes or jumping the tempo in a sung melody, slightly ahead of or behind the regimented cadence.
³ George E. Turner's and my coverage of George Terwilliger's *Ouanga* and the ordeal of its making can be found in *Forgotten Horrors: The Definitive Edition* (Midnight Marquee Press; 1999).
⁴ The title role of *King of the Zombies* had been intended for Bela Lugosi, who wound up starring instead in Monogram Pictures' production of *Invisible Ghost* (1941). A pairing of Lugosi with Mantan Moreland sounds almost too rich to bear contemplating.
⁵ Sally Hemming, of course, was the mulatto slave who seems ever likelier to have lived as an open-secret consort to the third President, and as mother to a handful of ill-acknowledged Jeffersonian heirs. Indignant rumors about such a sustained affair date from Jefferson's day.

# 8
# So Who's Bamboozling Whom, and to What Purpose?

>Wait a minute—wait a minute!
>—Mantan Moreland, 1941

Tough luck that none of this subversion-not-subservience approach of Mantan Moreland's had failed to register with Spike Lee when that capable, prolific and erratic filmmaker turned his slapdash artistry during 1999–2000 to a movie called *Bamboozled*. Provocative but wanton, not quite achieving the level of constructive satire, *Bamboozled* takes especial pains to sully the name of Mantan (though not specifically the name of Moreland) for the sake of a repetitive and ultimately unfunny gag. Lee's cavalier use of the name did not sit well with Moreland's surviving kin, who chose reasonably to interpret it as a pointless recurrence of the postwar blacklisting.

Lee's story, which seems a fusion-with-embellishments of Mel Brooks' *The Producers* (1968) and the Sidney Lumet–Paddy Chayefsky film *Network* (1976), has to do with a black writer who has found himself in a state of economic slavery to a suspiciously Fox- or WB-like television network. Under pressure to develop a hit program, Pierre Delacroix envisions a deliberately offensive throwback to minstrel-show caricature. Delacroix is portrayed by Damon Wayans, in a backhanded nod to the Wayans Bros.' own self-indulgent and perhaps ironic flirtations with stereotyping in commercial television. Lee's strategy here involves a thinly veiled lambasting of the Wayans-created teleseries *In Living Color* (1990–1994), with the punitive gimmick-casting of one of the parties responsible.

Delacroix, an opportunistic and cowardly intellectual snob, selects two hungry troupers (Savion Glover and Tommy Davidson) as his star players and rechristens them as Mantan—scarcely a mystery as to where Lee came up with that name—and Sleep 'n' Eat.[1]

Delacroix' predictably flawed strategy in *Bamboozled*—and thus a predictable flaw of Lee's scenario—is to concoct a program so offensive that it will trigger his firing; merely to quit would violate a lucrative contract. Against Delacroix' naïve expectations, the show proves tremendously popular across-the-board, reinstating images long believed vanquished. *Believed* vanquished, that is—until one examines the postmodern stereotypes that are part-and-parcel of modern-day gangsta'-rap society, which amounts largely to self-caricature, inflicted with big-business corporate encouragement for the sake of turning a trend-driven profit.

Lee's worthier attempt with *Bamboozled* is to mount a polemic with the mass audience's appetite for a lower common denominator in entertainment. This argument can only fall under the heading of So What Else Is New?—although Lee's motivating conceit is sufficiently audacious to make the argument appear somehow original. The attempt at satirization falls short, however, because it neglects to pitch anything resembling a remedy for an epidemic of questionable taste among the multicolored masses.

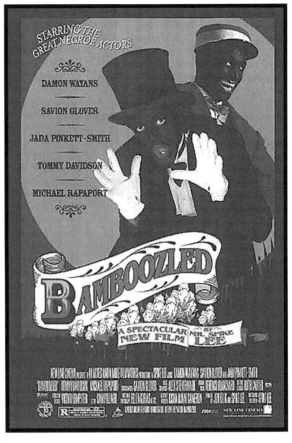

Lee explained himself, to an extent, in an interview in 2000 A.D. with *The Bergen Record* of North Jersey: "Ten years back, I thought Stepin Fetchit was an Uncle Tom...I've come to understand that, unlike us today, [such artists] didn't have a choice. And these guys were good artists. Mantan Moreland—that guy was funny. Bill 'Bojangles' Robinson—I don't think it was his choice to spend the best years of his life dancing with Shirley Temple. Hattie McDaniel had the famous quote, 'It's better to play a maid than be a maid.' So I've gained a much greater understanding... [N]owadays, we have choices—at least, more choices than Mantan Moreland or Stepin Fetchit."

*Time* magazine's Richard Corliss would cut somewhat deeper, in terms of perspective and context, by connecting *Bamboozled* with two turning points in the larger history of cinema: "The first great movie epic [1915's *The Birth of a Nation*] and the first talkie sensation [1927's *The Jazz Singer*] wallowed in racial derision." As opposed to *Bamboozled*, that is to say, which confines its wallowing to the embittered ironies implicit in derision. The redeeming grace of Lee's film, cemented by its confrontational gumption, is that Pierre Delacroix, who gazes casually into the Abyss for self-serving reasons, finds the Abyss not only gazing back but also drawing him inward—hook, line, and stereotype.

I have not trusted Spike Lee's tactics entirely since 1993's *Malcolm X*. Although that film turned out as an earnest and valid study of its intense subject and his troubled orbit, the picture had become Lee's assignment only after he had harangued its studio into favoring him as director-of-choice over a handful of comparably qualified white-guy talents. Or so Lee boasted to me during a pertinent interview in 1993, and other such published accounts convey this same attitude. This maneuver impressed me at the time as an outcropping of separatism, and it looks even more divisive when seen from a deeper perspective. The situation might bear interpreting as a Corporate Hollywood version of the naïve black protesters who descended upon one Southern mainstream newspaper after another during the 1980s, bearing placards reading: "If You Don't Look like Me, You Can't Write about Me!" Exclamation point.

The effect of that ill-advised newspaper-picketing campaign, of course, was to reinstate a separate-but-(un)equal system of personnel management within the journalistic arena, with black reporters consequently hired in greater numbers but assigned almost exclusively to cover black personalities and supposedly black issues. The upper management in mass media, meanwhile, has remained almost exclusively white, while taking condescending advantage of the illusion of ethnic diversification. To complicate matters, the Society of Professional Journalists—purportedly an inclusive organization—began during the 1990s to encourage the expansion of such splinter groups as the National Association of Black Journalists, the National Lesbian & Gay Journalists Association and so forth, in an ill-concealed push to restore the Old School white separatism of the general-purpose society. Better simply to hire reporters to report and then encourage their mingling on grounds of journalistic (not ethnic) solidarity, without attempting to fulfill some illusory and mercurial quota.[2]

This divisive trend can be traced with scarcely a detour to an altercation of the middle 1980s at the Dallas *Times Herald*, a once-lively, since-defunct newspaper. Here, the critic and humorist John Bloom, who also wrote under the pseudo-redneck name of Joe Bob Briggs, devoted an installment of his popular column, *Joe Bob Goes to the Drive-In*, to a frivolous spoof of a self-serious pop song called "We Are the World."

Now, "We Are the World" was just then garnering all manner of Socially Correct acclaim for its holier-than-thou opposition to hunger and disease in the Third World. Here was the grandstanding pose of the dilettante do-gooder, as struck by an assemblage of wealthy entertainers who might have accomplished results more helpful just by rolling up their high-fashion shirtsleeves on behalf of the Peace Corps. The backlash against Briggs (whom many people assumed to be an actual trailer-trash personage) was immediate, lethally well focused and utterly wrongheaded, for a contingent of Dallas' black citizenry chose to perceive Bloom/Briggs' spoof, "We Are the Weird," as a white-supremacist tirade. There followed a massed march upon the *Times Herald*'s newsroom, where the white-male majority of editors and publisher's lackeys responded by committing an impulsive act of applied bigotry in the name of Politically Correct mollification.

The newspaper's brass replied, in essence: "*Ooh*! Negroes! And they're *angry* with us! What can we give them that will make them go away?" The proper sacrifice of easy appeasement proved to be John Bloom's head upon a platter. Figuratively speaking, I mean. Whereupon the management cratered on a loyal and popular journalist and administered to its black readership an insult greater than any that had been imagined. Everybody went away with an inflicted delusion of relief and/or the happy fulfillment of a vengeful impulse. Everybody, that is, except for John Bloom. Bloom rebounded soon enough, retaining the Joe Bob Briggs identity as a free-agent satirist of greater honesty and ferocity than the *Times Herald* would have allowed him to become.

Now, Bloom was no more giving the razz to black people than he was advocating a perpetuation of Global Famine. But then, neither was Bloom offering a particularly well-considered parody with "We Are the Weird." A featured columnist staring a relentless deadline squarely in its ugly face will commit facile hackwork sooner than acknowledge defeat—yes, and I've sure-enough done so, now and again—and thus did that tossed-off column take on the unforeseen roles of a test and a turning point for the limits of *quid-pro-quo* tolerance within the popular culture.

And from that easily mimicked crisis, there stems the present day's odd amenity among newspapers of assigning reporters of any given color to specialize in topics of a matching hue. The tactic is guaranteed to placate the Human Relations bureaucrats who keep score on such matters.[3] But in fact, it amounts to nothing neither more nor less than *carte blanche* for the white-owned news-packaging companies to foster a strange and cynical system of internal segregation, while pretending to pay homage to some nebulous but fashionable concept of Cultural Diversity. This is what passes for progress in a reciprocally vain and selfish society.

## II

Spike Lee's *Bamboozled* remains a fascinating job of agitative propaganda, all the same. Its more incisive moments bear mentioning in the same breath with the artist's premature masterwork, *Do the Right Thing* (1989). The character of Mantan, as deployed in *Bamboozled*, proves less abhorrent a figure than even Lee might have intended, but Lee's use of the name itself verges upon gratuitous slander. ("How many fellers can there be named Mantan?" Robert Shaw had asked.) The cavalier deployment of the name also betrays a failed understanding of Moreland's body of work, which resists the watermelon grin at every turn in favor of a more ironic and *knowing* smile.

The evidence of Moreland's tendency to test the limits of the color bar can be found in even so early a film as *Riders of the Frontier* (1939), where

the comic turns the supporting role of a chuckwagon cook into a forward-thinking bit of buddy-casting with star player Maurice "Tex" Ritter. Ritter (1905–1974) clearly prefers Moreland's company over that of the white ruffians riding this particular frontier, and the actors share a brief discussion about the fallacies of prejudice before settling down to the business of singing a comical duet. Their reading of the traditional "Boll Weevil Song" bespeaks jovial friendship, although Ritter's extravagant use of a black-styled dialect also lends the scene an air of caricature that many viewers today would find in need of retroactive correction. As though such were possible, short of a film's suppression or destruction.

Marcella Moreland Young found *Bamboozled* particularly offensive, on a personal level.

"You'd think a big-shot Hollywood director would have the courtesy to call up and let me know he was about to slander my Daddy in some new movie," she complained in 2002. "But no. That picture came out without much fanfare, and somebody told me I should go and see it—and I was devastated. It was a humiliating experience, to see my Daddy's name appropriated for such purposes. And it *is* a unique name, y'know."

Apart from a tentative complaint to the Screen Actors Guild, however, Marcella pursued no approach to Spike Lee or his representatives.

"I just shouldn't've even gone to see that picture, that's all," she said.

---

[1] That second moniker wants a bit of explaining: The black comedian Willie Best (1913–1962) had billed himself briefly as Sleep 'n' Eat during the early 1930s. Best's work dealt almost entirely in facile and trepidatious stereotypes, however endearing, during a period when Moreland was confronting, inverting, and undermining such popular images in their own terms.

[2] The Texas journalist Chuck Jackson, who had been the editor of a *Sepia* magazine spin-off called *Soul Teen* during the 1960s, often told of his approach around 1969 to the *Star-Telegram* of Fort Worth, Texas, to apply for a general-assignments newsgathering job. "I want to be a reporter," Jackson informed the hell-bent-for-Status Quo editor, Jack Tinsley. Replied Tinsley: "We don't have any openings just now for porters." (Or so Jackson told it, occasionally in the presence of Jack Tinsley.) Jackson persisted, and he became only the second black reporter in the paper's history—gradually moving into management.

[3] I prefer to steer clear of any and all Human Relations Departments, except perhaps for encounters of a fixed purpose and a limited time-span. While collaborating with one H.R. executive around 1995 on a corporate-charity project, I sent an impatient memorandum to her office with the suggestion that "we should get cracking on this effort, A.SA.F.P." She showed up in my office the next day with the memo, having highlighted its "A.S.A.F.P." reference in livid red ink. "What is the meaning of this expression?" she asked. "Why, don't you know?" I answered, thinking faster than usual under such circumstances. "That's short for 'As Soon as Feasibly Possible.'" Content with this explanation, she left and promised to "get cracking" on our venture. The following week, I noticed that she had begun using "A.S.A.F.P." in her own memoranda.

# 9
# An Intolerance of Tolerance

Oh, yeah!
—Tim "Kingfish" Moore, 1951

Perhaps it is the very illusion of incorrectitude, the appeal of the officially or artificially forbidden, that has provoked in more recent times a dawning general rediscovery of Mantan Moreland. Such temptations lend themselves to an exploration of the cunning subtexts with which Moreland proved himself an artist of staying power and relevance beyond his time astride the planet. People want to understand, and an understanding requires a confrontation with controversy. Oftentimes, one comes away from such an encounter wondering what all the ruckus was about, in the first place.

The realm of cultural heritage remains the one combative arena where the agents of Political Correctness must be intolerant of tolerance, what with innumerable historical provocations for reactionary consternation, obfuscation and condemnation. The early 20th century novelist Earl Derr Biggers can be taken to task for creating "a Chinese Uncle Tom" (as *The Saturday Review* once put it, with all due self-seriousness) in his popular heroic character, the detective Charlie Chan. The most cursory reading of a Chan adventure will find the genial sleuth brimming with ethnic self-esteem, with the occasional militant outburst. Meanwhile, the Swedish-born actor Warner Oland comes in for a recurring posthumous harangue for "playing yellowface," as the saying goes, with his long-running Depression-era impersonation of that same Charlie Chan (to say nothing of Oland's earlier portrayals of Sax Rohmer's villainous Mandarin, Dr. Fu Manchu). And never mind that Oland claimed Asiatic ancestry via the Northlands incursions of the Khans.

Mark Twain, America's most enduring satirist, still drives the correctionists in our midst to a blithering outrage because he wrote humanely of class-and-color relations of the 19th-century Southland in the uninhibited terminology of his own 19th-century Southland.

Mel Blanc's affectionate polyethnic dialect comedy—notably, as the Warner Bros. cartoon character Speedy Gonzales and in the intermittent vocal impersonation of Eddie "Rochester" Anderson, Blanc's co-worker with Jack Benny's radio-and-television troupe—makes for a convenient whipping boy, generations after Blanc's innocent heyday. And entire careers and bodies of work of pioneering black performers have been compromised because they neglected to reckon with the retroactive armchair quarterbacking of P.C.-ism.

Mantan Moreland is the most significant casualty of this persistent movement, and hence the great near-tragedy. A more fully realized downfall, of course, was balked by the artist's refusal to fade away or to alter his style. The cultural bludgeonings of just the closing half of the last century include the forced demise of *Amos 'n' Andy,* a favorite in households of many colorations as a network-television showpiece during the earlier 1950s. Less noticeable, during the 1960s, was an attempt straight out of Ray Bradbury's *Fahrenheit 451* to destroy surviving prints of Dudley Murphy's "St. Louis Blues" (1929), a short subject containing the only moving-picture performance of the great singer Bessie Smith. This campaign was carried out by a mostly youthful and bourgeois-intellectual coalition of the National Association for the Advancement of Colored People.

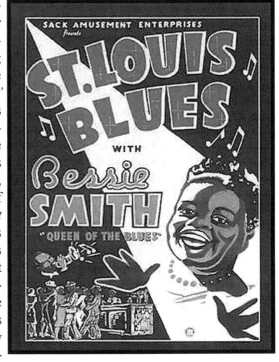

Moreland was among the few most gifted, and handily the most prolific, of many entertainers to be hounded into obscurity by such mid-century purges. Some might-have-been casualties would reinvent themselves, in curious ways: Jackie "Moms" Mabley retrenched successfully via a conspicuous political realignment as a champion of the Civil Rights movement; she wound up working opposite Moreland toward the ends of their lives.[1] Dewey "Pigmeat" Markham, who had performed in black-on-black makeup in perpetuation of the rapidly fading minstrel-show style, mounted a resurgence with more of a rock 'n' roller stance and benefited accordingly.[2] Paul Robeson—never a comedian as such, but capable of finding the humor in any role—nurtured a conspicuously prominent, duly embittered reclusiveness in response to a blacklisting bordering on house arrest from the political establishment and the federal government itself.

Moreland stuck with the dignity of honest work on his own terms, come what might and however large or small the opportunity.

---

[1] Moms Mabley and Mantan Moreland would appear together in 1969 in showcased supporting roles on the "Lovers' Quarrel" episode of network television's *The Bill Cosby Show*.
[2] Pigmeat Markham's recording of "Here Come de Judge," a parody of courtroom decorum, crossed over sufficiently well to mainstream acceptance to earn Markham a berth, or a bench, on *Rowan & Martin's Laugh-In* during the late 1960s.

## 10
# Work Is Work, and the More, the Better

> If everybody doesn't want it, nobody gets it.
> —Roger Price, *The Great Roob Revolution*; 1970

The foremost comedian of his ill-appreciated league of show business, Mantan Moreland was an all-'round entertainer first and a horror-movie star as a lesser priority. Work is work, after all, in Hollywood, and genre-fled typecasting is oftener a consequence of registering strongly in a particular type of film than of setting out to identify oneself with it. Examples are as diversified as Boris Karloff, ZaSu Pitts, Fay Wray, Erich von Stroheim, John Carradine, Bob Steele, and Bela Lugosi—who shared in common a great dramatic versatility that never quite could overcome their overwhelming identification with narrow areas of specialization.

Moreland's earliest movie, a short-subject diversion from 1933 called "That's the Spirit," is a supernaturally motivated entry—more musically and comically attuned, though, than out-and-out scary. And it is in such later spookers and offbeat mysteries as *King* (and *Revenge*) *of the Zombies, Phantom Killer, The Strange Case of Dr. Rx* and the diminishing last cycle of *Charlie Chan* features, with their ghastly episodes of wholesale homicide, that Moreland left his most resounding statements of an ultimately thwarted career as a studio-based actor.

One thwarting was hardly enough, of course. After Moreland's cultural enemies, gratuitously ill-provoked and self-appointed, had hogtied his prospects at the dawn of the 1950s, shaming the motion-picture industry into minimizing and marginalizing his brand of jive-talking humor, Moreland appears to have faced the tantalizingly unrealized prospect of membership in the Three Stooges at Columbia Pictures. Scattered returns of the 1960s and '70s—including a slight reassertion of his identification with horror pictures, with a showy but expendable role in Jack Hill's *Spider Baby, or the Maddest Story Ever Told* (1964)—found Moreland consistently well prepared for a more sweeping resurgence that should have happened.

His frustration had nothing to do with lapsed artistry, for Moreland's comic/dramatic timing in 1970 was as whiplash-accurate, despite an alarming raspiness that had taken hold of his voice, as it sounded formerly in 1940. The obstruction has everything, rather, to do with the ruinous myth of race, which insists upon dividing humankind into sub-sets from which preordained patterns of behavior are expected. The various races, thus falsely designated, have proved only too eager to buy into such divisive dogma, whose success relies upon a herd mentality in order to accomplish its dirty work. And there is no shortage of herd mentality among the Masses. To this day and probably beyond, the mass media continue to accept and promote race as a fundamental state of being, like Flat Earthers clinging to cherished beliefs long since proved false.

I resist herewith the temptation to digress further, and refer any and all to Nick Tosches' provocative and fascinating book *Where Dead Voices Gather* (2001)—and specifically to its concise discussion of the Human Genome Project of 2000 A.D.

The book overall is a bracing, argumentative consideration of the minstrel tradition, such as it was, as a warped and seductive mirror of class-and-color relations. Tosches takes especial pains to know the un-knowable story of a diehard minstrel singer and humorist, white-in-blackface, named Emmett Miller. Mantan Moreland does not figure in *Where Dead Voices Gather*, but his pivotal show-business teammate, Flournoy E. Miller (1887–1971), is a recurring presence.

# 11
# A Collision Between Good Fortune and Bad

> You want to know what racism is? It's the belief that there even is any such of a thing as *race,* to *begin* with. Whatever color you might be, if you believe that *you,* or anybody else, must belong to any sub-races within the *human race*—well, why, then, you're a *racist.*
> —Rudy Ray "Dolemite" Moore,
>    Backstage conversation; 1988

It had become Mantan Moreland's good fortune to learn early on that all manner of audiences loved his shenanigans and his wide-awake wisecracking patter, especially in counterpoint with supernatural terrors and what Moreland himself might have called "murder mo' foulest" if ever he had found himself afoot in an Agatha Christie picture. It was Moreland's misfortune to have become typecast as a black artist associated with finding humor in the midst of horror, at a moment in history when his entertaining and universally identifiable brand of juba-to-jive comedy would suddenly become the antithesis of Afrocentric uplift.

Thus do the Right-leaning and Leftward extremes of American culture and politics find more in common than either is often willing to grant: The hell-bent-for-witch-burning House Committee on UnAmerican Activities pronounced the mighty Paul Robeson (1898–1976) a menace because Robeson—quite apart from the naïve Soviet allegiances with which he had estranged himself from the U.S. of A.—had played a despot in Eugene O'Neill's *The Emperor Jones* (filmed in 1933) and therefore must have fancied himself "the black Stalin among Negroes." Or so a defrocked Communist named Manning Johnson testified, in all self-seriousness, during the H.U.A.C. hearings in post-World War II Washington, D.C.

Right around this same time, the N.A.A.C.P. pronounced Mantan Moreland a demeaning stereotype (and thus a threat to the Holy War for Social Parity) because he played most prominently a valet/chauffeur/porter/bellhop/elevator pilot who made no bones about his unwillingness to share his quarters with zombies, mad doctors or rampant killers. (Paul Robeson, for that matter, can be seen indulging something of a superstitious streak in *The Emperor Jones.*)

Moreland registered strikingly in practically any assignment, of course. It was while working on the now-comical, now-creepy *The Strange Case of Dr. Rx*

**As a fugitive from a chain gang, Paul Robeson radiates menace in Dudley Murphy's *The Emperor Jones* (1933).**

with Samuel "Shemp" Howard—a founding member of the family act known as the Three Stooges, long since gone solo by the time of this movie—that Moreland inadvertently announced himself as a favored candidate for membership in some eventual configuration of the Stooges. Which never happened, of course, but not for want of trying on the part of brothers Shemp and Moe Howard and their "adopted cousin," as Moe called him, Larry Fine. This, according to a late-in-life reminiscence from Moe Howard.

With the magic of Photoshop we can imagine how Three Stooges would appear with Mantan as the third stooge. If only...

But we're getting ahead of the game, so Moe about that later. So would an integrated Three Stooges ensemble have proved uncomfortably progressive for the culturally stodgy Hollywood establishment of the 1950s? Fearful on the one hand of plunking a black Southerner such as Moreland amidst the traditionally white-guy *Yiddishe* Stooges, and, on the other hand, of incurring the embargo-happy wrath of Moreland's influential Nemesis, the N.A.A.C.P., Columbia Pictures took a Big Pasadena on what would appear to have been an earnest proposal by Moe Howard—and in the process denied both Moreland and the Three Stooges a promise of resurgence.

Only one's imagination (with a little nudging from a *faux*-Stooges film of 1942 called "Phoney Croneys") can reveal the fuller potential of such a teaming. But imagination is amply fueled here by a popular rediscovery of Mantan Moreland as a dependably busy talent of Old Hollywood: He was a ticket-selling mainstay of the tiny studio known as Monogram Pictures Corporation, which afforded him a stable home-base situation with a long-term contract as actor and improvisational writer. He was a celebrity within the demimonde of black Vaudeville and the black-ensemble movie companies, which kept their "All-Colored" attractions in circulation for years at a stretch as opposed to the few-months' shelf-life of most of the major studios' productions. And Moreland was a favored character man and bit player at most of the major studios.

# 12
# Everything To Gain and Nothing To Lose

> From here on down, it's uphill all the way.
> —Walt Kelly, ca. 1950

His overall body of work, and its general survival to newfound recognition, argue persuasively that Mantan Moreland probably accomplished more good for the advancement of civil rights in America—and for society as a class—than any of the self-serious forces of rejection and censorship whose agents ultimately stood athwart of his career.

Like the more prominent but less prolific Hattie McDaniel and Louise Beavers, like Matthew "Stymie" Beard in his short-lived span of *Our Gang* stardom, Moreland demonstrated to the dominant-by-economics culture all that it had to gain by embracing its black citizens as equals. White people in a forcibly segregated America could come away from *King of the Zombies, Up in the Air* or *The Strange Case of Dr. Rx*, or most of the *Charlie Chan* pictures of 1944–1949, thinking not necessarily what a terrific movie they had seen—far from it, in too many instances—but rather what a likeably funny fellow that guy Moreland was.

It helps not to dwell upon the social standing of his roles, the janitors and valets and chauffeurs, or upon their *de facto* subservience to white players who weren't half as much fun to watch: Moreland undermined the reality, and the social-mirror realism, of typecasting and commandeered the moment to such an extent that he might as well have been calling the shots.

As Marcella Moreland Young has noted: "Daddy was a painstaking writer of his comedy routines, okay, but he also had a gift for making up precisely the right saying on the spot, especially when the cameras were rolling. He'd come up with these out-of-the-blue lines and exchanges, there, at Monogram Pictures, and the directors—Phil Rosen was a favorite of ours, and Jean Yarbrough—would keep on rolling with the scene, oftener than not.[1] The bigger studios were less encouraging, in that respect. But Monogram, it seems, just sort of let Daddy direct himself, and he always came up with something finer than what had been written for him to do or say."

In a particularly forward-thinking series of buddy pictures including the murder mystery *Up in the Air* (1940), Moreland and Frankie Darro, a glib and personable white-guy comedian, played characters with two qualities in common. They shared second-class citizenship and an amateur-sleuth talent for beating the law to the solution of any case.[2]

And as heard earlier from Hattie McDaniel: Better to *play* a maid, or a manservant, than to *be* one, indeed. Moreland was nobody's servant off-camera, and indeed he made something of a chronic joke of the recurring complaint that he couldn't keep good housekeeping help in wartime Los Angeles.

"Mantan Moreland... would rather build a new house than dust the furniture in his old one," declared a press release circulated during 1945 by Monogram Pictures' publicity department.

The prefabricated news story continued: "The only trouble was that there was no such thing to be found in Los Angeles. After many weeks of unsuccessful apartment hunting, [Moreland] finally decided to turn carpenter to remodel a five-car garage into living quarters."

Further, the notice quoted Moreland: "It makes my bones ache to do so much work, but it's better than cleaning up those seven rooms every time a new maid shoves off to work in an aircraft factory." The anonymous publicist capped the story with this: "Moreland, who has finished the interior of the garage behind an apartment building he owns, has named his new home 'Monogram Ranch.'"

In another of Monogram's stop-the-presses news dispatches, from 1949, Moreland declared: "Hollywood has been very good to me. If I had it to do all over again, I'd come to Hollywood sooner." The quotation continues:

> I own a house in Los Angeles, an apartment in New York, a cabin near Lake Elsinore, California, two dogs, and two cars, and I'm married to a very wonderful woman. That's pretty good for a fellow who got his start in show business as a barefooted dancer, because he didn't have money for shoes.'

Yes, and that prosperous-sounding press release had been prepared to accompany the picture with which Hollywood would cease being very good to

Mantan Moreland. The film was *Sky Dragon*, the closing installment in Monogram Pictures' *Charlie Chan* series of 1944–1949.

Moreland would not grace the screen again until the middle 1950s, with a brief run of in-concert music-and-comedy showcases (*Rock 'n' Roll Revue*, *Rhythm & Blues Revue*, and so forth, from 1955–1956) and a network-television revival of *The Green Pastures* (a 1957 installment of the *Hallmark Hall of Fame* series). *The Green Pastures* derives from the densely dialectified Bible stories of Roark Bradford (1896–1948)—a white Tennessean who had predicated his career upon the pleasant-natured exploitation of something resembling a Black Narrative Voice.

---

[1] Philip E. Rosen (1888–1951) was a pioneering camera artist in the moving-picture industry, and founding president of the American Society of Cinematographers. Rosen became a prolific director of low-budget thrillers, as early as the 1930s. Jean W. Yarbrough (1900–1975) came to the cinema as an assistant director during the 1920s, working his way into a key identification with comedies and horror films—often combining the idioms to striking effect within a single picture, as with 1940's tongue-in-cheek *The Devil Bat* and 1941's *King of the Zombies*, Mantan Moreland's signature picture.

[2] A pertinent aside from Moreland enthusiast William F. Chase: "Speaking of Darro and Moreland, I have a print of a David Sharpe cheapie called *Social Error*, made in 1935. Sharpe's valet is played by Fred 'Snowflake' Toones. And it really does look like a blueprint for the Darro & Morelanders." North Carolinan Fred Toones (1906–1962) was a busy player in Hollywood from 1928 into the post-WWII years, with a winning personality but little inclination to undermine any stereotypes.

# 13
# A Mantan for All Seasons, So Long as the Seasons Keep Coming

> Lawd, you made the night too long.
> —Sam M. Lewis & Victor Young, 1932

> Sam, you made the pants too long.
> —Milton Berle, 1940

Mantan Moreland was born on September 3, 1903,[1] in the town of Monroe, in Northeastern Louisiana—the locals pronounce the name as "*Mun*-row"—and became enchanted as a child with the act of provoking laughter.

Just as *Yiddishe* America had its Borscht Belt, which blended itself into the cultural mainstream with such significant artists as the radio comic Menasha Skulnik, Milton "Mr. Television" Berle and the movies' Jerry Lewis, the black Southland had its Chitlin' Circuit. This distinctive mutation of medicine-show minstrelsy-into-Southern Vaudeville, often borne on circus trains and highway caravans, brought before Moreland a procession of comical troubadours (whites imitating blacks, blacks imitating whites imitating blacks, and infinitely so forth back-and-forth), blues singers of rustic, folkloric origins and citified, commercialized ambitions and melodramatic troupes. A saying common among Northern black entertainers who toured the Southland allowed as how one might travel South via Greyhound—but head back Northward by bloodhound. More of that laughin' to keep from cryin'. From such nomadic talents, Moreland can only have taken the inspiration to hit the road in search of larger opportunities. He could make his own household laugh, so why not the rest of the whole wide world?

He had not become Moreland yet, or even Mantan, except within a very close family circle that contained a distinct element of rip-snorting outlaw legendry. And so any description of the earliest stages of his career requires a different name for the protagonist. Who *was* this guy, anyhow?

Both *Moreland* and *Mantan*, to say nothing of their memorable combination, amounted to his birthright. But he had been born with the comparably resonant name of Jesse James Brodnax.

His mother, Marcella Brodnax, and her Louisiana kin had descended from the 18th- and 19th-century West Virginia plantation lineage of Bordeneaux-become-Brodnax. The name and its streamlined variant are of French-settler origins, of course. The captive-immigrant Africans who lived and multiplied as slaves to the Bordeneaux clan had been assigned that surname as a matter of paternalistic feudal custom.

The teenaged Marcella Brodnax had become involved early on in the last century with an otherwise married family man named Frank Moreland. Jesse James Brodnax was their offspring—scarcely acknowledged by his father until the child had begun skirting his teen years.

"The only thing Daddy really ever told me about my grandfather Frank Moreland, aside from his having this whole other family that was off-limits to my Daddy, was that Frank was a violinist," Mantan's daughter, Marcella Moreland Young, recalled in 2004. "Not a fiddler, but a classical violinist, and an accomplished one, at that. So Daddy told me.

"Now, Frank Moreland was married, and he had these four other kids with his legal wife, and he just left Daddy's raising, pretty much, to my Daddy's mother and her mother," continued Marcella Young. "My Grandmother Marcella died young, at about the age of 24, when Daddy would have been, oh, about 10 years old. And my great-grandmother, Mandy Brodnax, who was my Grandmother Marcella's mother, continued on with his raising until *she* died, when Daddy would have been about 14."

Pertinent official records have proved lacking, if any such documents had existed or had been maintained in the first place. Such vacancies in the public record might be ascribed to such factors as an out-of-wedlock birth, the rural Southland's quaint custom of ignoring the day-by-day comings and goings of its black citizens unless trouble was afoot, and the geographical immensity of a provincial parish—Old World Catholic Louisiana's term for *county*—that once had covered the state's northeastern corner. This sector has long since been divided into the parishes of Ouachita (containing Monroe as the county seat), and Madison, Tensas, East Carroll and West Carroll, Morehouse, Union, Caldwell and Franklin.

Incorporated as a municipality in 1871, almost a century after its emergence as a civilian settlement branched off from Colonial Spain's Fort Miro, Monroe had taken its name in 1819 from the *James Monroe*, the first steamboat to navigate the Ouachita River.[2] The town is the commercial hub of an area whose economy rests upon a basis of soybeans, cotton, rice, cattle and lumber. Monroe's population was swelling toward a solid thousand by the arrival of the 20th century. The discovery in 1916 of the Monroe Gas Field brought about a sweeping boom-town industrialization, but the decline of such resources in times more recent has seen a dramatic shrinkage—from 60,000 residents in 1980 to 53,000 in 2000.

Ouachita Parish has an unstable history of maintaining its historic courthouses. A stucco annex to the original 1816 courthouse proved itself sturdy into modern times, but a more imposing courthouse, raised in 1860, stood for only four years before its burning in a gunboat siege from the Northern Army—an episode of the Civil War, of course. Ouachita waited some 20 years, then, before its local government built a third courthouse that stood finished in 1883—the one that might most likely have contained vital statistics pertaining to Mantan Moreland's more immediate ancestors. Most of the Hall of Records documents did not survive the transfer to a fourth courthouse, which was raised during 1924–1926 and served chiefly to end a cherished tradition of public hangings with the installation of a Gallows Room adjoining the upper-story Ouachita Parish Jail.

So we can learn, here, to get along without the stock-in-trade biographical shinplaster of blurred copies of microfilmed birth-and-death certificates. Assuming that any of the reigning authorities of the day had bothered with such niceties on behalf of its lower-tier citizenry, in the first place.

Denied much of a formally recognized family by circumstance, the boy who would become Mantan Moreland set out to develop a family on what terms he could control.

"Now as he got older, Daddy then came to have quite a bit more contact with his father, Frank Moreland," said Marcella Young. "He didn't exactly get rejected, there, but neither did he get welcomed into the Morelands' household."

Somewhere along about this point, now, the question of nomenclature becomes complicated. Why Jesse James?

"Daddy was christened with that name by his grandmother, Mandy, in honor of Jesse James," Marcella told me.

Okay, then, and would that be *the* Jesse James?

"None other," said Marcella. "You know—the *outlaw*, the one they made up all those songs about."

A pause to allow this revelation to sink in, then: "Or so Daddy's own personal family legend goes, and it'd be a shame to dismiss all that as just a tall tale when my Daddy could tell the story with such conviction."

The James legend runs deeper yet, though. Conventional wisdom holds that Jesse James had met his Maker in 1882, when ambushed by a fellow owlhoot, Robert Ford, who had given in to the temptation of a bounty promised by Governor Thomas Crittenden of Missouri.

The more fascinating and problematical lore, however, maintains that James, then, used that ambush to feign his demise—and then carried on for decades more, hiding out under a variety of aliases in Louisiana and Texas. The most extravagant version finds James living on to the age of 103 in 1951 and traces his final resting place to a graveyard in North Central Texas.

And that's what I like about the South, if I can get away with stealing a line from the minstrel-turned-jazzman Andy Razaf. The Southland's heritage of storytelling, I mean to say, is its most likable aspect—more so, even, than hoedown fiddling and/or the blues, the scent of magnolia sweet and fresh, or the entrenched custom of eating a mess of barbecue and guzzling red soda-water down in Navasota, Texas, on the 19th day of any given June. This appreciation applies in particular to those whoppers of a caliber so outlandish that they would inspire my own storytelling grandmother, Lillian Beatrice Ralston Wilson Lomen, to wrap up any such yarn with this declaration: "Well, it's all true, 'cept for the parts that's not, and if *they* ain't true, then they *ought* to be." And naysayers need not apply, because most tales worth the telling require an instinctive suspension of disbelief.

The long-term-survival version of Jesse James' strange and flamboyant story tends almost by accident to bear out, or at least to dovetail with, Mantan Moreland's account of his christening. Moreland also would tell his daughter that the owlhoot Jesse James (having survived the assassination attempt of 1882) was a family friend who spent much of his time on the dodge with the House of Brodnax in Monroe, Lousiana. A big personality requires a big autobiography, even if the medium is confined to the privately spoken word. Not unlike John Henry or Stagger Lee—or Jesse James, or Mantan Moreland.

**Jesse James Brodnax, a.k.a. Mantan Moreland, was named after infamous outlaw Jesse James.**

"Jesse and Frank James and their gang, so Daddy told it, lived on very friendly terms with the black settlers in rural Louisiana," Marcella Young continued with her account of her father's account. "There was always the opportunity for shelter, there, and a place to lay low, where the white law wouldn't think to go looking for them. The blacks down there would hide Jesse out and feed him, and he'd leave with them some money when he headed back out for parts unknown. And Jesse James had a standing welcome at my grandmother's house. Supposedly, anyhow.

"And so Daddy grew up in the company of his namesake, Jesse James, as a frequent houseguest. Daddy spoke very fondly of the man he had known as Jesse James."

The telling sounds almost like a prototype for a *Forrest Gump* scenario. A recurring line from Moreland's Hollywood years bears mentioning here: "I saw what I saw when I *saw* it!"

**An 1880 census purports to document a fixed abode, and a prototypical alias, for Jesse James. So much bureaucratic busy work, of course, and irrelevant to anyone immune to Obsessive-Compulsive Disorder.**

And so much, at any rate, for the christening as Jesse James Brodnax, and for the eventual reclamation of the paternal surname of Moreland. But whence the name of Mantan?

Once again, Marcella Moreland Young invokes the name of that more notorious Jesse James:

"Daddy's grandmother, who essentially had raised Daddy, had given him this nickname, Mantan, when he was little. She made up a rhyme with this name, and it became their own personal song: 'Mantan the Funnyman,' she called him," said Marcella. "Because he *was* a funny man. I think my Daddy must've been *born* laughing.

"But now, as to the context or any deeper origins of that name, Mantan— well, don't ask *me*, because I haven't a clue. Daddy never had a clue, either, about where such a name might have come from. Just something that his grandmother made up, I suppose."

Is it coincidental that the grandmother's name, Mandy, shares a syllable in common with *Mantan*? Just wondering. Then there is the self-evident truth that Mantan was by nature a tan man. Which summons to mind the only other prominent instance of a like-sounding proper name: A cosmetic product called Man-Tan, introduced during the 1960s as a virile combination of scented shaving lotion and skin-bronzing solution, served chiefly to turn its users an embarrassing shade of streaked orange, assuming that a user had started out fair of complexion. Which has no bearing here, beyond a homonymous resonance and a bit of gratuitous absurdity. So did the manufacturer of Man-Tan skin balm owe a licensing fee to Mantan Moreland?

But Marcella Young has the floor: "And here's where Jesse James comes back into the picture, the way my Daddy told it," she added. "His version has it that Jesse was moving back-and-forth, gallivantin' hither and yon through Louisiana, during those early years of the 20th century, and he and my Daddy got to be great pals.

"Daddy had this natural eye-rolling thing that he'd do, that little facial-expression business that he grew up with and then made into a kind of trademark in his movies, and he'd tell me how he used to make Jesse James laugh that way. Daddy was doin' the 'google-eyes' business before there was any *Barney Google* character in the funnypapers.[3]

"So it seems that Jesse picked up Daddy's grandmother's song about 'Mantan the Funnyman,' and made up more words to it—you know, like a little rhyming thing. I don't suppose anyone ever wrote down any of the words to that song—probably too busy laughing to bother with keeping a written account of it."

Moreland was about 14 when he ran away to join the circus. His Grandmother Mandy had died, and Frank Moreland, though not exactly estranged from his extracurricular son, offered nothing in the way of encouragement for Mantan to stay planted in Monroe.

"Daddy had no one, really, in Monroe," said Marcella. "His immediate family, such few of them as there had been, had all died out, and Frank Moreland just wouldn't put himself in any position to be nurturing or even helpful, beyond maybe some well-intentioned advice. And so my Daddy took it upon himself to find his own way. And yes, he did run away to join the circus."

And here, Jesse James Brodnax became Mantan Moreland for the long haul.

It would be tempting to add that he never looked back, apart from the recurring fond reference to his hometown in his monologues. But he did look back with sufficient frequency to keep up with friends, including a local family by the name of Henry, whose daughter Mantan eventually would marry. But not in Monroe. Mantan was gone from there for good.

## II

Various published accounts have had Moreland running away to join the circus (the phrase, and the concept of liberation that it represents, are so generally over-familiar as to sound merely figurative) as early as age 12. But as Marcella has insisted, Mantan would never have left his grandmother alone. And as long as Mandy Brodnax lived on, Mantan can only have known a stable household and at least a shred of hope of gaining something more from his father than token recognition.

Such casually researched accounts never specify the finer points of *which* circus, in *what capacity* of employment or for what motivating reasons Moreland would have hauled out in search of finer prospects. A sideshow or carnival troupe might seem the likelier prospect, whether attached to a larger circus or self-contained in the manner of an itinerant medicine show.

"Daddy was looking for a family, that's all," said Marcella. "And he had been fascinated since his baby days with what little taste of show business Monroe could offer him. He spent his life trying to build himself a family, and then trying to hold together what family he could. The circus became his family, there, after he'd given up on the old hometown."

A personality-profile type of article, published in the October 1946 issue of a New Orleans-based magazine called *The Negro South*, cites a combination of "minstrel shows and the Hagenbach-Wallace (*sic*) Circus" as Moreland's escape hatch from Louisiana. The anonymous author misstates the name, which is *Hagenbeck-Wallace*, but the meaning is obvious. And the naming of that one particular hippodrome, misspelled or not, is persuasive enough as a partial account of Moreland's early meanderings.

"Daddy just called it 'the circus,'" said Marcella, "as if it were the *only* circus worth mentioning. And as far as his experience was concerned, it *was* his only circus. But Hagenbeck-Wallace is the name that he had put down on this one early application I've seen for his employment in a Broadway show, there during the 1920s. And he had practically a lifelong friendship with Red Skelton, who had started out clowning in the same Hagenbeck-Wallace troupe that Daddy wound up working with."

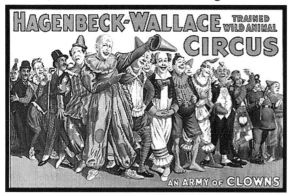

Hagenbeck-Wallace was a major-league company among the circuses that bridged the 19th and 20th centuries, bigger and grander in its heyday than the circuses of Barnum & Bailey or the Ringling Bros. Hagenbeck-Wallace had provided, around 1900, a springboard to the legitimate stage for the eccentric comedy team of Bobby Clark & Paul McCullough. Red Skelton became a clown with Hagenbeck-Wallace during the 1920s. The big-cat handler Clyde Beatty perfected his act with that same formidable outfit. Both Skelton and Beatty then followed a path akin to Moreland's into the movies—Skelton settling into a major-studio milieu, and Beatty portraying, essentially, himself in a few low-budget jungle-adventure thrillers while sustaining his circus roots. Moreland, meanwhile, accepted all the work the large or small studios could offer. In 1933, while Moreland was easing from Broadway into the cinema, Hagenbeck-Wallace became the launching-pad for Emmett Kelly's famous clown personality, Weary Willie. The history of Hagenbeck-Wallace also includes one legend-inspiring disaster, a train wreck that claimed approximately 60 lives in 1918 in Indiana.

It seems as likely that Moreland, given his periodic references to an early career as a dancer, might have joined up with a minstrel company attached to the Hagenbeck-Wallace Circus. A late-in-life collaborator of Moreland's, Roosevelt "Livinggood" Myles,[4] once said that Moreland's first job in show business had been with a unit descended from the Rabbit's Foot Minstrels. This organization was the same outfit that had given a start to the Louisiana-bred playwright and actor Augustus Smith, whose work in filmmaking includes such fascinating big-screen backwater melodramas of the Depression years as *Drums O' Voodoo* and *Chloe (Love is Calling You)* (both dating from 1934).

"Being very ambitious," reads the article in *The Negro South* magazine, "Mantan decided to try his luck in New York, and landed in a famous stock company at the Alhambra Theatre, where he stayed for two years. From that show, he was selected for... *Lew Leslie's Blackbirds of 1928*. After a long run, he went abroad and was the rage of the continent."

And here is where *The Negro South* becomes a tad thick with the hyperbole. *Blackbirds of 1928* enjoyed a long run, all right—518 documented performances, beginning May 9, 1928—leading to a sequel with the streamlined title of *Lew Leslie's Blackbirds*, which saw 57 performances beginning on October 22, 1930. This production begat 1931's *Singin' the Blues*, which brought Moreland to the back-to-back presentations of *Blackberries of 1932* and *Yeah, Man!* Moreland joined a revival of 1921's *Shuffle Along* for a December-of-1932 première. All of which would seem to leave little time for an up-and-coming artist to travel abroad and become "the rage," whatever that fatuous reference is supposed to mean, of whatever continent the unsigned author might have had in mind. As pleasing as it might appear to see a magazine devote its cover and four interior pages to Mantan Moreland, this spread in *The Negro South* is more puffery than journalism or biography and appears to have been cobbled together from fannish assumptions and movie-studio press releases.

Sheet music for *Blackbirds of 1928*

What is patent, is that an exhaustive concentration of major-league experience during the 1920s and early '30s—including a hitch with his Broadway mentor-turned-collaborator, Flournoy E. Miller, at Warner Bros.' East Coast satellite moviemaking studio—enabled Moreland to polish his natural talents. These crucial gifts included a command of slapstick agility, a taste for cerebral wordplay, and jazz-like improvisational timing and phrasing.

### III

The Harlem Renaissance, a movement rooted more deeply in the arts than in politics, was in full flower, however brief, by the time of Moreland's arrival during the middle 1920s in that "Mecca of the New Negro," as a black-centered journal called *Survey Graphic* termed the district.

Mantan Moreland (front row, right-of-center) is pictured with the ensemble cast of his Broadway breakout *Blackbirds of 1928*. Front-and-center is Tim Moore—the Kingfish-to-be of *Amos 'n' Andy*. At far right is dancer Clayton Bates.

"[O]ur problem is to conceive, develop, establish an art era," wrote one key figure, Aaron Douglas, in a letter to the poet Langston Hughes. Douglas' attempt here was to define the spirit and the purpose of the Harlem Renaissance in concise terms while leaving room for improvisation. Douglas added as a cautionary note: "Not white art painted black." What was true, and truly a widely shared problem, in that first quarter of the last century, remains so today, despite persistent tendencies all along toward the upholding of black artistic integrity.

"Be real black for me," Roberta Flack and Donnie Hathaway sang back-and-forth to one another in one of the more persuasive jazz-to-pop crossover duets of the early 1970s. The singers' earnestness rings true in the words alone, and truer yet in the context of an easily grasped melody and chord structure that could have worked just as well if, say, such a team as Dinah Washington and Brook Benton had tackled the tune. (Patti Page and Vic Damone need not apply.) But any lasting influence for Flack and Hathaway's episode of harmonizing proves to have been limited. Just a few years before the appearance of their recording—its lyrical hook also is its title, "Be Real Black for Me"—even such black-self Deep Blues singers as Chester "Howlin' Wolf" Burnett and McKinley "Muddy Waters" Morganfield had begrudgingly played along with a hyper-commercialized dilution of their work, delivering record albums patently calculated to appeal to the same white-kid audience that was devouring the imitative, blues-like rock 'n' roll of Eric Clapton, early Fleetwood Mac and the Rolling Stones.

Mantan the Funnyman 71

Nor were Muddy and the Mighty Wolf the first such artists to capitulate, grudgingly or not. Johnny Otis, a born-white entertainer who had rendered himself black by assimilating into Los Angeles' South Central scene during the 1940s, has spoken regretfully in recent times of his flirtation with mass-market rock-and-roll during 1957–1959:

"I tried to chase the almighty dollar," Otis told the researcher George Lipsitz during the 1990s, "and I listened to bad advice from profit-motivated sources [at big-time Capitol Records] when I should have been my own black self, recording my own black R&B sounds and not gone into contrived rock-and-roll…

"With a few exceptions," added Otis, "…I am quite ashamed of some of the directions I took in those days." Otis spent the 1960s making up for lost time, and even the most desultory of his '60s-into-'70s recordings—including the improvised background accompaniment for one of Mantan Moreland's comedy-routine albums—will demonstrate how thoroughly Otis had reconnected with what he called, in all earnestness, "my own black self."

In the benighted *déjà vu* milieu of the present day, the so-called *urban culture* (a marketing-industry euphemism for black and/or Latinate influences, rather like the earlier mass-merchandising term *soul music*) hinges largely upon a superficial blackness that the likes of Aaron Douglas, Langston Hughes *et al.* could only have found repugnant. (Certainly Bill Cosby, whose career over the longer term has been something of a sustained follow-through to the spirit of the Harlem Renaissance, has found the hip-hop scene less than uplifting.) A popular home-décor item among black middle-class households during the early years of this new century was a mass-produced and gaudily framed reproduction of a Renaissance (Italian, not Harlem) painting of two Euro-honky cherubs—digitally transmogrified into a state of blissful mock-Negritude. And so much, literally speaking, for Aaron Douglas' *caveat* against "white art painted black." And what, in turn, would the cutting-edge thinkers of the Harlem Renaissance have made of Michael Jackson, if not a grotesque instance of black art rendered white?

## IV

The narrow window of time commonly employed to demarcate the Harlem Renaissance allows for a persuasive view, if only one will accept the historian Richard Powell's argument that the movement had begun in 1915, coinciding symbolically with the death of Booker T. Washington.

Now, Washington, though an influential black leader, essentially had accepted second-class citizenship as a tolerable way of life and embraced the Imperialistic Paternalism of the 19th century as a basis of his attitudes toward fellow black Southerners. Too, Washington's concerns lay more strictly with Southern provincialism and entrepreneurial Southern commerce than with any artistic or literary inspirations.

By 1915, meanwhile, the National Negro Committee, founded during 1909–1910, was rapidly evolving into the National Association for the Advancement of Colored People. In 1913, the organization had mounted vigorous protests against President Woodrow Wilson's introduction of segregation as a mandate of federal policy. The Harlem Renaissance had less to do, however, with the N.A.A.C.P. and its more genteel intellectualism and middle-class strivings, than with the creative radicalism of a youthful black citizenry. This Renaissance addressed primarily an audience of kindred black thinkers. Here was a concerted campaign of preaching to the converted: A majority of black Americans remained unaware of the Harlem Renaissance until many years after that movement had come and gone—leaving vivid traces and after-effects to preserve and broaden its visionary impact beyond its naturally finite span.

**Flournoy Miller and Aubrey Lyles in** *Shuffle Along,* **1921**

By the time that *The New Negro*, Alain Locke's confrontational and naturalistic anthology of upstart writings, had seen publication in 1925, the Harlem Renaissance already had yielded the musical-comedy breakthrough of *Shuffle Along* (1921). *Shuffle Along* holds pride of place as the first all-black production to grace Broadway. The show would provide, in turn, the inspiration for a *Ziegfeld Follies* set-piece of 1922 called "It's Getting Dark on Old Broadway." The authors and composers responsible for *Shuffle Along* included Flournoy E. Miller, who was destined to become Mantan Moreland's most nurturing and steadfast team-comedy cohort. And yes, it was the December-of-1932 revival of *Shuffle Along* that would involve Moreland as a member of the cast.

The Harlem Renaissance ended, in a practical sense, during the 1930s with the emergence of the black athletes Jesse Owens and Joe Louis to a state of mainstream celebrity; and of the author Richard Wright as a distinct literary voice. The distinction lay in Wright's greater concern with crossing over without compromise to reach a generalized readership, than with writing about black life for an already-attuned black readership. And yet a Renaissance-like attitude persisted throughout the 1940s in such isolated pockets as a Southern movie company called Sack Amusement Enterprises. Here, the white-Jewish proprietor, Alfred N. Sack, dealt largely in black-ensemble comedies, melodramas, religious pictures and even the occasional Afrocentric horror movie, all designed expressly for distribution to black neighborhood theaters. Sack entrusted money, and autonomy, to black creative talents—primarily, the actor and turn-key writer-producer-director Spencer Williams, Jr.—in exchange for products of saleable authenticity.

Mantan Moreland would owe a great deal of his decisive beginnings in film to such small-time companies and their niche-market productions. Moreland had experienced a false start at cracking big-league Hollywood in 1933, when he and Flournoy E. Miller graced a short musical film called "That's the Spirit" (made by Warner Bros.' East Coast subsidiary, Vitaphone), impersonating night watchmen on duty in a haunted pawnshop.

The black-ensemble Western, *Harlem on the Prairie*, had originated as a starring vehicle for Herbert Jeffries, with Mantan Moreland as a supporting player. Later on during the 1940s, Moreland's burgeoning popularity inspired a new advertising campaign emphasizing his presence.

Miller had carried on a song-and-dance-and-comedy partnership with Aubrey Lyles since the early 1900s. Their characters proved a key inspiration for the whites-in-blackface teaming of Charles Correll and Freeman Gosden, who performed as Sam 'n' Henry before assuming the more lasting team-identity of Amos 'n' Andy in March of 1928 at Chicago's WMAQ-Radio.

Following Lyles' death in 1932, Miller joined with the somewhat younger Moreland to carry on with such an act. The roles of Miller & Moreland in "That's the Spirit," enacted with the lily-gilding of minstrel-show blackface makeup, require the artists to do little more than exchange quips and react to various ghostly music-making manifestations. The larger point of the film is a se-

Mantan Moreland and Joe Louis in *Spirit of Youth* (Photofest)

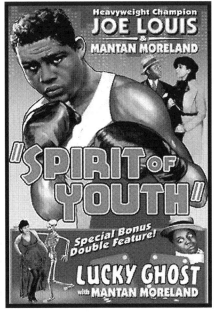

quence of jazz tunes, performed by Noble Sissle's orchestra, whose large-ensemble sound foreshadows that of the more lastingly prominent Duke Ellington.

Moreland gained a more decisive foothold in Hollywood in 1937, leaving a sharp if fleeting impression with a comic-relief role alongside Flournoy Miller in the black-ensemble Western *Harlem on the Prairie*, part of a short-lived series starring the jazz singer Herbert Jeffries as a cowboy-crooner hero. Then in 1938's *Spirit of Youth,* a fanciful bio-picture about the rise of prizefighter Joe Louis starring Louis himself, Moreland would emerge as a more dramatically attuned screen player alongside the Baltimore-born actor-composer Dr. Clarence Muse.[5]

Moreland's stage-honed gifts, as refined and embellished in his movies, would place him handily on a par with W.C. Fields, Charles Chaplin, the Four Marx Bros., Laurel & Hardy, Abbott & Costello, Buster Keaton, Joe E. Brown, or any other acknowledged masters and/or brilliant also-rans whom one might care to mention. The measure of such artistry lies in qualities including inventiveness, both studied and spontaneous; stealthy and rhythmic timing; mannerisms that invite and then defy imitation; and a certain readiness to deflate pomposity while laughing at oneself. Moreland's approach has less in common with such pioneering black comedians as Lincoln "Stepin Fetchit" Perry and Willie "Sleep 'n' Eat" Best. Fetchit and Best specialized in lazybones or flaccid portrayals of subservience, a quality of court-jester figurative impotence, and a predisposition to panic. Perry's Stepin Fetchit act was particularly anomalous to his intellect. Surviving examples of his correspondence convey an assertive, professorial tone—especially when applied to the business of negotiating performance contracts and backstage amenities with theater managers.

Moreland's Broadway-into-Hollywood years found him settling down gradually, at last, from the rambling life of Chitlin' Circuit Vaudeville. His friend of long standing, the Texas-born guitarist T-Bone Walker, had made Los Angeles his base as a recording artist and nightclub entertainer. Along with such cohorts as the popular L.A. barbecue chef R. Bob Cooper and a numbers-racket entrepreneur named Elihu "Black Dot" McGee, Moreland and Walker became well-known habitués of the nightclub scene in the city's then-thriving South Central district, known as Sepia Town in the black newspapers of the day. *Move over, boys—I'm one of the gang, now.*

---

[1] Scattered other sources cite 1901 and 1902, but Marcella Moreland Young marks 1903 as the year of her father's arrival.

[2] *Ouachita*: Just in case anyone might be wondering how to pronounce that mouthful, the phonetic reading is "*Wash*-uh-tah."

[3] The term *google* is nothing so much as a mispronunciation of *goggle*. You could look it up—or just Google it, as it were. The exaggerated term denotes an ocular protrusion, as seen in the face of Barney Google, the bug-eyed cartoon character created by Billy DeBeck. DeBeck's *Barney Google* feature of the 1920s served in turn to inspire a popular song: "Barney Google—with the goo-goo-googly eyes."

[4] Roosevelt Myles varied the spelling of his stage name—sometimes as *Livingood*, and sometimes as *Livinggood*.

[5] Muse (1889–1979) was a towering figure of dignity and musical-dramatic-literary artistry in black Hollywood, with a singing voice as resonant as that of Paul Robeson and a mastery of boogie-woogie piano comparable with that of Meade Lux Lewis or the team of Pete Johnson & Albert Ammons. Muse's robust singing voice can be heard in George Melford's jungle-horror melodrama *East of Java* (1935). Muse's keyboard prowess underscores a memorably tense scene in Will Jason's *The Soul of a Monster* (1944), a modern-dress *Faust*.

# 14
# Like Father, like Daughter

> What happened to divide us all so bad as a society was that we got so all caught up in desegregating—that we forgot to *integrate*.
> —Ozell "Larry" Reynolds, 1996

Mantan Moreland had fallen in love while still a school kid in Monroe, but the object of his affections was scarcely old enough to notice. Hazel Henry was the pampered daughter of a Shreveport, Louisiana-born merchant and entrepreneur named Will "Chip" Henry. This ambitious go-getter had befriended Mantan while the boy was still going by the name of Jesse James Brodnax, gradually rechristening himself with the unique nickname of Mantan.

"It was Mom's father, Mr. Henry—'Chip' was all anybody ever seems to've called him, maybe because he went around with a chip on his shoulder, I guess—who brought Daddy into the family," recalled Marcella Moreland Young in 2005. "Now, Hazel, my Mom, she was just a little-bitty one when Daddy first became acquainted with the Henrys, there in Monroe. She might not've even been born as yet, when my Daddy had met up with Mr. Henry. Anyway, Mom was 11 years younger than my Daddy. But Daddy kept track of her, even after he left Monroe for a life in the circus.

"And he kept up with the Henrys, too—well enough to know that Chip Henry, who had a history of getting himself run out of town for being what the white people called 'uppity,' wasn't too likely to stay put in Monroe long enough for my Mom to finish growing up there.

Chicago, 1936: Marcella Moreland at age two with her maternal grandfather, Will "Chip" Henry.

"And sure enough: Now, this grandfather of mine was a respectable businessman, and a restless businessman, too. He had what they'd call a franchise today, with the B.F. Goodrich Rubber Company. A tire business, it was. And then a restaurant, and then a tailoring shop. And then a restaurant, again. Kept thinking up new businesses to get himself into. Mr. Henry *worked*, and he worked *hard*, for what his family had, and he considered himself fully the equal of any white man. This attitude, of course, kept him in a world of trouble, in the South in those days," said Marcella.

"Chip, now, he seems to have been a regular Dapper Dan, with that air of 'I *am* somebody' about him. His family would urge him, like, 'Oh, *please*, do what the white folks tell you to do—just try to get along,' but Chip Henry just flat-out *would not do it*. Wouldn't step off the sidewalk to give a white man the right-of-way, wouldn't tip his hat, just that refusal to comply. Very selfish, I believe, in the sense of putting pride before the safety and security of his family, and it wound up costing them all—although the family wound up in a better place, in Chicago, after all.

"The story goes that Mr. Henry had gotten into a disagreement with the son of the town mayor, there in Shreveport, and the mayor's people had Mr. Henry run out of town, under threat of violence. That's the version handed down by my Daddy and my Mom, at any rate," she said.

"So Chip Henry ended up, then, in Monroe. But he still wouldn't put up with any of that Jim Crow nonsense, havin' to bow and scrape or havin' to ask for 'Mr. Prince Albert' whenever he'd go into a general store to buy himself an ordinary tin of Prince Albert tobacco. There were some crazy rules of conduct in those days, and the few black people who objected to them were considered to be troublemakers in need of punishment.

"So my Grandfather Chip Henry, he stayed in trouble, there in Monroe, and never you mind that he was a respectable and taxpaying businessman," Marcella continued. "Finally, so the story goes, the [Ku Klux] Klan sent 'em a delegation to his house in the middle of the night and announced that Mr. Henry was going to have to leave Monroe—or *else*. And he said, well, y'know, like, 'Well, I was gettin' fed up with this little ol' town of you-all's, anyhow,' and he just packed up the family and moved 'em straight on to Chicago.

"Daddy had stayed in touch with the Henrys, of course, all during his years on the road, and so he made it a point to check in on 'em every time he'd come touring through Chicago.

"Daddy liked Chicago, of course, and Chicago liked him—a good *show* town. And he had made it up in his mind that he was going to wed that pretty little daughter of Mr. Henry's, once she had attained a marriageable age.

"And so they got married in Chicago, just like that, in 1933, when Daddy was 30 and my Mom was 19. He was already a star, I guess you could say, from his experience with some shows on Broadway, and he and F.E. [Flournoy Miller,

Mantan's mentor-become-partner from the Vaudeville-to-Broadway days] had just recently made their first short-subject movie together [1933's "That's the Spirit," for Warners-Vitaphone].

"And my Mom, of course, she liked the idea of Daddy's becoming famous, one of these days. But there was also never any question as to whether she was in love with him, no matter how difficult things were bound to turn out between them."

Marcella was born to Mantan and Hazel Moreland on April 5, 1934, in Chicago. By 1937, the family had resettled in Los Angeles, there to begin following through in earnest upon Mantan's moviemaking ambitions. He connected first with the low-rent producer William J. "Jed" Buell (1897–1961), an exploitation-film impresario who prized ticket-selling gimmickry and sensationalism over dramatic substance. Buell had recently signed the jazz singer Herbert Jeffries—whose greater fame as a featured vocalist with the Duke Ellington Orchestra was yet to come—to begin developing a series of black-ensemble Westerns.

For Jeffries, the project bespoke a mission of cultural integrity that might also help him to earn a living. For the less sociologically enlightened Buell, the notion of a Negro-cowboy movie was more nearly akin to the dwarves-as-cowboys stunt that he and director Sam Newfield would accomplish with a movie called *The Terror of Tiny Town* (1938). If their artistic and/or commercial imperatives were essentially in conflict, Jeffries and Buell nonetheless made things click—and each man derived a measure of success from the venture.

Moreland landed, as a consequence of fortunate timing, among the ensemble cast of Buell and Sam Newfield's co-directed *Harlem on the Prairie* (1937). This film and its companions hold up as more-or-less conventional horse-opera entries in the manner of such

Mantan the Funnyman

Dominant Culture buckaroos as Gene Autry, Ken Maynard and Buck Jones—but Jeffries' series is distinguished by a tacit acknowledgment that yes, after all, there had been many black settlers on the American frontier.

"I knew that Mantan had the makings of a movie star, the moment he arrived to begin shooting," Herb Jeffries told me in 2003 upon his induction—at age 92—into the Cowboys of Color Hall of Fame of Fort Worth, Texas, an institution that also would enshrine Moreland the following year. Jeffries added: "Mantan and I also made for a good, striking contrast, what with his being short and stocky and my being tall and lanky, and he was generous enough to stick around for a follow-up [1938's *Two-Gun Man from Harlem*] while some bigger prospects were beginning to open up for him in the movie business."

The small start with Jeffries' horse-opera series pointed Moreland toward richer opportunities, indeed, with the major studios, but Moreland consistently hedged his bets by remaining aligned with the Poverty Row sector of Hollywood.

"Daddy had no airs of self-importance about him, not at all," said Marcella. "He never felt that his Broadway credentials had entitled him to any special star treatment in Hollywood, and he was grateful for any and all of the movie work that came his way, big-time or small-time. Now, as to my Mom—she liked the whole reflected-glory business, fancying Daddy to be a movie star and all that, but for Daddy it was just honest work that he took very seriously. He never expected any special treatment—just a chance to do what he loved doing, and to keep getting better at it.

"Which is, I believe, why he had wanted to get me involved, too, in the acting profession. The business of acting can provide a person with tremendous mental and physical discipline."

## II

Marcella Moreland weighed in, very briefly, as a player in black-ensemble independent cinema, finding her one such assignment to be a stepping-stone to a promise of greater prominence. In a review of Sam Newfield's *Am I Guilty?* (a.k.a. *Racket Doctor*; 1940, from Supreme Pictures), the influential trade publication *Variety* hailed six-year-old Marcella as the "cutest kid performer since Shirley Temple" and averred that Mantan's daughter "would make a top-notch bet...on any major lot."

Her role in *Am I Guilty?* serves to confront a renegade physician (Ralph Cooper) with a crisis to test his courage and skill: "Now, my character, there, she gets run over in traffic," recalled Marcella, "and so it's up to this doctor to come through and save my life in order to prove and redeem himself."

And so she lived up to *Variety*'s prophecy, for a spell: By the following year, Marcella had become a contract player at big-time MGM, with an unbilled but noticeable role in Frank Borzage's *The Vanishing Virginian* and a more substantial part in Wells Root's *Mokey*, both sentimental family-style pictures that saw release early in 1942. Marcella also graced a few of MGM's *Our Gang* comedy shorts, appearing as a supporting presence for Billy "Buckwheat" Thomas.

*Mokey*, for that matter, had provided an interlude between *Our Gang* assignments for both Thomas and Mickey Gubitosi, who was in the process of changing his professional name to Bobby (and later, Robert) Blake; the strategy would help him to survive the pitfalls of child stardom and make a transition to adolescent and grown-up roles. Marcella, like a great many other child players, had formally retired as a screen presence at about age 10—although she would maintain credentials with the Screen Actors Guild for the long term. (She last dealt with that trade union in 2001 when seeking in vain an apology, at least, from the writer-director Spike Lee, in view of his Mantan-bashing movie *Bamboozled*.)

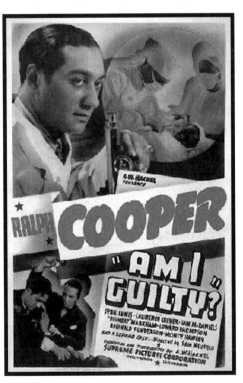

Mantan was, of course, the busier bearer by far of the Moreland name to the sacrificial altar of Show Business.

"That was Daddy's idea, the notion of my becoming an actor," Marcella explained. "And although

I enjoyed the experience and all that good friendly camaraderie—Bobby Blake and I were 'specially good friends on the *Our Gang* lot, back when Bobby was still trying to outgrow the name of Mickey Gubitosi—I didn't really enjoy the whole process of acting. The training served its purpose, though. I mean, it helped me to understand more thoroughly what it was that my Daddy was doing with his life.

"I just wasn't cut out for it. Acting was not my niche," she said. "But my experience, there, helped me to help my Daddy, even as young as I was at the time. I'd sit on his lap whenever he'd get a new assignment, help him study his scripts and—so he told me—help him get a handle on whatever character it was he'd be playing on this or that occasion. Of course, I always liked Daddy best when he was just being himself, in whatever role might come his way.

"And that was why his years at Monogram Pictures turned out to be so important: The association with Monogram just let him *be* himself, and it set him up with a studio whose production values, while still very low in the budget department, were a cut above the even smaller Poverty Row studios that bankrolled those black-theaters-only productions. Monogram gave my Daddy his best exposure for a long time and he loved having the creative freedom that Monogram extended to him.

"Anyhow, that background, that professional life in common that we had, I believe, drew us closer together as a family—a family of just us two, as it would eventually turn out," Marcella added. "For all of our lives, except for a few years after Mom and my Daddy had first parted ways and she dragged me off to New York City for a spell, he and I were always together.

"And so what do you make of all that?" she asked. "Here, he's an only child from a marriage that never had existed—just an affair that had ended with his arrival. He has lost all his own people, in one way or another, and all he wants to accomplish, really, is to hold on to what family he can, however he can manage a way to do so.

"You can draw that picture yourself, and you don't need any highfalutin' psychology to get to the bottom of it, either. Daddy spent his entire career trying to *go home*, or to find whatever home-and-family life that he could, that had been denied him, to start with. And it turned out that he and I were just about *it*.

"When all else had started to slip away—what with the acting partners who'd up and die in the midst of things, with my Mom's temperament and volatile nature or with one personal agent, some guy named Fischman or something like that, who took off with some money owed to Daddy, or with the N.A.A.C.P. and its attempts to 'purge' the culture—my Daddy and I still had each other. And we were grateful for that.

"Had I said that Daddy and I were very protective of one another? Well, we *were*. I was his toughest critic, professionally speaking, but I also was his most receptive audience. And sure, I was what they'd call a Daddy's Girl. But I never felt as though either my Daddy, or the world itself, ever owed me a living. We supported each other, that's all.

"And of course, when things could come down to a disagreement between Daddy and my Mom—well, then, she had to fight the *both* of us. Emotionally speaking, I mean."

This deteriorated newspaper clipping from the early 1940s shows, from left, Hazel (Mrs. Mantan) Moreland, Gladys Snyder, Marcella Moreland, Pete Webster, Dorothy Dandridge, Marguerite Whitten and Jeni LeGon. The occasion was a Christmas party staged by the *Los Angeles Courier*.

Such simmering disagreements came to a rolling boil during the closing half of the 1940s.

"It really hit with full force when I was 14 or 15, in 1948," said Marcella, "but the family troubles had started as early as 1945, when Daddy started feeling too weak for his own good—he'd always been a very energetic man, and he was just hitting his stride with the *Charlie Chan* pictures, there at the Monogram Pictures lot. And he found himself diagnosed with a diabetic condition.

"He got *really sick*, there, and it demoralized him terribly—not that you could tell that from the *quality* of his work. The treatment of diabetes in those days was not particularly well advanced, and a diagnosis of diabetes might as well have been a death warrant for a lot of people. Luckily for all of us, Daddy wasn't much of a drinking man, not to any excess, and he kept himself in strong physical condition, as a requirement of his work and the slapstick routines that his work sometimes entailed.

"Now, Daddy never did as much out-and-out slapstick comedy in the movies as he'd do on the stage, but he was an *expert* at these big-scale acrobatical routines that he and Ben Carter would do," Marcella digressed. "He had this one routine, with Ben, where they'd have 'em a few drinks of whiskey and pretend to go into these fits of frenzy, like, 'That *sure enough* is some *good* whiskey!'—Daddy, now, he'd spin on his head, spin on his back, then get up and crow like a rooster, take himself another sip of that whiskey, and go through all that spinning routine, all over again.

"Anyhow," she resumed the train of thought, "Daddy's sudden outbreak of illness, and some of the professional and political disappointments he went through, later on, during those several years—well, they all left Mom thinking that he'd probably never work again. She was torn between caring for his well-being and her own very spoiled nature. Her wants were more important than anything else, to her, and she began leaning toward the idea of a divorce while Daddy was just finding out how sick he was and figuring out how he was going to deal with it.

"My Mom, now, she'd always had just about anything she had wanted, and what she wanted *most* was a famous husband who could support her in the style she'd become accustomed to.

"Now, being a Daddy's Girl, myself, which I admit to being with some pride, I never really forgave Mom for that attitude—although, as young as I was, I didn't really understand all the deeper currents going on there," added Marcella. "I was just bewildered by it all. My Daddy had gotten sick, and he experienced some devastating losses on other fronts, such as losing two of his favorite acting partners.

"Ben Carter, whom Daddy considered his best comedy-team partner after F.E. Miller, took sick of a strep infection and died, very abruptly," she explained. "Then, Sidney Toler, who had almost single-handedly revived the *Charlie Chan* pictures, there at Monogram, as their star and guiding talent, after [Twentieth Century] Fox had dropped the series—well, he died. Not so unexpectedly as Ben's death, for Mr. Toler was on along into his 70s and had been in failing health. But such terrible losses so close together [during 1946–1947] worked a bad effect on Daddy, who had been Mr. Toler's own personal choice to co-star with him in the *Charlie Chan* pictures.

"Daddy was able to carry on with the *Chan* series, then, and he got along just fine with the new Charlie Chan player, Roland Winters. But the series just wasn't as much fun for him as it had been with Mr. Toler and the occasional appearance by Ben Carter."

Monogram Pictures' revival of the *Charlie Chan* franchise in 1942, two years after Fox had discontinued its *Chan*s, was a mixed blessing for Moreland. Although it assured him of a steady procession of assignments, it also placed him in a fixed characterization and a narrative formula (assorted conspiracies involv-

ing murder), with few variations. *Chan* at Monogram was patently a comedown from *Chan* at Fox, but for Moreland—who had not been involved with the Fox *Chan*s—the assignment signaled a stretch of continuity and stability.

The renewed franchise also benefited from Sidney Toler's continuation of the title role—he had succeeded Warner Oland (1879–1938) as Chan at Fox, and handled the role ably for the longer term—and from Toler's proprietary stake, as well, in the *Chan* trademark.

The advantage of the Monogram *Chan*s over the more polished Foxes lies in Mantan Moreland's finely wrought portrayal of chauffeur-turned-sleuth Birmingham Brown. This is not so much a string of isolated portrayals, as it is a single portrayal, sustained and enriched from film to film, in which the comedian develops the character so thoroughly well as to help obscure the dreadfully uneven quality of the film series.

"Daddy worked on Birmingham—his speech, his mannerisms, his attitude—in precisely the way he had polished and re-polished the *Indefinite Talk* routine with F.E. [Miller]," said Marcella Moreland Young.

*Indefinite Talk*? Well, we haven't quite reached that milestone yet in this story.

"*You* know," explained Marcella. "The *Indefinite Talk*—that's the routine, the two-man routine, where each partner finishes the other's sentences for him and it feels as though they're making all that business up on the spot." (The impatient reader is referred herewith to Chapters 16 and 17.)

"It was just Daddy's style to *work* a routine, like a silversmith shaping a fine art object to the *n*th degree, standing back and looking at it, and then going back in there and *shaping* it some more," continued Marcella. "We didn't have the convenience of tape-recording devices or any such thing, not back then. But Daddy'd test out everything he'd come up with, with me as his sounding-board.

"And he'd go, like this: 'Now, if Birmingham was to react like *so*, to such-and-such a situation, how do you think that'd go over?' And I'd tell him either, yes, that should work just fine, or no, that's *old* business and how about trying something *new*—or else a flat-out *N–O, no*, that's laying things on too thick with the dialect and caricature.

"For you see, my Daddy knew better than to play a part too broadly, and he tried to keep things dignified amidst all the funnyman business. That's why he was able to do all those explicitly color-conscious gags with Frankie Darro [in their pre-*Chan* series of comedy-mysteries at Monogram] and make things come off so *friendly*, as a friendship between equals. And for the *Charlie Chan* pictures, Daddy wanted to establish Birmingham as a guy who'd be smart and resourceful enough to be accepted into Charlie Chan's circle as a colleague—more in Chan's *employ* than in Chan's *service*. Birmingham had an outspoken distaste for murder and murderers, of course, and he knew how to make a conspicuous exit when he needed to run off and summon help—but Daddy never played Birmingham as any kind of a superstitious Negro scaredy-cat. *That* had been done to death, ever since the minstrel-show and silent-picture days.

"The *Chan* pictures, themselves, now, were pretty much assembly-line productions," she said. "Quick schedules of a couple of weeks or shorter per each picture, crank 'em out and move on to the next one—except for that long, dry spell [from late 1946 to late 1947] between the death of Mr. Toler and the tedious waiting period to see if the series could be continued, since Mr. Toler's estate owned the *Chan* movie rights.

"Daddy had grown to like Birmingham so well that he was glad to keep on going with the series, and of course he grew very fond of working with Roland Winters, the new Charlie Chan, and the various guys who played Charlie Chan's sons, like Benson Fong and Victor Sen Yung. These were friendships that prevailed, on down through the years.

"But Daddy would get very *down* over the losses that he sensed: 'I lost my comedy partner,' he'd say to me. 'I lost my first and best Charlie Chan. I feel like I'm losin' your Mom. I *know* I'm losin' too much weight." Naturally plump for all his quick-on-his-feet vigor, Moreland in his prime of health had carried 185 to 190 pounds on a five-foot-seven frame. He dropped to a range of 165-175 pounds in the midst of coming to terms with his diabetic condition.

The greater blow, however, came from Hazel Henry Moreland.

"And when Mom just hauled off and had him served with the divorce papers [in 1948]," said Marcella, "Daddy felt he was losing his family, all over again. Monogram Pictures ended the *Charlie Chan* series about then, too." (The December 1948 production of *The Sky Dragon*, which went unissued until April 1949, marked the series' closing.)

"And right around that time, then, the forces of 'racial uplift,' as they called themselves, started assailing Daddy with this nonsense about how he was presenting what they called 'a negative stereotype,'" she added.

## III

Now, Marcella Moreland Young reserves no fondness for blatant stereotype or overt caricature, and she recalls taking her father to task for his heavy-dialect readings of several of Roark Bradford's *Ol' Man Adam* Biblical stories for a record album of the 1950s. Her contempt for the cultural purges of the National Association for the Advancement of Colored People, however, is rooted in a belief that her father was unfairly singled out as a sacrificial goat: "Daddy was opening doors for black artists, I believe—not contributing to any forces of oppression. I believe that Birmingham Brown was quite enough, all by himself, to make white audiences take a more sympathetic view of black people, like Rochester [Anderson] with Jack Benny or, in later times, Redd Foxx with his Fred Sanford character [on the *Sanford & Son* teleseries; 1972-1977]."

Moreland might have mustered a greater defiance toward the N.A.A.C.P.'s campaign of suppression, if not for the demoralizing effect of his wife's defection.

"Mom just took him to the cleaners, that's all," said Marcella. "She didn't take anyone's side against him—there was nothing politically or culturally motivated about her actions, because she thought he was a real artist—but she sensed that Daddy's failing health and the attempt to boycott his work might leave him incapable of babying her any longer.

"And so, yes, Daddy was pretty well beaten down, but nobody ever managed to break his spirit—try as they might. He just set his mind on getting well again, and on making the best stab he could at a comeback. He never retired, not once in his life, from any job, and Daddy wasn't one of those men who just *goes* to work. He *was* his work.

"So anyway, after Mom had him served, she moved to New York—I guess I was too flabbergasted to do anything else but just go on along with her—and I went to a finishing school up there, and, for a while, there, to a private Catholic school in Missouri.

"Daddy stayed based in Los Angeles, more or less, and he hooked up with a popular radio show called *Duffy's Tavern* after the N.A.A.C.P. had bullied the film studios into putting him off to one side. He stayed with this other lady—I don't recall her name—who helped to nurse him back to health, and later on, he had a girlfriend, whose name hasn't stuck with me, either. She worked on, or maybe owned, a ranch, out in Oklahoma. I wasn't around during all that.

"But Daddy never got over his love for my Mom. What few other women he ever took up with, it was just a matter of his trying to ease the pain of being abandoned. The love was just too strong, between my Mom and my Daddy, even if it took *her* a long time to admit as much.

"When I got out of school," Marcella went on, "I didn't want to live with my Mom any longer. And so Daddy and I were reunited for the long haul, for all the good times and all the rest of the bad times, and then some good times, again. Back and forth, like that.

"After he had started to get well and get his [diabetic] condition and his blood pressure under control, and after he'd started his comeback as best he could, he called up my Mom and told her things were starting to look better again. Of course, at this, here she comes back again, wanting to jump right back onto that bandwagon—because nobody ever had spoiled her, not even her own very indulgent father, like my Daddy had spoiled her. She showed up again, just as if their divorce hadn't even become final. And just when things had started to look up on that domestic front, she took up with some other man, right under my Daddy's nose. I was already mad with her, but this stunt really sealed it for me."

Mantan Moreland, in a practical sense, dropped out of sight during the early 1950s, although he kept his own personal funnyman-for-hire business anchored with the influential William Morris Agency in Los Angeles.

The radio-production company responsible for *Duffy's Tavern* came looking for Moreland, via the Morris Agency, following the unexpected death in 1950 of a mainstay player named Eddie Green, another prominent black comedian of the day. Green had appeared with Moreland in *Mantan Messes Up* (1946), and they had made solo appearances on wartime broadcasts of the Armed Forces Radio Services Network.

Green, like Moreland, had possessed a gift of gab well suited to radio comedy. Green's shriller and more nervous-of-manner style[1] lent itself well to stammering monologues, often having to do with a demanding wife and an overbearing mother-in-law. Moreland's speech ran more toward a contemplative tone, with an ability to make a painstakingly composed story sound as though it might be a stream-of-consciousness ramble. Moreland seemed a likely successor to fill the barroom-waiter role suddenly left vacant at *Duffy's*—if Mantan could be located. As abruptly as Green had cashed in, so had Moreland just as suddenly slipped from public view. Recalled Marcella: "Daddy just quit everything for a while, trying to get himself back together."

The William Morris Agency contacted Marcella Moreland in New York. Her approaching graduation coincided approximately with her determination to rejoin her father. The agency's plea to her went like this: "You've got to help us find that little man—we've got the role he's been needing," as she recalls it.

---

[1] In an interview with George E. Turner and Mike Price around 1970, Don Knotts acknowledged Eddie Green as an influence—"a master of the 'nervous' style of comedy."

## 15
# Down at Duffy's Tavern —Puerto Rican Branch

Duffy ain't here.
—Ed "Archie" Gardner, 1940 and onward

"Godsends are where you find them—or where *they* find *you*, don't you think?" asked Marcella Moreland Young during one of our earlier visits at the beginning of the present century. "And *Duffy's Tavern* came looking for my Daddy at precisely the time he needed to see something happen for the better.

"It was a breakthrough, all right—the right job, at the right time, and in a really spectacular, kind of a magical, place for us to retreat to, just when Hollywood, or the movie business, had turned its back on Daddy," continued Mantan Moreland's daughter.

"Now, when the Morris Agency got hold of me and told me they had a job lined up for Daddy on *Duffy's Tavern*," she explained, "I had it in mind that they'd be wanting him to either come up to New York, or else retrench in Hollywood. The show had been broadcasting [over network radio] from one and then the other of those cities since—what?—1940 or thereabouts, I guess.

"Well, now, New York sounded like a mixed blessing for Daddy, since it was *far* away from Los Angeles—but it also was where my Mom had resettled, after the breakup. And Daddy was *very* mixed about whether they could ever get back together again and make things work, as much as he loved her and missed her needing to be with him.

"But as it turned out, *Duffy's Tavern* didn't need Daddy in New York *or* Hollywood—because Mr. Ed Gardner [the producer-director-star and supervising scriptwriter] had already moved *Duffy's Tavern* to Puerto Rico. So not only was Daddy going to get fixed up with a new job to help him get back into action—but also I was going to accompany him on the job, since I was about finished with school and had become old enough to make up my own mind as to which parent I'd choose to be with. And we were going to get ourselves a three-year tropical vacation out of the deal! Sad as it was to lose Eddie Green, it was heartening to think that Ed Gardner appreciated Daddy well enough to see him as a successor to Eddie."

*Duffy's Tavern* had proved a popular success from the start—yes, in 1940—as a favorite with both the critical brethren and a massed audience. The imaginary establishment of the title was a joint at Third Avenue and Twenty-Third Street in New York City, touted by its raspy-voiced manager, Archie (Ed Gardner), as "Duffy's Tavern—where the elite meet to eat." Having answered any and all telephone calls thusly, Archie would continue: "Duffy ain't here. Archie, the manager, speakin'."

Gardner interpreted Archie with a classic-manner tough-guy tenderness of the Damon Runyon straight-outta-Brooklyn school. Gardner was a master of wordplay (mangling the language with straight-faced, gruff-friendly aplomb) who shaped *Duffy's Tavern* as a star-making and guest-starring vehicle for any number of friends and colleagues. Gardner's wife, Shirley Booth (1898–1992), was a *Duffy's* regular in the beginning, playing a bubble-headed daughter of the perpetually absent Duffy.[1]

Recurring characters on *Duffy's Tavern* also included career barfly Clifton Finnegan, played by Charlie Cantor; a loquacious if tongue-tangled waiter named Eddie (Eddie Green); and a flatfoot patrolman named Clancy (Alan Reed). Guest artists ranged from Boris Karloff and Vincent Price to Shelly Winters, Lucille Ball, and Dinah Shore—not to mention Alan Ladd, Mickey Rooney, boxer-turned-actor Slapsie Maxie Rosenbloom, Bert "the Mad Russian" Gordon, and Gloria Swanson and Marlene Dietrich. A movie version of *Duffy's* had surfaced in 1945—Gardner's only big-screen effort, also featuring Bing Crosby, Eddie Green and many other marquee names.

Gardner, who had directed such radio-serial standbys as *The Burns & Allen Show* and *Ripley's Believe It or Not*, shaped *Duffy's* over the long haul as a smorgasbord of styles—from hard-boiled cynicism to heartwarming schmaltz—unified by a command of brisk, spontaneous-sounding banter that accommodated one-liner gags without sacrificing character development. More a forerunner of *Archie Bunker's Place* than of, say, *Cheers* (to cite some more nearly modern examples of mass-appeal barroom camaraderie), *Duffy's Tavern* benefited from a crackerjack writing team that included, at one time or another, such Broadway gadabouts as Dick Martin, Abe Burrows, Larry Gelbart and Larry Marks. Gardner retained final-edit control of the scripts, ensuring a consistency of narrative tone.

Gardner produced *Duffy's Tavern* independently for CBS, at first, and over the longer term, for NBC. The programs originated as in-person, real-time broadcasts from New York and, later, NBC's Sunset-at-Vine studio in Hollywood, until 1949. During that year, Gardner began casting an eye toward two prospective developments. One was the notion of moving *Duffy's* onto television. The other was the temptation of a tax-incentive program that the

*Duffy* beer ad from magazines in 1950

Puerto Rican government had established, as a means of luring American industry. Gardner chose to continue the serial on radio, the better to take advantage of this 12-year moratorium on taxes known as the Puerto Rico Development Act. Gardner moved his ensemble cast to Puerto Rico, continuing the relationship with NBC, and scrapped the real-time broadcasts in favor of a recording-transcription process that would allow him to employ canned musical scores in place of a studio orchestra. A resort to prerecorded music, if attempted in the United States, would have brought Gardner some unwelcome attention from the American Federation of Musicians, a powerful trade union that since 1947 had orchestrated conspicuous crackdowns on the pop-music recording industry and the emerging medium of original-for-television production.[2]

The 10th season of *Duffy's Tavern* marked the Puerto Rican début. So low of profile was the relocation that even some of the actors auditioning for steady roles were caught off-guard.

Hazel Shermet, upon completing a successful audition in 1949, was informed: "We're going to send you tickets on Monday for the first rehearsal," as Miss Shermet once told the culture-of-radio historian Martin Grams, Jr. "What do you mean?" she replied. "I have to have a ticket to go to NBC? I go there every day." Came Gardner's reply: "No, a ticket to Puerto Rico."

The tax-advantage ploy ultimately backfired for Gardner, who faced criticism within the domestic U.S. broadcasting industry for dodging his responsibilities as a taxpayer, and who found big-name Hollywood players increasingly reluctant to undertake the travels necessary for guest-star appearances—the paid-vacation prospect notwithstanding. *Duffy's* stumbled on into 1952, and then ceased production.

"But it was very nice while it lasted," recalled Marcella Moreland Young. "Daddy and I loved the country, the climate, the friendships with Ed Gardner and all the regulars, and once in a while they'd get a guest-star player in from Hollywood, like Maxie Rosenbloom, who'd be very encouraging to Daddy about his maybe taking another run at the movie business."

*Duffy's Tavern* resurfaced briefly on network television in 1954 as a production of Hal Roach, Jr. Mantan Moreland was noticeably missing from the ensemble cast. Ed Gardner found himself sidelined as to the TV version's script approval and casting, although he prevailed in his insistence upon continuing to play Archie. White-guy comedian Jimmy Conlin (1884–1962), a Vaudeville-to-Hollywood veteran, stepped into the headwaiter's role, marking a pre-emptive sop to Political Correctness in view of the recent sacrifice of *Amos 'n' Andy* to the borderline book-burning tactics of the N.A.A.C.P. (Ed Gardner died at 62 in 1963.)

## II

Moreland likely would have had a crack at co-starring in the foredoomed *Amos 'n' Andy* television series—had he not been working in Puerto Rico at the time. Moreland's longtime colleague Flournoy E. Miller had served, after all, as a paid casting consultant for *Amos 'n' Andy* in its leap from radio to television. Miller had been recruited by the white actor-entrepreneurs in charge of *Amos 'n' Andy*, Charles Correll and Freeman Gosden, as a behind-the-scenes symbol of further ethnic validation for the televised version's thoroughly black array of leading players.

And Flournoy Miller saw to it that his colleague Spencer Williams, Jr. should land the pivotal role of Andy Brown, and that another Chitlin' Circuit-to-Broadway crony, Tim Moore, be cast as the bombastic-but-henpecked George "Kingfish" Stevens. But Miller made no such case for himself as a prospective cast member. While *Amos 'n' Andy* was entering the spreading province of television and Moreland was working offshore in a practical alternative to a movie-studio blackballing, Miller contented himself with an ensemble role in a low-budget minstrel-revival movie called *Yes, Sir, Mr. Bones!* (1951), featured along with the white-in-blackface minstrel man Emmett Miller (1900–1962).

Explained Marcella Moreland Young: "Well, F.E. Miller, by this time, had become more interested in writing than in performing, it seems. But F.E.'s friendship with my Daddy abided."

Back in America after the discontinuation of *Duffy's Tavern* on radio, Moreland found readier opportunities on the stage than in the movies. He renewed a partnership with fellow comedian Redd Foxx (John Elroy Sanford, a.k.a. Chicago Red; 1922–1991) for occasional forays into Harlem's Apollo Theatre. Moreland also appeared with Earl Jackson at the Apollo. A standard routine was the *Indefinite Talk* trade-off of rapid-fire non-sequiturs, as developed by F.E. Miller for the act of Miller & Moreland and then passed along to Moreland with all due blessings.

Marcella Moreland found her father to be "inordinately patient with anyone to whom he tried to teach the *Indefinite Talk*. And none of his team-partners, after his time with F.E. and Ben Carter, ever quite lived up fully to that standard of perfection. Some picked up on it well enough, but Daddy had become accustomed to that higher level of accomplishment. Of course, Daddy couldn't just drop the routine—because his audiences had grown to expect to be treated to some of that *Indefinite Talk*. So he kept it going and taught it to whoever could grasp its finer points."

Off-Hollywood's black independent picture-making sector had all but withered by now as segregated film going gradually became obsolete and the spread of television began to alter mass-audience movie-going patterns across-the-board. My uncle, Grady L. Wilson, was among the first Southern theater bosses to yank down the bar during the 1950s, bucking the hard-line segregationists who owned his Dallas-based company and eliminating the Interstate Circuit Theatres' customs of Negroes-to-the-balcony and Colored Only Night, at least in Amarillo, Texas. Grady's rationale to the brass was that the box office would rake in more and greener money if anyone could come see any movie at any time one pleased. The Civil Rights movement might have covered more ground, more rapidly, if only it had appealed strategically to the acquisitive instincts of the Dominant Culture.

Tough luck, then, that the black independent cinema did not flourish apace with such an opening-up of the mainstream theaters. But Art in its more genuine forms is born of repression and dies of freedom, subsidized into compromise and tempted away from creative subversion by the absence of any restrictions worth flouting. It was easy, during those days of broad-sweep striving to purge stereotypes from the mass media, to slap the Uncle Tom label upon an actor who played blue-collared and liveried servants and caused audiences to chuckle. And a hard-pressed movie industry found it easier to forget about Mantan Moreland than to broaden or even sustain his opportunities.

### III

Four short-feature motion pictures boasting Moreland's presence—the back-to-back productions of *Rock 'n' Roll Revue, Rhythm & Blues Revue, Rockin' the Blues*, and *Basin Street Revue* (1955-1956)—are in fact stagebound concert movies, interspersed with comical interludes. These films illustrate Moreland's retrenching onto the stage more so than they bespeak any newfound opportunities for him in mainstream narrative cinema.

Those four revue-styled films, however, are emblematic of a greater influence that Moreland would prove to exert—an impact upon the emerging idiom of rock 'n' roll, as a trailblazing force in popular music. If Moreland had hinted at a pop-jazz inclination with his late-'40 Cyclone Records platter ("Laffin' Song" b/w "What Did It Getcha?"), then his rock 'n' roll bearings manifested themselves more strikingly in the work of several other artists of Top 40 prominence. And this influence, though often without due attribution to the inspiration, shows up as early as 1956.

Moreland's purported nephew, Prentice "Prince" Moreland, spent a portion of that year as a substitute tenor with a harmonizing group known variously as the Cadets and the Jacks. This outfit was under contract to Saul and Jules Bihari's Modern Records Company of Los Angeles, an aggressive independent label strategically positioned amidst the rise of rock 'n' roll. The Cadets' version of the composition "Stranded in the Jungle" (Modern No. 994; 1956) is one of the first great comical novelties of the rock 'n' roll movement.[3]

The Cadets' rendition contains an imperishable line from Prentice Moreland: "Great googly-moogly! Le'mme outta here!" The exclamation had long since been in popular usage—the blues artist Willie Dixon often explained that "Great googly-moogly!" is a bowdlerization of the commonplace oath "Great God A'mighty!"—but Prentice's application of the phrase accounts for a watershed moment within the popular culture, however nonsensical the context. The line, in spirit and letter, also is closely akin to Mantan Moreland's signature performance in 1941's *King of the Zombies*.

The Cadets' Modern Records edition of "Stranded in the Jungle" cropped up on the pop-music radio stations in my South-by-Southwestern hometown at about the same time its title surfaced on a widely distributed roster of songs forbidden by the Roman Catholic Church's hellfire watchdog/lap-dog group, the Legion of Decency. This *verboten* status, naturally, contributed to the popular success of the recording among a young-and-defiant populace just now beginning to feel its oats. The spectacle of hundreds of grammar-school children, cavorting about a campus playground while hollering, "Great googly-moogly!" must have driven any number of teachers to a state of google-eyed distraction, if not necessarily to drink.

More about that connection surfaces in a telling aside from Marcella Moreland Young: "Prentice—or *Prentiece* or *Prentis*, as he sometimes spelled the name—is supposed to be the only one of many alleged show-business

Prentice Moreland record

kin that we actually recognized as family. Now, we couldn't quite confirm the lineage that he claimed, but he said he had some folks from Daddy's hometown of Monroe, Louisiana. And he called Daddy his uncle.

"And Daddy always called Prentice his nephew—there was that longing for family ties, y'know, that Daddy always had in him. That is to say, Mom and my Daddy always accepted Prentice as a member of the family. Prentice knew some of the same Louisiana people that Daddy knew, and of course Prentice obviously took a great pride in bearing the name of Moreland. I'll never know just how well authenticated the family connection was—but we were all crazy about Prentice, anyhow."

"Stranded in the Jungle," representing Prentice Moreland's only recording session with the Cadets, provides indelible evidence of the lasting influence of Mantan Moreland. The song's very scenario, for that matter, is reminiscent of the establishing scenes that had set *King of the Zombies* in motion, 15 years earlier:

> I crashed in the jungle while trying to keep a date
> With my little girl, who was back in the States.
> I was stranded in the jungle, afraid and alone
> Trying to figure a way to get a message back home...
>
> The boys in the jungle had me on the run
> When somethin' heavy hit me, like an atomic bomb.
> When I woke up and my head started to clear,
> I had a strange feeling I was with cookin' gear.
> I smelled somethin' cookin', and I looked to see—
> That's when I found out they was a-cookin' me...
> (Great googly-moogly! Le'mme outta here!)

> I jumped out [of] the pot, and I finally got away—
> Frantic and worried 'bout what my baby'd say.
> So I jumped in the ocean and I started to swim,
> But my chance of survival was gettin' mighty slim.
> So I thumbed down a whale who was a-headin' my way,
> And I reached the States in 'bout a half a day...

Prentice told Modern Records' Joe Bihari that he improvised "Great googly-moogly! Le'mme outta here!" and that was inspired in part by Mantan, and in part by some disc jockey whom Prentice had heard in Cincinnatti. The Bihari family encouraged Prentice to remain with the Cadets, but the singer moved along to other doo-wop harmony groups, eventually becoming a solo artist for such labels as Edsel, Del-Fi/Donna, and Challenge, during 1959-1962. Prentice Moreland died in 1988.

Elsewhere within the bedrock of rock, the Robins (who would mutate more famously into the Coasters at Atlantic Records' ATCO subsidiary, with the Cadets' Will "Dub" Jones as their droll bass voice) appropriated Mantan Moreland's contemplative expression, "Mmm-mmm-*mmm!*" to striking effect. That escalating spiral of throaty hums, though inarticulate on the face of it, conveys by itself a greater depth of meaning than, say, the entire Life's Work of Elvis Presley, along with a sense of bemused humor that proves lacking in most of the more celebrated rock-star *poseurs*. And in their 1964 recording of "Bad Detective" (ATCO Records No. 6300)—hardly a runaway hit, but then who's keeping score when the music can stand on its own merits?—the Coasters paid an extended homage to Moreland's character, Birmingham Brown, of the *Charlie Chan* films. Atlantic Records might just as easily have hired Moreland to vocalize a cameo appearance.

The South Texas balladeer and preacherly monologue artist Joseph Arrington, Jr., who became Joe Tex only after he had put his native state behind him, worked a cascading variation upon Moreland's high-pitched chuckle into his singing. Tex seemed almost to *become* Moreland in such rambunctious recordings of the waning 1960s as "Skinny Legs and All" (Dial Records No. 4063; 1967), "Men Are Gettin' Scarce" (Dial No. 4069; 1968), and "Go Home and Do It" (Dial No. 4083; 1968). Joe Tex seemed delighted to find himself likened to Moreland when several fans-of-Mantan and I visited with the singer backstage in 1966, during a show at the Tri-State Fairgrounds in Amarillo, Texas.

## IV

Flash back to the early 1940s, and one finds various articles in the tradepaper *Variety* hailing Moreland for outbursts of the quirky spontaneity that would become essential to the rock 'n' roll youthquakes of the following decade: "He

works with remarkable ease and at all times is natural." And: "His eye-white exposures, general laugh-mugging, and scene-swiping go over all the time." And: "[He] never fails to garner a laugh, no matter how feeble the line."

That laugh-getting impulse appears to have been essential to Moreland's personality, on- or off-camera. An anecdote from Monogram Pictures' publicity department has been preserved in the press kit for one of Moreland's *Charlie Chan* pictures, *Shadows over Chinatown* (1946). The text bears reprinting, more-or-less intact:

**Comedian Loves To Pull Gags on Theatrical Pals**

Give comedian Mantan Moreland half a chance, and you'll either be the victim of one of his jokes or be laughing at him. He's a true comedian, without a doubt…

Mantan gets a big kick telling some of the tricks he has pulled on his friends. One time, he was umpiring a [baseball] game in which a number of celebrities were participating. At bat was Cab Calloway, the famous bandleader.

"Strike one!" Mantan yelled when the swing baton-waver missed the first ball. "Strike two!" shouted Mantan with glee as Calloway let the next pitch go by without a swing.

"That was this high," argued Calloway. "You're blind."

"You're another!" retorted umpire Moreland.

The bandleader promptly got his dander up. He swung with all his might at the next pitch, and a resounding crack echoed across the diamond as the ball went sailing over the fence.

"Ha, ha, ha!" laughed Cab as he went running around the bases, and just to add to the merriment he slid into home base, covering Moreland with dust.

"That," he said, "is for calling them the way they ain't."

"And this is for you," roared back Moreland as he threw his thumb into the air. "You're out!"

"What do you mean, I'm out? I hit the ball over the fence!" yelled the irritated bandleader.

"Sure, you did," returned umpire Moreland, "but you stepped out of the box when you hit the ball. So you're out."

"Why didn't you tell me that before I started running around the basis?" demanded Calloway.

"Oh," snickered Moreland, "I just wanted to see you get some good outdoor exercise."

Yes, well, and if it ain't true, then it ought to be—just like the old-time tale-spinners would insist.

That same publicity department turned the tables on Moreland—as if to demonstrate that his prankish nature worked reciprocally—in an incidental story from the press kit for 1948's *The Shanghai Chest*. To wit:

### Jokes Played on Comedian

If Mantan Moreland didn't possess a good sense of humor, he might have been a very nervous man when he completed his role…in Monogram's The Shanghai Chest…

Since the film comic likes to perpetrate gags, the other members of the cast decided to beat him to it. Moreland is a constant cigar smoker, but whenever he put [a cigar] down on the set he couldn't pick it up again because somebody would nail it down.

The comedian lost so many cigars that he finally took to his pipe. But he found it very unpalatable, since one of his fellow actors had covered the mouthpiece with mineral oil.

Later, when Mantan had to rehearse his lines, he was squirted with cold water; and on another occasion, after doing a long dialogue scene which involved lots of action on his part, he was told there wasn't any film in the camera.

Moreland sheepishly promised to have the last laugh some day.

### V

So able a hand was Moreland, so infallibly entertaining in large pictures and small (but more generously deployed in the smaller films), that the abrupt cratering of his career left a bewildering void. The National Association for

the Advancement of Colored People issued no mass-media pronouncements of its spiteful victory over the laugh-making imperative. Of course, careers are as cheap and expendable as life itself as far as Establishment Hollywood is concerned.

The filmmaker Melvin Van Peebles, who would cast a resurgent Moreland to memorable effect in the 1970 satire *Watermelon Man,* has called it "a tragedy...that Mantan was left out in the cold in his prime, that the studios let themselves be bullied into agreeing that his image fostered some sort of racism.

"Now, Stepin Fetchit—I could see him causing white people to think the less of black people," Van Peebles told me in 1996, during a visit in Dallas. "But even Stepin Fetchit didn't pretend to represent any class beyond his own sense of humor. Mantan, now, *his* gift was simply, brilliantly, that of finding the humor in *any* given situation. He was not a political being, and he was no apologist, either.

"To my thinking, he actually brought out the resilience and the resourcefulness in the characters he was assigned to portray. His speaking voice was no exaggerated dialect—that was the way he talked, just as deep-Southern as you please. Nowadays, we'd call it Ebonics. The entire so-called New Black Cinema, from Spike Lee to Eddie Murphy to my own son [the actor-turned-director Mario Van Peebles] owes a great deal to trails that were blazed by Mantan." (Van Peebles did some back-pedaling from this stance in a documentary film of 1998 called *Classified X*. Though respectful of the black-talent pioneers, Van Peebles conveys here more of an indictment of the portrayals themselves.)

A more conservative and inclusive force in black-origin show business, Bill Cosby, also cut Moreland a significant length of slack in 1969, enlisting him for a showy guest appearance on network television's *The Bill Cosby Show*. Moreland's character, teamed with Jackie "Moms" Mabley (1894–1975), cropped up just long enough to inspire Cosby to begin thinking about a spin-off program centered upon their uncle-and-auntie characters. Which never developed.

"Mantan was a throwback to that broader school of comedy, y'know, and he had what I'd been brought up to consider to've been a disgraceful history," Cosby told me in 1990 in Los Angeles, during a promotional tour on behalf of his and Sidney Poitier's collaborative film *Ghost Dad*. "But Mantan was a brilliant comic actor—and had he lived on, I'd've liked to've worked all I could with him."

Today Mantan fans can easily find his work on DVD, such as his TV appearance on *The Bill Cosby Show*.

The visit with Cosby took place during a business-as-usual press event, although Universal Pictures had taken the uncommon step of inviting several black-readership newspapers in addition to the customary mass-market dailies. While Cosby and I spoke, a novice journalist from one of these Afrocentric publications came barging into the interview suite without so much as a knock on the door: "Bill! Bill!"

"*What?*" answered Cosby, glancing up but remaining seated, as impatient as you please.

"Bill! Remember me? I interviewed you, just a little while ago, for my newspaper—and I *forgot* somethin'!"

"Okay," said Cosby. "Then *what?*"

"I forgot to get you to autograph these movie stills, Bill," answered the reporter, flashing a fistful of 8-by-10 glossies from the movie's press kit while taking for granted a first-name familiarity with an artist too dignified for such an assumption. Then he explained: "They're for my *Mama!*

"And my Mama, she'll *kill* me if I don't bring her back some autographed *pictures* of you, Bill!"

Cosby stood, walked toward the youngster, and fixed a withering stare upon him.

"Don't *ever* talk that way about your mother," said Cosby, ignoring the urgent demand for signatures. "Your mother most certainly *would not* kill you—and *certainly* not over anything so insignificant as a photograph of a movie actor."

"Yessir," came the reply, in a suddenly timid voice.

"Now," said Cosby. "It certainly goes against all professional protocol to ask for an autograph in a formal interview situation, so perhaps you'll be good enough to re*mem*ber that, the *next* time you should find yourself granted such a privilege."

"Yessir."

"Now, hand me one of your photographs, there—just *one*—for your mother," said Cosby, "and I'll be glad to inscribe it for her." Which he did, with an emphatic flourish.

The reporter left, then, cowed but perhaps contented. Or perhaps not.

"That boy was prob'ly intending to haul off and sell a stack of autographed photos," Cosby turned back to me with a conspiratorial grin. Then he continued:

"Now: And what was it that we were talking about? Oh, *sure*—Mantan Moreland. A *fine* comedian, I'll say! Came from a very civilized and somehow appropriate, for its time, school of comedy, however old-fashioned he might have seemed by the middle of the century.

"Not at all like some of these ill-mannered little snots nowadays," Cosby added, glancing over one shoulder as if anticipating another intrusion.

---

[1] Shirley Booth went on to land an array of Tony Award and Oscar citations; she is best remembered for the anguished leading role in *Come Back, Little Sheba* (filmed in 1952), and as the assertive housekeeper on network television's *Hazel* (1961–1966).

[2] An A.F. of M. embargo upon employment offered by the hit-record industry had inspired the jazz singer Dinah Washington to deliver a defiant, satirical piece called *Record Ban Blues* (Mercury Records No. 1592) in 1947. The same union's ban on prerecorded musical accompaniment for post-WWII television serials served essentially to put a good many American musicians out of work—for the suppliers of such underscoring resorted as a consequence to the employment of foreign orchestras.

[3] Ernestine Smith and James Johnson had composed "Stranded in the Jungle" for Johnson's singing group the Jayhawks (Flash Records No. 109; 1956)—but the Cadets beat the Jayhawks into mass-market distribution, and onto the hit-record charts, with a prompt cover-version performance ordered by Modern Records' director of artists-and-repertoire, Joseph Bihari.

# 16
# Moe on Moreland—and Hoodooing the Hoodoo Man

Nyuk–nyuk–nyuk.
—Jerome "Curly" Howard

Moe Howard lamented thusly to me in 1973: "We really should'a' made Mantan Moreland our next third Stooge, back when my brother Shemp [Samuel Howard] cashed in [in 1955]. They'd worked together, y'know, and Shemp actually had recommended Mantan if the need should ever, God forbid, arise.

"Mantan was responsive, when Larry [Fine] and I talked the idea over with him. I mean, we'd *all* seen our better days by that time, but ol' Moreland—now, *there* was a talent that could'a' invigorated the whole act! He had the wordplay—you ever heard him do that 'anticipation' routine, where he and one or another of his partners finish each other's sentences?—and he had the physical *shtick,* the jive moves and the double-take reactions that would'a' filled in the gaps that Jerome [Curly Howard] and Shemp had kept covered.

"But of course Columbia [Pictures' management] demanded a white guy, because they'd apparently been scared off of Mantan, and we ended up stuck with that prissy damned Joe Besser, who was whatcha might call a pain... I've always thought what a great act the Stooges could'a' stayed for a while, if only we'd'a' gone with Mantan."

Per the wise old Oriental saying: *Nevah hoppen.* And 'way off in some Alternate Reality, maybe it all transpired just that way and Everybody Lived Happily Ever After.

This slight revelation of a bit of that Stuff of Which Dreams Are Made should have seen print when new, when I had chanced to

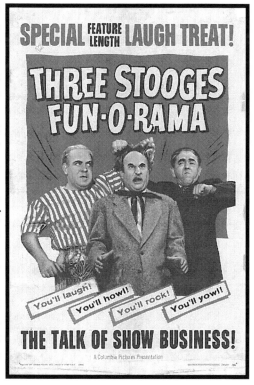

Mantan the Funnyman

interview the more-or-less retired Moe Howard while he was visiting friends within the Jewish mercantile-district community of Northwest Texas. (I had an inside track, here, having spent my high-school and early college years as a store manager and fashion buyer for several such retail-clothier families.) The incidental news-hook, on this occasion, was that Howard's last film—1973's *Dr. Death: Seeker of Souls*, in which he has a small role—had just come into play at a local drive-in theater. My supervising editor was not sufficiently concerned with Howard's reminiscent ramblings to allow the story more than a few column-inches of space. So there lies the scoop, as rescued from the cutting-room floor at the Amarillo *Daily News*. Make of it what you will.

It develops that Columbia Pictures *had* dabbled with a mixed-color comedy team as early as 1942, when it assigned a short-subject script called "Phoney Croneys" (which had been pitched, but rejected, as a Three Stooges project) to a sub-Stooges lineup. The assigned players included gruff Tom Kennedy as the Moe surrogate; El Brendel, a sweet-natured Scandahoovian-dialect comic, in the rough equivalent of a Larry Fine-type role; and the black comedian Dudley Dickerson in something resembling a Curly Howard part. The scenarist-director, Harry Edwards, seems to have exhausted his deeper reserves of wit in establishing Dickerson's character as a bookkeeper named Petty Larsen. The teaming failed to persist beyond just the one film, although the key players sustained ties to Columbia's short-comedies department. Even so, the picture packs a wealth of lowbrow nonsense into a headlong rush of 18 minutes, and to rediscover "Phoney Croneys" today is to find a tentative, isolated foreshadowing of the strategy that Moe and Shemp Howard had envisioned.

Such a development would have meant as much to Moreland as to the surviving Stooges, for Moreland's stardom had long since been foiled despite his abiding willingness to work.

## II

Moreland returned in 1957 to Broadway, scene of the black-and-tan jazz-baby productions that he had served during the late 1920s, for a black-ensemble presentation of Samuel Beckett's Existentialist tragicomedy *Waiting for Godot*. Moreland handled the role of Estragon in a significant departure, serene but alert and wary, from the overtly nervous style that Bert Lahr had brought to the part a year earlier.

"*Godot* Is Back" declared the *New York Times*, heralding a vaguely appreciative but nonetheless sarcastic review by J. Brooks Atkinson, long the most influential-and-don't-you-forget-it critic in the market.[1] Atkinson had reviewed Moreland's work as early as 1928, allowing at the time that "humor such as *Blackbirds of 1928* affords comes chiefly from Tim Moore's [the Kingfish, in embryo] threatening personality and robust physiognomy, and Manton [*sic*] Moreland's nervous card-concealing act [in a poker-game scenario]."

**Mantan Moreland and Earle Hyman in *Waiting for Godot* (Photofest)**

Moreland may well have found the baffling ironies of *Waiting for Godot* ideally matched with his own prevailing view of life as a sustained absurdity. Or does anyone really comprehend the intended meaning of *Godot*? Atkinson of the *Times* believed not, anyhow.

"Since no one knows what Beckett's rigadoon means," snarked Atkinson, "one should not say that the new version misinterprets the theme. Obviously, a play has to be understood before the actors can be suspected of having muddled it."

This dumbfounded bluff of a review finds Atkinson on something less than the leading edge of criticism attuned to a revolutionary concept in the legitimate theater. Composed in 1948 as *En Attendant Godot*, the play was published in 1952 before its first staging in Paris in 1953. Beckett translated *Godot* into English for two London productions of 1955, followed by the American début in 1956 at the Coconut Grove Playhouse in Coral Gables, Florida (where the promoters touted it, in a bait-and-switch manner, as a laff-riot comedy) as a prelude to a Broadway opening.

*Godot* foreshadowed and encouraged the coining of the phrase *Theatre of the Absurd*, a course of thought set forth by the influential professor and London-based broadcasting executive Martin Esslin (1918–2002). But Beckett, balking at such categorical thinking, declined to consider *Godot* as a part of any larger movement. The play remains consistent, however, with the Absurdist Theatre standard of disorientation in its avoidance of conventional plotting, readily identifiable characters (the titular Godot, like the absentee landlord of *Duffy's Tavern*, never appears) and any palpably meaningful sense of attempting to make any sense at all. If there are, indeed, "many here among us who feel that life is but a joke," as Bob Dylan would put it, then Beckett and Moreland must be early arrivals at such a conclusion.

The disheveled Estragon, or Gogo (played by Moreland in Michael Meyerberg's 1957 revival), and Vladimir, or Didi (Earle Hyman), travel to a lonely site to await the arrival of Godot, whoever Godot might be and whenever he might be coming along. Hoboes, these two might be, or war refugees—Beckett's tale leaves such an interpretation entirely to the absorbed viewer. Gogo and Didi conversate and argue, pondering the inexplicable nature of their sojourn, until an intruder named Pozzo (Rex Ingram)[2] arrives, accompanied by a servant known as Lucky (Geoffrey Holder). Pozzo, purportedly the owner of the land where this lonely vigil takes place, puts Lucky through some humiliating paces as if to entertain Gogo and Didi. Pozzo feasts, as if picnicking, and throws the scraps to his companions. Pozzo and Lucky depart at length, and a boy (Bert Chamberlain) shows up with word that Godot will coming along later than anticipated. Pozzo reappears, blind, and Lucky, mute. The boy returns with word that Godot will not be coming, after all. Didi turns to Gogo with this: "Well, shall we go?" To which Gogo replies: "Yes. Let's go." (Reads Beckett's closing stage instruction: "They do not move.")

Brooks Atkinson, did, despite his stated intentions, tend to accuse the actors of muddling Beckett. He wrote such words as these, which contain a surprising degree of insight into the style of Mantan Moreland:

> *Waiting for Godot* is not so much of a minstrel show as it has become in Herbert Berghof's new style of direction. The actors are good enough in their own right. Mantan Moreland...has all

the mournful humors of the traditional Negro Vaudeville actor—a suspicious joyousness of manner, a crack-voiced laugh, a teetery walk, a general feeling that he is the one who is going to get slapped.

Since [Moreland] is short and stubby, he is a comic-looking figure in the company of Earle Hyman, who is tall and skinny and plays Didi...an excellent actor who knows how to speak a sentence.

...Throughout the animated first act, Mr. Moreland and Mr. Hyman put on a funny show. That would seem to be a consummation devoutly to be wished, for Mr. Beckett needs actors. But...*Waiting for Godot* cannot be laughed off. In some elusive fashion, it is concerned with the suffering of humankind...more of a dirge than a Vaudeville turn...

The black-ensemble Godot played for six days, January 21–26, 1957, at the Ethel Barrymore Theatre—hardly a runaway success, but an assurance, nonetheless, that Moreland had regained some momentum.

Then in nightclubs large and small, mostly small; on phonograph records that ranged wildly from smutty-joke routines to readings of Roark Bradford's dialect-laden Biblical fables; and in the occasional niche-market movie assignment or mass-appeal network-television appearance, Moreland would continue to perform for as mixed an audience as he could find, and for those pocketed black audiences who understood that his art needed no correcting. It bears remembering the subtext of punishment that the cultural historian David J. Skal has perceived and isolated as the motivating basis of any attempt at correction.

### III

Around the close of the 1960s, still game after suffering a series of strokes, Moreland toured the nationwide network of Veterans Administration Hospitals with fellow comic Roosevelt "Livinggood" (a.k.a. "Livingood") Myles, with whom he also recorded two comedy-routine albums: *Elsie's Sportin' House* and *That Ain't My Finger!* (Scandalous in their day, those recordings play out almost quaintly in the here-and-now, their bawdier excesses notwithstanding. Moreland's delivery leans more toward the explicit than the merely naughty, but his tone-of-voice is not so much calculated to shock as it is merely crass, in a playful way.)

I learned after the fact, around 1970, that the stops on the Moreland & Myles tour had included the V.A. Hospital in Amarillo. I was still a citizen of the old hometown, working by now as a newspaper reporter responsible for covering the public schools' long-delayed process of integration. Had my blues-enthusiast uncle, Grady L. Wilson, not died (in 1968), I'd probably have received notice in time to catch the un-publicized Moreland appearance. For Grady often occupied a ward at the V.A. Hospital, thanks to lingering maladies from his wartime tour of duty in the scenic and vermin-infested Pacific Theatre of Operations.

The Amarillo Independent School District had ignored for over a decade a sweeping order to remove its barriers of segregation; this, in passive-aggressive defiance of 1954's *Brown vs. Board of Education* decision, which proved more a mollifying sop than the revolutionary action that wishful-thinking hindsight has made it out to be. Amarillo's educational bureaucracy now found itself under the gun and moving with a federal-fiat haste that only stirred up long-dormant, reciprocal resentments and polarized the city ever further. As the reporter-of-record on this chronic story for S.B. Whittenburg's Globe-News Publishing Company, I struck up a cordial acquaintance with Dr. Richard W. Jones, the longtime president of Amarillo's N.A.A.C.P. branch and my Uncle Grady's dentist of years gone by.

Jones, a wiry, intense fellow of light complexion and brooding demeanor, became a crucial voice in the news coverage. He warmed, more or less, to my eagerness to give his organization a forum despite his wariness of a Dominant Culture newspaper company. The Whittenburg publications, after all, had historically steered clear of the town's sharply defined black district, except when reporting crimes that happened to cross the color line in one direction or the other, or when publishing obituary notices for the official record.

While speaking with Dr. Jones one evening after a meeting of the entirely white-folks School Board and administrative staff, I mentioned my disappointment over having missed Moreland's show at the Veterans Administration Hospital. This was probably not a good time to attempt anything in the way of small talk—much less, as it turned out, to make a reference to Mantan Moreland—for Jones and his entourage usually came away fuming, whether on principle or in specific indignation, from any gathering of the Amarillo School Board.

This occasion had been especially combative, with a sustained bit of face-to-face animosity between Dr. Jones and Robert A. Ashworth, the self-important superintendent of schools, whose public-speaking vocabulary still included the archaic and dismissive Southern term *nigra*. The encounter had peaked with an out-of-nowhere apocalyptic reference from Dr. Jones: "…It's going to be the *fire* next time," he had said, apropos of nothing much more than the urge to antagonize, "and as y'all *know*, I *never* go *any*where without a pocketful of *match*books!"

So when I caught up with Jones after the meeting and dropped the reference to Moreland in an off-the-cuff remark, nothing more, I received a harangue—and an unanticipated revelation—in reply:

"What?! Mantan Moreland? Here in *town*? Why, that man is a dis*grace*! I thought we'd put the wraps on his career, *years* ago!" Dr. Jones fumed.

Say *what*?!

*Well, yes, and I suppose you-all had put the wraps on his career, Dr. Jones. It's a pretty steep drop from even a low-budget Hollywood studio, smack-dab into the pits of obscurity and the frustrations of one almost-comeback after another. Once I lived the life of a millionaire...*

And here follows a fantasy sequence, far from gratuitous: In a screenplay treatment called *Harlemwood*, dating from 1996, Josh Alan Friedman writes of a backstage meeting in 1947 between a black comedian named Hog Jowl Powell—loosely based upon Moreland's contemporary Dewey "Pigmeat" Markham—and a young, idealistic officer of the N.A.A.C.P. named Mr. Warden. Warden heads a delegation on a visit to the backstage dressing-room of Hog Jowl Powell, who still performs in black-on-black greasepaint, minstrel-style. The aim is to initiate a confrontation:

> **Mr. Warden:** Mr. Powell, we've laughed at your jokes since we were children. As our mothers laughed before us. But we've made great strides since then. We've fought in the last war. We have a man about to enter major-league baseball...It's a time for uplifting our people. That blackface you [are] wearin' demeans all of us. It brings no credit to our race. It's old, it's tired, it's worn out. We come to you with hopes for positive change.
> **Powell:** What chu mean?
> **Mr. Warden:** It's time to lay off the shoe polish, Pops.
> **Powell** (*after a long pause*)**:** Now, you listen here, son. I been makin' up every night, since the heyday of Vaudeville, goin' on thutty years. I can't get my laughs without my makeup. No colored comedian could...
> **Mr. Warden:** Sammy Davis, Jr., does. Bill Robinson never wore it. Cab Calloway [is] funny without it.
> **Powell:** I don't make no Cab Calloway salary. I don't play no Cab Calloway nightclubs in New York. I works the Chitlin' Circuit. I'm an old minstrel, and I knows how I gets mah laughs, and dis here tin of *shoe polish*, as you call it, [has] been travelin' wif' me all mah days.

Mantan Moreland had long since "laid off the shoe polish," as it were, at such a time in history as Friedman half-recaptures and half-imagines. But the siege of correctionism targeted any qualities or characteristics that might strike its adherents as caricatured. Thus does Friedman's scenario capture the conflicted imperatives that polarized a society at precisely the moment it should have been, as the voguish saying goes, celebrating its own diversity. Or at least practicing a bit of live-and-let-live philosophical tolerance.

But to get back to that encounter with the N.A.A.C.P.'s Dr. Richard Jones: By this time, now, I had become cordially conversant with the West Texas honchos of the National Association for the Advancement of Colored People, but this was the first occasion on which any member had hinted to me at "putting the wraps" on anybody's career—not that we made a habit of talking about any such agendas. Our discussions had strictly to do with my business of harvesting immediate-issue information for the local newspaper-of-record, and with the organization's interest in telling its side of the school-integration story to anybody who might prove attentive.

But now, T-Bone Walker's passing remark of several years earlier came rushing back to mind, as if no time at all had passed between those words and Dr. Jones' grouchy outburst. What was it that Walker had said about his old-time pal Mantan? *"Hollywood's been scared off of him by pressure from our own bless*é*d N.A.A.C.P."*

Things were beginning to make a bit more sense in a sudden combination of early insight and newly shed light. And I hadn't any better sense than to press the issue.

So I asked: "What do you mean by 'put the wraps on his career,' Dr. Jones?"

"Have you ever watched one of that man's moving pictures?"

"All of 'em I can get a look at," I answered. "Mantan Moreland is a great comedian."

"He's an Uncle Tom, is what he is—a symbol of the Negro as a laughing-stock."

"Well, sir," I said, "all due respect, but I've always found Mantan to be pretty darned heroic and quick-witted. Closer to Paul Robeson than to Stepin Fetchit, if you're talking about dignity and resourcefulness."

"Yes, well, and even Robeson has committed a crime or two against racial uplift."

I didn't inquire at the time as to what performances of Robeson's Dr. Jones might have had in mind, but I suspect he was thinking of the 1936 *Show Boat*, where Robeson and Hattie McDaniel carry on a pure-stereotype domestic relationship, perfectly in keeping with the condescension fundamental to Edna Ferber's original story. Or maybe Jones was recalling Dudley Murphy's 1933 filming of *The Emperor Jones*, in which Robeson, playing an American hoodlum who installs himself as dictator over a Third World protectorate, throws off the occasional "Feets, do yo' duty" type of line with no perceptible tone of irony.

"Well, I think Mantan Moreland was a positive force. Might even still be," I told Dr. Jones, "and I'm sorry to learn that you claim a hand in any blacklisting of him."

"Oh, it's not as though I brought him down, personally," Jones came back. "These are times of change, and times of correction."

Frankie Darro, left, and Mantan Moreland struck up a lasting friendship as stars of a forward-thinking buddy-picture series of the early 1940s.

"Nothing personal, huh?" I said, disregarding the customary barriers of formality that exist (for right and proper reasons) between a journalist and the subject of an interview. But Dr. Jones and I were 'way off the record at this moment, as far as my newspaper bosses, or Jones' higher-ups with the N.A.A.C.P., might have been concerned.

"Well," I added, "I doubt that anybody subjected to a blackballing would consider the experience anything *but* personal."

Dr. Jones could deliver a "*Hmph!*" capable of chilling the blood, and when in a state of high dudgeon he wielded a withering evil-eye glare to match, cloaking himself in a radiant fog of cigarette smoke and seething like an unventilated pressure-cooker. He summoned this ocular mojo to intimidating effect, now, while I fought off another onrush of memory lest I appear amused at the direction our conversation was taking: I was thinking of an exchange between Jack Benny and Eddie "Rochester" Anderson in a movie from 1943 called *The Meanest Man in the World*. Rochester is describing the rituals basic to his fraternal lodge, and Benny seems unimpressed. He tells Anderson that the organization doesn't sound especially appealing, and Anderson replies that Benny would be ineligible for membership, in any event: "You'd be whiteballed!"

Whiteballed, blackballed—same meaning, just inverted according to whichever side one might occupy along the Iron Curtain of Racialism. Blacklisted, excluded, declared unfit, 4-F'd. *Move over, boys, I'm one of the gang, now*—but not for blasted long enough to navigate the intended course.

Dr. Jones winced at my use of the term *blackballing*, which packs no ethnic denotation but sounds, instead, grim and punitive.

"Well, it's not as though we had tried to kick him out of the race, or any such thing," Jones said, mellowing slightly. "The organization's lobbyists merely discouraged his employment among the moving-picture companies and urged him to apply his talents to a higher calling.

"That was a long time ago," Jones added, as if to suggest that such acts of character assassination and career sabotage came equipped with a statute of limitations. "Last time I heard of Mantan Moreland, he was reciting those *Green Pastures* Bible stories for some record company—minstrel-show dialect stuff that should have gone out with Mammy songs and Mr. Bones."[3] (Jones' reference here was to Moreland's Caedmon Records album of 1958, *Ol' Man Adam and His Chillun*.)

"Sounds to me like your bunch put a hoodoo on him," I said. "What'd you-all do—hire a conjure man to slap a whammy on his career?" I was speaking facetiously, of course, but Dr. Jones was in no such mood.

"I'll have you know, Michael Price, that the N-double-A-C-P is an *enlightened* organization," he said, in an oblique sort-of rebuttal to my tongue-in-cheek accusation.

"Okay, then," I pressed the taunt, "but y'all ought to get your money back from whatever conjurer you used—'cause it looks like Mantan's still working and still making people laugh. Maybe he done hoodooed the hoodoo man."

"Wherever did you learn to *talk* like that?" Jones asked, vaguely startled.

"Well, sir, us white folks listen to the blues, too," I said.

"I like you, boy," Jones said, shedding the severe demeanor for a moment. "You speak right up."

We left it at that, then, and never again raised the topics of Mantan Moreland or even show business in general, except to compare observations occasionally on this or that favorite jazz artist.

Dr. Jones' condemnation had at least the saving grace of earnestness: He seemed genuinely to perceive villainy in such entertainment as Mantan Moreland represented.

Jones would live on for another decade or so, a loyal, honest and unfailingly controversial newsgathering contact to the end.

I was nonetheless surprised to find myself mentioned in Dr. Jones' will. Following his death in 1979, I received a telephone call from his widow, Hessie Mae Jones, informing me that Dr. Jones had intended that I should inherit his collection of phonograph records.

This formidable batch of pressings numbered into the thousands and spanned a period from the Depression years into the present day. Right there alongside

Fats Waller and Billie Holiday, John Coltrane and Miles Davis and Dizzy Gillespie, sat a matched set of Mantan Moreland's party-record albums, along with his disk of readings from Roark Bradford's *Ol' Man Adam and His Chillun*, that "minstrel-show dialect stuff that should have gone out with Mammy songs and Mr. Bones."

---

[1] Brooks Atkinson was prominent among the mass-media reviewers whom the journalist and dramatist Ben Hecht (1894–1964) had in mind when he composed a scathing poem called "Ode to Critics." Here, Hecht dismissed the critical brethren as those ' you who come to drama not to drink or sup / But to shine your little egos up'." Hecht's springboard lay in a similarly conceived "Ode to Critics," by the satirist Hugh Henry Brackenridge (1748–1816).

[2] Rex Ingram (1895–1969) was one of Old Hollywood's godlier presences, having portrayed De Lawd in 1936's *The Green Pastures*, and having turned full-circle to handle an explicitly Satanic role in 1943's *Cabin in the Sky*—with Mantan Moreland as a lesser demon. Ingram's range bridged the sacred and the profane, a casting agent's dream-come-true, all together in a tidy package and at your beck and call.

[3] Dr. Jones' reference to "Mr. Bones" calls for a bit of context. In a trailblazing fellowship treatise (dating from 1979 and circulated under an assortment of titles including *Black Humor from Slavery to Stepin Fetchit*), the historian Mel Watkins sets forth this persuasive argument: "Perhaps the most apt way to describe the public humor of black Americans prior to the middle 1930s is to say that it was nearly always masked…, [not only literally, as in face-painting] but also figuratively and psychologically. As an old blues tune put it: 'Got one mind for white folks to see / 'Nother for what I know is me…'" The structure of a minstrel show, explains Watkins, found the performers "on stage in a semi-circle facing the audience with a [master of ceremonies] called the Interlocutor seated in the center. Characters called Mr. Bones and Mr. Tambo were seated at each end. The repartée among these three characters provided most of the humor, although the End Men were the most important performers. Their antics, dances, and sharp wit established basic prototypes that became standards for American humor…[T]hey were anything but the "authentic" representations of blacks that they were advertised to be…Minstrel arts, then, were initially performances featuring whites parodying the amusing antics of black slaves. It was a curious phenomenon, since the behavior being satirized was itself a parody of white behavior. It became even more convoluted when black performers, wearing blackface, formed their own minstrel shows…" Mel Watkins' *On the Real Side: A History of African-American Comedy* (1994) is an essential resource.

# 17
# Indefinite, Most Definitely

History breeds and seeds in strange ways and places.
—Elithe Hamilton Kirkland, *Precious Memories*; 1987

By the early 1970s, a multicultural but studiously un-cultured television serial called *All in the Family* was beginning to foster a more caustic and confrontational strain of Mantan Moreland's brand of class-conflict humor—though without Moreland's participation. Moreland himself faced little prospect of furthering such renewal, despite well-received guest appearances on such network-television standbys as *Adam-12*, *Love, American Style*, *The Dating Game* and Bill Cosby's first foray into the situation-comedy arena.

Moreland had appeared particularly vigorous and ready for resurgence on a late-1960s installment of *The Dating Game*, vying for the attentions of a still-girlish Butterfly McQueen (1911–1995), the Georgia-born actress most vividly remembered for a spirited contribution to *Gone with the Wind* (1939). When asked a qualifying question as to what attribute he prized most highly in a prospective sweetheart, Mantan responded without missing a beat: "Cooking, honey!"

Recalled Marcella Moreland Young: "That slacks-and-jacket outfit that you see Daddy wearing on *The Dating Game*—well, I picked out that ensemble for him. He was a man who knew how to look *dashing*, I mean. Of course, he seldom got to dress up all dapper and flashy in his movies, because so many roles called for him to wear a serving uniform or a janitor's overalls."

In an interview at around this same time on San Francisco's local-television showcase for low-budget movies, which aired under the fashionably snarky name of *The Worst of Hollywood*, Moreland reminisced fondly about a too-brief sojourn on the perimeter of a larger fame, guardedly acknowledging the movement that had labeled him a bad influence.[1] The appearance inspired the cartoonist Kim Deitch to concoct a comic-book story called "Two Old Birds" (published in Robert Crumb's *Weirdo* magazine in 1988). Here, Deitch re-

Flip Wilson, left, with Mantan Moreland and Eddie "Rochester" Anderson in a 1969 episode of *Love, American Style*

imagined Sidney Toler, title-role player of Monogram Pictures' *Charlie Chan* films, as a bigot who delighted in bullying co-star Moreland. "This was a matter of pure irresponsible speculation on my part," Deitch told me in 1999.

That odd scenario scarcely could have veered any farther from the truth, Marcella told me, adding this: "Mr. Toler and Daddy got along famously well with one another, a regular partnership-of-equals situation, and Daddy mourned Mr. Toler's passing, of course." (Moreland's appearance on this *Worst of Hollywood* program served to introduce a telecast of Jean Yarbrough's *King of the Zombies*—a film that, though modestly conceived, falls far from the purportedly "worst" that Hollywood has foisted onto the movie-going masses.)[2]

In his run of motion pictures dating from the late 1930s until the tail-end of the '40s, Moreland had succeeded without straining at the task of endearing black America to the cultural mainstream, neither homogenizing his style nor attempting to mimic any stereotype. Any number of jazz musicians had accomplished such a feat, most notably the New Orleans trumpeter Louis Armstrong (who appears in cahoots with Moreland in 1943's *Cabin in the Sky*) and the New York-based pianists Fats Waller and Duke Ellington. Theirs, however, was an idiom in which they were—artistically, if not economically—in charge. Moreland's vehicle was primarily the Hollywood studio system in all its large and small manifestations, and a black comedian in mid-century Hollywood hadn't a prayer of tailoring a picture to suit his strengths. That is, unless that comedian happened to be Mantan Moreland, under contract to a studio that gave him *carte blanche* to say whatever might come to mind while the cameras rolled.

W.C. Fields, Charles Chaplin, Bob Hope, Buster Keaton, and Stan Laurel & Oliver Hardy—such bankable artists could assume any social station they chose in their scenarios, and often it suited their purposes to assign themselves the role of outsider-looking-in. *Gone with the Wind*'s Hattie McDaniel, Jack Benny's butler-become-sidekick Eddie "Rochester" Anderson, and even the bombastic Paul Robeson were obliged to find what authoritative voices they could in servant-or-subject roles. Moreland's very coloration sublimated his vast gifts in the eyes of the larger corporate studios, which nonetheless supplied him with steady work in addition to his standing commitment to small-time Monogram Pictures.

Most of Moreland's more brilliant showcase pictures find him ingrained in the social underclass, with a notable exception in the black-ensemble independent production of *Mr. Washington Goes to Town* (1940). Here, Moreland inverts the usual casting to play an heir to a windfall fortune, moving about incognito as a bellhop and elevator operator while assuming the ownership of a haunted hotel; only the film's just-a-dream finale derails the inversion of social and economic circumstances. Though usually lacking the creative authority that the acknowledged Great Comics wielded during a film's pre-production stages, Moreland instinctively imposed upon his films-in-progress an insurgent, real-

time control that makes a good many of his assigned pictures quite his own. Even when deployed in the background of a scene, he could upstage the principals. Such episodes of nonchalant scene-stealing can be seen in *Tarzan's New York Adventure* (1942) and *Bowery to Broadway* (1944), the latter also granting some showcase time to Moreland and teammate Ben Carter. The camera liked Moreland just fine and dandy, and he returned the affection a hundredfold.

As a physical comedian, the rotund and moon-faced Moreland—chubby in his prime of health, noticeably leaner as he rebounded from an onslaught of diabetes—possessed a springy grace to rival the conspicuously slimmer Charles Chaplin, Harold Lloyd and Stan Laurel. Moreland also indulged a broader roughhouse streak, and a more overtly flirtatious manner with his leading ladies. And he practiced a whiplash double-take reaction as extraordinary as those of Edgar Kennedy, Oliver Hardy and W.C. Fields, with particularly expressive use of the eyes.

A nickname that appears to date from childhood, "Google Eyes," was popularly applied during the 1920s and onward as a means of likening Moreland to Barney Google, the bug-eyed white-guy comic-strip character created by the cartoonist Billy DeBeck. As daughter Marcella has observed, of course, folks in Louisiana were calling Moreland "Google Eyes" well before the introduction of the *Barney Google* feature as a newspaper attraction.

Like W.C. Fields, like the brusque-and-breezy cowboy star Ken Maynard and like Billy Costello's and Jack Mercer's off-screen voicings of the animated cartoons' Popeye the Sailor, Moreland made an art of commenting upon the passing parade of human absurdity in a way that only *sounded* as though he might be muttering to himself.

Moreland's surrealistic wordplay is in a class with that of the Marx Bros. or Bud Abbott & Lou Costello. Like his fellow born-Southerner Oliver Hardy, Moreland had a musical air about him that manifested itself in a rhythmic chuckle here, a spot of improvised shuffle-dancing there and an occasional outburst of song. Moreland's emphatic speech patterns, that habit of be*labor*ing *cer*tain *syl*lables, made his voice suit his animated physical presence.

An independent-label phonograph record from the postwar years, "Laffin' Song" (Cyclone Records No. 517; 1947) is sufficient to vindicate T-Bone

Walker's appraisal of Moreland as a "good blues singer, too, when he lets it out"—except that "Laffin' Song" is a tune of wordless eloquence, bereft of any utterances that might be considered to rhyme or hew to a fixed meter. Moreland does not *sing* this composition, so much as he uses his high-pitched laughter as a musical instrument: From intimate chuckle to primal shriek, the voice darts and dodges among an obstacle-course maze of brass and reed horns in a three-minute symphonette of hilarity, peaking with an *a cappella obbligato* and then rejoining the combo for a finale leading to a spoken punch line—a perfectly reasonable explanation for that seizure of giggling.

Moreland utters the word *baby* early on in "Laffin' Song," as if addressing a child or perhaps a sweetheart, then soars into a snickering fit that becomes the very music of the piece. Finally, he chuckles his way back into coherent speech with this punch-line of a coda: "Baby, stop…ticklin' me!" So *that* is what was causing this fugue of hilarity—not to give away too much, y'know.

The flip-side of "Laffin' Song" is more strictly a song: "What Did It Getcha?" plays out as a backhanded eulogy to some decrepit, if not defunct, acquaintance who has become "premature'y old/slavin' for gold." The piece might be considered a foreshadowing of rap, built as it is upon Moreland's sardonic recitation of rhyming couplets about the lethal futility of greed. Except that rap as a class is more a matter of *lurching* than of *swinging*, and rap has seldom exhibited much of a sense of ironic humor.

The band accompanying Moreland on "Laffin' Song" and "What Did It Getcha?" is that of the Dallas-bred saxophonist Budd Johnson (1911–1984), a pivotal figure in the post-WWII transition from swing to bebop, and an artist of rare growth and staying power over the long stretch. Though no doubt marketed in its time as a novelty item—more so than as any manifesto of straight-ahead jazz—the platter today bespeaks a progressive approach to music and comedy alike on the part of Moreland. His billing on the label is as Mantan "Birmingham" Moreland, invoking the name of his chauffeur-turned-sleuth character of the final cycle of *Charlie Chan* movies.

It is in the movies, of course, and in his Monogram Pictures assignments in particular, that Moreland's legacy is most vividly defined.

"Mantan seemed to be better served by Monogram than by Universal Pictures," as the Cleveland-based researcher William F. Chase has pointed out, adding that Monogram positioned its Moreland pictures onto a strategic fulcrum where they could be leveraged either as general-appeal fare for the mainstream shirtsleeves audience, or, as Moreland starrers for a predominantly black audience.

Two such Monograms, 1941's *King of the Zombies* and 1943's *Revenge of the Zombies*, distill the Moreland *oeuvre* to an essence. These are only ostensibly horror movies, thanks to Moreland's talent for benevolent subversion and rambunctious caricature. The artist is, in both, a servant traveling in the company

of paternalistic white men, who stumble onto campaigns to raise the dead as indefatigable soldiers of the Third Reich.

Throughout, Moreland protests his lower-berth citizenship with wisenheimer joviality, and he appraises the menaces-at-large with a philosophical, sensibly indignant trepidation—the reasonable response of a man who subscribes to the old saw about discretion in proportion to valor. He scrams like a bandit when danger looms, not to flee but to summon backup assistance from the ranks of disbelieving white-guy expeditioners. He retains his wits and seems ready enough to fight if cornered, indulging in none of the scared-silly reactions that would afflict the portrayals of Stepin Fetchit, Willie Best and Fred "Snowflake" Toones (the surname occasionally appears as *Toomes*, perhaps a studio-publicity misnomer). And Moreland's aggressive approach to the occasional leading lady, particularly Marguerite Whitten in *King of the Zombies*, gives the comedian more in common with the romantically robust portrayals of Paul Robseon (in the likes of 1933's *The Emperor Jones* and 1936's *Show Boat*) than with any other comedian of color. The limber foolishness of Stepin Fetchit—a strategic posture, derived from the Old World's *commedia dell'arte* and court-jester traditions and designed to leave the audience laughing *at* and not *with* the character—becomes irrelevant in Moreland's manner of bearing.

Thus does Moreland become the very point of these two *Zombies* films, overshadowing even such intense Grand Manner actors as Bob Steele and John Carradine in *Revenge*. Moreland's lines, embellishments upon the script if not outright improvisations, are calculated to make moviegoers of any coloration understand his way of confronting panic and laugh along with him, never at

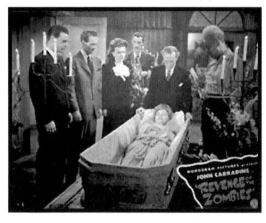

his expense. Moreland's contract with Monogram Pictures was an actor/writer deal, involving no original scenarios but rather his ability to inhabit his characters' very streams of consciousness. Upon hearing a disembodied voice moaning, "Where am I?" Moreland answers: "I don't know where you [are] at, but 30 seconds from now, I'm gonna be 'leven miles away from here!"

And likely no other comedian could have turned the reporting of a murder into a defining characterization, simply by describing the victim's wounds as "long, deep, wide and con*sec*utive." The line-reading, more so than the phrase itself, is distinctive.

Moreland's more memorable sayings from *King of the Zombies* include these: He pretends to mistake the gaunt and baleful Leigh Whipper (1876–1985) for a fellow lodge member, then mutters, "Harlem never was like *this*." (Whipper and Moreland had worked together on Broadway toward the final stretch of the Harlem Renaissance cycle.) Of the similarly cadaverous Mme. Sul-Te-Wan (1873–1959), Moreland observes, "I know a *mu*seum that would give a *for*tune just to have *her* under *glass*." Upon learning of an industrial fatality caused by "a revolving crane," he comments "Mmmm-*mmm*! Y'all *sho'* have some fierce *birds* around this country!" When (to all appearances) mesmerized into believing himself a zombie, he joins the ranks of the living dead with that single most imperishable line: "*Move* over, boys—I'm one of the *gang,* now." Later, when he finds his zombiehood challenged on grounds that "zombies can't talk," Moreland replies, "Can *I* help it 'cause I'm lo*qua*cious?"

Monogram's *Phantom Killer* concerns a confounding case of serial murder. The likely culprit (played by John Hamilton, the Perry White-to-be of postwar television's *The Adventures of Superman*) is a clinically deaf-and-mute big shot who seems unaccountably to have conversed with bystanders. Moreland is the first of these witnesses, a janitor who reacts to the shock of discovering a corpse by downing a quart bottle of liquor in a sustained guzzle. While poring over a book of known criminals' mug shots at a precinct station, Moreland renders a desultory scene at once hilarious and poignant: "Well, looka *there*—High-Pockets Johnson. I *wondered* what happened to *him*. Ol' High-Pockets. He wasn't a bad boy, at that. He was *awful* good to his mother." In court, he works the witness stand like a nightclub stage:

"Do you ever drink anything?" he is asked under oath.

"Sho'. *Anything*."

"How much whiskey did you drink that night?"

**Mantan Moreland's show-stopping scene-of-the-crime sequence from *Phantom Killer*.**

"Not a *drop.*"

"Now, *think*: That was six weeks ago. How can you be so sure?"

"Sure that I didn't drink any *whiskey*?"

"Yes."

"Well, *that* night, I was only drinkin' *gin.*"

*Phantom Killer* is a remake of a Depression-era picture called *The Sphinx*, from an earlier incarnation of Monogram Pictures.[3] Moreland's role is substantially the same as that handled in *The Sphinx* by Luis Alberni, who had applied to it his signature enactment of the Italian-immigrant stereotype. Where *The Sphinx* (1932) is entirely Lionel Atwill's show, a masterful display of predatory villainy, *Phantom Killer* has no such trump in the dignified but far less intense John Hamilton. Alberni performs his amusing scenes in *The Sphinx* and then vanishes, leaving no particular void. Moreland performs his extended showstopper in *Phantom Killer* and then vanishes, leaving the absorbed viewer to wish for more of Moreland.

Universal's *The Strange Case of Dr. Rx* finds another madman-at-large shockeroo usurped by Moreland, who plays a butler to crackerjack detective Patric Knowles. Moreland has any number of crucial details of which to keep track, and when he wants to remember an urgent task he resorts to a free-association monologue that makes perfect sense out of nonsense: "Airport—airplane—clouds—birds—nests—eggs—*breakfast*!"

It is in *The Strange Case of Dr. Rx* that the collaborative moment with Shemp Howard occurs. Howard can only have come away from the experience with an appreciation of Moreland's potential worth to the Three Stooges.

Moreland catches Howard, who plays a boozy plainclothes cop, prowling about the kitchen, and demands: "What're *you* lookin' for?"

"Just a little drink," replies Howard.

"No, you *ain*'t—this is the *boss*'s. This costs six dollars a *pint* and four dollars a *quart*."

"I'm a man that pays," insists Howard.

"I can't help *that*," snaps Moreland, asserting a sterner authority.

Howard proposes a deal: "I'll tell you what I'll do: I'll toss you for it."

"I don't gamble—," Moreland protests, halting when Howard produces a pair of dice. "On second thought, maybe I *might*."

Howard loses a throw, then has a sudden change of attitude: "I gotcha—*gamblin*', huh? And with an officer of the *law*!" Howard gives Moreland a classic-manner Stooge slap upside the head. ("I winced at Moreland's stooging for Shemp Howard," writes film enthusiast Bill Chase, and indeed this one bumpy spot in the routine plays out more harshly than the push-and-pull camaraderie between the actors would lead a viewer to expect.) Moreland objects with a bewildered indignation, much as the Three Stooges' Larry Fine might have responded, but suddenly the matter is dropped when Howard is called away

**Moreland and Shemp Howard indulge in a spot of reciprocal stoogery in *The Strange Case of Dr. Rx*.**

on business. It is an odd scene, overall, and it might not work if not for the roughhouse joviality of the players and the sense that each exercises a certain sway over the other.

Moreland's most arresting routine overall (as mentioned during that long-ago conversation with Moe Howard as overheard in Chapter Sixteen) is a jewel of a team-piece, created by Flournoy (or F.E.) Miller for his formal teaming with Moreland and then bequeathed to Moreland by Miller for long-term use with subsequent partners. Miller called the basic routine *Indefinite Talk*, for reasons that will become plain in a moment.

Moreland performed hundreds of variations upon *Indefinite Talk* on stage with Miller and then refined it with further embellishments in the movies and

Mantan Moreland and Ben Carter do their *Indefinite Talk* routine in *The Scarlet Clue*.

on radio. Moreland gave the routine its most polished and sustained form with fellow comedian Ben Carter (1911–1946) in the *Charlie Chan* series, and while guest starring with the Armed Forces Radio Service's *Jubilee*. *Jubilee* was a series of radio transcriptions, jazz interspersed with comedy, produced for the troops stationed overseas during World War II and thereafter.

This masterful routine is worth mentioning in the same breath with Abbott & Costello's most famous exercise in mind-boggling miscommunication, that epic-caliber outpouring of misperception called *Who's on First?* A striking example of *Indefinite Talk* comes from an Armed Forces Radio Service transcription disk of 1945:

"I'm *sick*," Moreland declares. "I'm sufferin' from—"

"No, no—not that, Mantan," interrupts Ben Carter.

"No?"

"You're *over* that. Don't you remember? You went to—"

"That doctor wasn't no good at *all*...Why, he made me take a—"

"Well, you weren't supposed to *drink* that stuff. Didn't it say, 'For external use only'—?"

"Well, I drank it *outdoors*."

And all this, and more, with no over-obvious rim-shot effects from the orchestra pit as a cue for strained laughter. The laughs come of their own spontaneous accord.

As a general rule, Moreland and a teammate would stretch an *Indefinite* conversation to the breaking point, then wrap things up on a say-*what*? parting note: "That's why I like *talkin'* with you—we *always* seem to *agree* 'bout *ever*'thing!"

"Yes, F.E. [Miller] wrote the basis of that *Indefinite Talk* routine for himself and Daddy to do, starting on the stage and then bringing it into the movies," explained Marcella Moreland Young. "F.E. was very exclusive with that routine—wouldn't teach it to hardly *any*body—but he also was very generous with Daddy. And when F.E. decided, later on, that he'd rather be doing more in the way of writing than of acting, he encouraged Daddy to develop new partnerships, and to take that routine and run with it. Daddy was as good a teacher as he was a performer, as long as he could have himself a receptive protégé to work with.

"Now, F.E.'s daughter, Olivette Miller, decided at one point, there, that all that *Indefinite Talk* business must be worth some money to somebody, so she started making a whole bunch of noise about how she deserved a piece of it, a copyright or a trademark, what with her father having concocted it, to begin with. But F.E. stood firm. He said, 'No, I wrote that for 'Tan, many years ago, and it's *his*—to do with as he pleases.'"

So there.

Moreland clearly enjoyed this demanding form of repartee, sharing the *Indefinite Talk* spiel as early as 1940 with a white-guy teammate, former child star Frankie Darro (1917–1976).

"If you could have just *seen* my Father's face when he was working on an *Indefinite Talk* routine with, well, with whom*ever* he might've chosen to try teaching that business to," said Marcella Moreland Young, "well, why, you'd've been awestruck—I mean, really in awe—at the dedication that went into performing this patter.

"Not to mention that the *expressions* on my Daddy's face, while teaching some routine, would be worth a million dollars if they could've been captured on a reel of movie film," she continued. "Now, if some pupil of Daddy's was *just not getting it*, then Daddy's brow would just furrow itself into knots, and you almost could hear him thinking: *I don't want to pound this person too much, because then he'll just get all flustered.* And a fellow couldn't perform the *Indefinite Talk* if he was all nervous and fearful of getting it wrong.

"Daddy'd never give a person too many times to flub the *Indefinite Talk*. He'd rather drop the routine entirely, than see it ruined by mixed-up timing or incompatible thinking. He wanted to honor the generosity of F.E. Miller, and then with Ben Carter he found a partner in that ability who was as good as F.E. Or so Daddy maintained, and I agree.

"Daddy was tolerant of Frankie Darro's attempts in this regard, during the time they were making their movies together. But Daddy never really liked doing the *Indefinite Talk* with Frankie—although he *did* really like Frankie as a friend and a co-star—because Frankie always tried to take things too fast."

And the *Indefinite Talk* is, in its truer form, a great deal like the rarified musical idiom of ragtime—both rely upon nuance and the power of suggestion more than upon punch-lines and easy yocks, and both draw the absorbed listener onto uncharted pathways *en route* to some perfectly reassuring conclusion. Both forms also require a leisurely deployment, in keeping with this warning, dating from 1908, from the pioneering ragtime composer Scott Joplin: "Never play ragtime fast at any time."

Added Marcella: "Daddy was a *very* pleasant person, very pleasant, and he could turn just about anything into a joke. But he never took that gift lightly, and he *worked* on his material, constantly.

"That is, of course, why Ben Carter proved so precious to him. Ben had that natural *something*—so teachable, so pliable. Daddy could *work* with Ben on stuff, I mean, and Ben would get to working *with* it, right off the bat.

"There were other partners, after Ben, right on down to Nipsey Russell in the 1950s and Livinggood Myles in the 1960s, who fared okay with that one special comedy routine," she said. "But Daddy measured everybody else by F.E. Miller and Ben Carter. The ones who approached that standard, now, they were the ones who *cared* about learning the bits of business, and learning them *right*. 'Let's get the *timing* down,' Daddy would say, 'and *then* we can work on the *words*.'

"You see, for most comedians, the ones who care and who matter, being a comedian is more difficult than being a conventional dramatic actor, *per se*. To be a real comedian, now, you have to make people laugh on multiple levels, all at once. It's easy by comparison to provoke a sad response, or an angry response, from an audience. Some artists can make people laugh. Some can make 'em cry. Few can make an audience do both, connecting on that level of intimacy that covers all the extremes of emotion.

"So I believe that comedians are, as a class, a little underestimated," she went on. "Red Skelton, who remained a friend of Daddy's all along after their circus years together, often likened his style to Daddy's—and said that he, I mean Red, and Daddy, and Jackie Gleason must've all been cut from the same bolt of cloth. In Red's opinion, anyhow. And I believe that they all had that same willingness to throw themselves, bodily and emotionally, into their work." (Red Skelton's celebrated *Guzzler's Gin* routine, performed innumerable times on stage and on television, bears elements in common with the "*good* whiskey" routine mentioned by Marcella in the preceding chapter.)

In 1940's *Up in the Air*—part of Monogram Pictures' unwittingly progressive comedy-thriller series—the impulsively Irish-tempered Frankie Darro teases Moreland about being afraid of ghosts while they are scouring the scene of the slaying of a *prima donna* entertainer. The progressiveness at work here is not a matter of the fallacy of colorblindness, but rather of the friendship that allows Moreland and Darro to pry, consciously, at the color bar until something shakes loose. This small scene is a curious confrontation, rather than an exploitation, of stereotype: "It ain't the ghost," Moreland snaps back, inverting Darro's taunt with practical indignation. "It's the person that *made* her a ghost—that's what's botherin' *me*."

Darro's brief appearance in blackface, later on in *Up in the Air*, is not a matter of lampooning black sensibilities but rather of trying (a bit too strenuously) to *become black*, while playfully acknowledging a fraction of a cultural debt. As the pals prepare to rehearse a comedy routine for an audition, Moreland asks, indignantly: "You don't expect me to speak in no *dialect*, do you?" When Darro's rapid-fire delivery proves *too* rapid for Moreland's tastes, Mantan halts the routine to demand that his overeager partner slacken the pace. (Yes, and Muddy Waters, who preferred a loping temp over a precipitous cadence, found it necessary to rein in the come-lately white-guy bluesman Paul Butterfield, too, when they integrated their styles during the 1960s.) When Moreland and Darro's boss in *Up in the Air*, played by Tristram Coffin, angrily swipes at the black makeup on Darro's face and then glances at Moreland, Mantan snaps: "Don't touch me! *I* don't rub off!" In such subtextual insights into a cross-cultural shadowland—perhaps more so than in its conscious humor—the Darro-Moreland combo is a marvel of quick-wittedness and spontaneous patter.

## II

Mantan Moreland died on September 28, 1973, following a heart attack while hospitalized for an onslaught of blood-pressure disorders and a respiratory infection. His funeralizing ceremony in Los Angeles included as honorary pallbearers Frankie Darro and T-Bone Walker; comedians Eddie "Rochester"

Anderson and Booty Green; Moreland's son-in-law, Gilbert Young and *Charlie Chan* series *alumnus* Benson Fong. The active pallbearers included Redd Foxx, Benjamin "Scatman" Crothers (1910–1986) and Matthew Beard (1925–1981), forever to be known as "Stymie" despite his forced retirement from that role while still a child during the Depression years.

The funeral was a tense but controlled occasion, complicated by the influence of two old-line religious denominations. Moreland had been raised a Roman Catholic in predominantly Catholic Louisiana, but he had become a practicing Baptist during his last few years, while his family remained Catholic. Then there was the intrusion of a cult-like organization, the Los Angeles-based Temple of Love & Christ, which had recruited the artist as a member during the 1960s.

"Daddy had just sort of fallen into step with the Catholic Church as a boy," said Marcella. "He was not particularly a sanctimonious person, but then neither was he a non-believer or an atheist—nothing like that. He got to being more serious about his religion about five years before he passed, but that was when he fell in with this so-called Temple of Love & Christ outfit. I was never very comfortable with that bunch, although they had some pretty well-known Hollywood figures, like Tab Hunter, amongst 'em.

"But Daddy just bought into that bunch—hook, line, and sinker, I mean to tell you—and then after a few years he decided it wasn't all that it had cracked itself up to be, and dropped right out. He had become a Baptist just shortly before he died. My Mom, now, she died a Catholic, steadfast to the end, and that's the way all our little family has remained.

"The funeral, now, it was no big problem reconciling those two brands of religion, because we all wanted to see Daddy off in an honorable fashion. Daddy's old lodge-hall had to have a hand in things, too."

And no, this lodge hall was not the Mystic Knights of the Pink Goddess—that imaginary fraternal bunch whose name Moreland invokes in *King of the Zombies*. Moreland was, in fact, a Thirty-Second Degree Mason within the Negro Masonic Order. This separate but officially acknowledged tradition had been established in 1787 by a Revolutionary War veteran named Prince Hall, following the approval of a petition by the Grand Lodge of Masonry in Great Britain.

The concept of Negro Masonry is the inspiration for the *Amos 'n' Andy* series' fraternal order, the Mystic Knights of the Sea, as well as Moreland's vaguely subversive-sounding Mystic Knights of the Pink Goddess. Real-world Masonry in general has, of course, integrated itself long since on an official basis—but there have remained isolated pockets of Old School Negro Masonry.

Marcella continued: "The turnout of mourners at Daddy's funeral consisted more of show-business folks than of church folks, in any case. But of course, then here comes this Temple of Love & Christ organization, wanting to take a hand in the memorial service—on account of, y'see, they still claimed Daddy

as one of *their* lot—and they raised such a noise about it that we finally allowed them to have a guest minister to say a few words. Yacked her head off, she did, and we were thinking, 'Oh, my goodness! What kind of weird people have we allowed in here?'"[4]

"But of course, Daddy was very accepting of all *kinds* of people. That's the kind of an attitude that comes from his being a generous soul—and sometimes people will use your generosity as leverage to impose more than they should on you."

Frankie Darro recalled Moreland, not long after the funeral, as "anything *but* a stereotype." Darro brought up that issue voluntarily and somewhat defensively, as if accustomed to hearing accusing questions about his old-time pal's alleged embrace of typecasting. Once assured that no one in the present company was seeking to chasten the memory of Moreland, Darro warmed to the line of inquiry:

"He was the boss of *our* act, there at Mono Pix," Darro continued, invoking the showbiz-shorthand term for Monogram Pictures Corp., "and he taught me more about the generosity essential to any comedian's worth than any other actor or any director I've ever worked with.

"Talk about a *patient teacher*!" said Darro, whose voice sounded just as boyish and gee-whiz eager in advanced age as it had during his youth. "Y'know, I never *did* get very good of a handle on that routine he called the *Indefinite Talk*—and Mantan just kept tolerating my feeble stabs at trying to make it work.

Mantan Moreland in a pensive moment.

"You have to have some kind of a fifth-dimensional brain, I think, to make that kind of calculated absurdity sound like natural conversation, and Mantan's thought processes were too highly evolved for Hollywood to know what to do with.

"The movies, of course, were his best vehicle toward his greater objective of just making people laugh themselves silly," added Darro. "Yeah, Mantan was unique among humanity, all right—and as great a pal as he was an artist."

Steve Brigati, an enthusiast from Los Angeles, became cordially acquainted with Moreland during the actor's later years and found him "as delightful in his supposed decline as he must have been in his prime."

"Actually, Mantan never was *out* of his prime," Brigati told me in 2001. "It was the *society* that declined—not Mantan. He took exception to the showier, more flamboyant black comics who had come up in his wake, but it never was out of resentment or bitterness.

"He just knew what was funny, and what wasn't, and he was one righteous family man. I'll never forget one thing that Mantan told to Richard Pryor, back when Pryor was showing off, one time, in front of us: Mantan stares Pryor down, draws back, and says, like this: 'Yeah, boy, you may have all the dope and all the white hookers your money can *buy* for you, but you gotta *know* one thing: Ain't *none* of that stuff makes you *one bit funnier*!'

"Mantan also knew what made *people* tick, and he understood the so-called racial barriers and what it took to prove them false," added Brigati. "It's like Mantan told me, one time, he says: 'Now, white people and black people may have different skin colors, all right, and they may talk differently from one another—but they *all* find the same things funny.'"

One of the more ostentatious come-latelies whom Moreland had found worth encouraging is Rudy Ray Moore, also known as a tougher-than-leather character of foulmouthed eloquence called Dolemite.

Born in Arkansas in 1927, Moore had entered show business during the 1940s as an amateur-night contender in Cleveland and Milwaukee, billing himself at first as Prince Dumarr and working as an *adagio* dancer, then as a ballads-and-blues singer under his right name and, at length, as a stand-up comedian.

Though embraced since around 1990 by the hip-hop underground (and he hardly has discouraged the attention), Rudy Ray Moore owes his essential style to the Chitlin' Circuit-and-earlier comedy traditions of two and three generations before his own. His deployment of rhyming couplets as a narrative medium is not borrowed from rap—quite the opposite, in fact—so much as it descends from a Southern-black custom of speaking in improvised doggerel verse while tossing off playful insults in the direction of one's companions. (Usually, one's drinking companions.)

As Moore has explained: "There's this old-time black tradition, called *toasting*—rhyming insults, exchanged back-and-forth amongst friends. Got to be done amongst friends, lest somebody take it the wrong way."[5]

I had been instrumental in Rudy Ray Moore's emergence from an unwanted retirement, in 1988, after a Texas-based fine-art-dealer friend named Thomas C. Rainone and I sought him out on a whim. Moore was living in obscurity in Los Angeles, traveling to Texas occasionally to visit kinfolks, and occasionally administering his more mannerly, G-rated scriptural humor at some Flat-Rock Washfoot Mount Zion Baptist African Methodist Episcopal church-folks outpost in Dallas. When Rainone and I finally caught up with him and pitched some comeback prospects, Moore wondered aloud whether any commercial venues in North Texas might have an interest in his Old School black-on-black comedy routines.

Moore had exited the low-rent moviemaking business after *Disco Godfather* (1979), he said, dropping a broad hint that that snakebit production had left him in the debt of some investors with criminal-underworld leanings. A decade had passed, then, without much prospect of a resurgence for Moore.

"Only reason I went the comedy route in the first place [during the 1960s]," Moore said during one of our earlier conversations, "was on account of I'd been tryin' for some 20 years to get myself a hit record, singin', for one record label after another, and couldn't get a hit to save my worried soul. Influenced some others, like Chuck Willis, who had him some hits time and time again. But not me. Not to go to feelin' sorry for myself or any such thing, y'know.

"So then this bum, this wino, called himself Rico, he kept comin' into the record store in Los Angeles where I was workin', pushing other people's hit records instead of havin' some of my own.

"Now, Rico, he was this toothless ol' bum, and he was always panhandlin' for money. He spoke in rhymes. Like this: "Dolemite is mah *name*," he'd say, "an' eff-in' up mo' fo's is mah *game*."[6]

Moore continued: "Now, I thought this was a very funny rhyme, and Rico, he would drag it out with these long story-poems about how this Dolemite cat was the toughest badman the world had ever seen, and never mind those legendary badmen like ol' Willie Green from New Orleans and Stagger Lee, who was so bad that he even whipped Satan and took charge of Hades.

"So I'd get ol' Rico to tell me all he could think up to say about this guy he called Mr. Dolemite, and I'd give him some money for his trouble. People'd hear him, there in the record-store showroom, and they'd be crackin' up all over, fit to bust. Probably as much at this shabby and down-and-out bum from down in the gutter, talking tough, as over the material itself. One of the record clerks, he told me this, he says: 'Rudy, you're a recording artist'—which I was, of course, 'cept without any hit records to show for it—'You oughtta make you a record of that "Dolemite" thing.'

"So I wrote it all down, took it on with me into a recording studio, and made me a record. Pressed up a hundred copies, out of my own pocket. Brought 'em into the store and put one of 'em on the record machine while I was there behind the counter. Some customer hears the first line that goes, like this [raising his voice and assuming a raspy timbre]: 'Some folks say Willie Green from New Orleans was the baddest man you ever seen...,' and that customer, he says, 'I'll take *that* record!'

"So he bought it, paid me a dollar for it, and walked on out of the store, and an hour or so later here come 50 people, maybe more, all comin' in to buy that record about Dolemite. Took me a while to convince a record distributor—the record business hasn't got a clue as to what people really want—but once the word-of-mouth caught on and people started clamorin' for copies of that one little record, I had me an order for a thousand copies and more, and more, and still more after that.

"Ended up makin'—what?—18 or 20 raunchy party records before 1975, when I started makin my *Dolemite* movies, self-financed from the record-makin' business. And I *am* the *first* comedian, I know, to make commercial records containing four-letter words with no mealy-mouthed flinching or bait-and-switching—Lenny Bruce had only done that in live performances, which got him busted. And Redd Foxx and Mantan Moreland, God rest his soul, had mostly just been risqué and let it go at that before I raised the bar on the rawer stuff.

"Mantan told me that it was *my* party records that had inspired him to try *his* hand at the game," Moore continued. "And I had run some heavy risks doin' mine, too. How were we goin' to sell records that you couldn't get played on a radio station and had to sell out from under the counter, like contraband? Word-of-mouth, that's how. A powerful force, that word-of-mouth."

As to Dolemite's larger cultural origins, Moore explained: "Now, the dictionary word *dolomite*—they spell it D-O-L-O-M-I-T-E, like that—is a name for a mineral substance, and in the poem that represents *stren'th*. I just changed the spelling to a different way—still means 'strong as a rock.'

"Mantan Moreland—now, I *worshipped* the man, considered him a *big* influence," continued Moore. "And I think he accepted me, if not as a colleague in that funny ol' corner of our business, then certainly as somebody who admired him and had never turned away from the kind of black-and-proud-of-it—I don't mean that in a political or militant way, but, well, *you* know what I mean—style that he rep'esented."

Rudy Ray Moore in *Petey Wheatstraw* (1977)

During a later visit, backstage in 1998 between shows at a comedy club in Texas called Hyena's, Moreland's name came up once again. Moore said: "I can tell you this much, right off the bat, and you can tell 'em Mr. Dolemite sent you: Mantan Moreland was the *funniest* funnyman of his generation—he caused a sensation to astonish the nation—and the way he's been forgotten is an abomination, 'cause there ain't been nobody come along since to challenge his station." Moore's ability to conversate in improvised rhyme is only slightly less astonishing than Moreland's gift of say-*what?* banter.

"Mantan was—well, Mantan *was* Mantan, in that he never pretended to be anybody he wasn't," continued Moore. "What you see, there, in the movies, is what those of us who were privileged to know Mantan Moreland, we saw in Mantan as we dealt with him in regular life. He knew when to turn off the funny business and be a civilian, and *vice versa*. But he also relished his life, and he laughed his way through it—even when times turned tough, and even after his health started letting him down.

"It was a *stren'th* that kept Mantan going, despite the best efforts to put him down by people who refused to understand. And it's time somebody honored Mantan Moreland as one of our great comedians. Not just somebody, I mean. *All* of us owe him a debt."

That old devil Obscurity is a tough customer, whether one is an artist attempting to break free of its clutches, or just someone attempting to excavate its strata of sediment in search of buried artistry.

Rudy Ray Moore had succumbed at one juncture to a form of obscurity. This was not so much a forced blacklisting, as it was his own perception that his career had played itself out and that no one wanted any more of what he was peddling. Moore's cue to exit had come around 1980, seven years after he had attended the funeral of Mantan Moreland and had sworn that he would carry on a semblance of that artist's legacy. Moore didn't so much dig himself out, as he merely encountered a few people willing to help him regain a measure of popular recognition. The upshot is that Moore has become more widely known at the start of a century than he had been as a self-launched star of Hollywood's postmodern Poverty Row district.

So here we have another battle-against-obscurity scenario—mirroring (however warped) both Mantan Moreland's experience, and Mantan Moreland's determination to keep laughing within earshot of an audience. Most such onslaughts of obscurity are not met by much of a meaningful protest from the artists thus affected.

Texas-born Lee "Lasses" White (1888–1949), as a pertinent example, had started out in the show world as a white-in-blackface impersonator during the time of Mantan Moreland's parallel ascent. White's career as a comic and singer-songwriter was a matter of feigning Negritude with crowd-pleasing impunity, from New York to Nashville—and then dropping that act, for the most part, in order to register in Hollywood as an all-'round character actor.[7]

White fared well enough, then, with his own natural-born whiteface complexion, specializing by the waning 1940s in Western-sidekick characters—the "ol' funny geezer" stereotype, in seeming perpetutity—at Monogram Pictures, where he also appeared with Moreland in a *Charlie Chan* picture of 1948, William Beaudine's *The Golden Eye*. All seemed to be going to suit White's long-term prospects, until Monogram abruptly dropped him at age 60 in favor of younger, more energetic backup players. White retrenched, after a fashion, with a handful of last-ditch assignments, but he died before he could assert a more emphatic case against the age discrimination of a forcibly premature retirement. Most of White's final backup-role pictures were issued posthumously.

Blackface entertainer Lee "Lasses" White ponders an investment, ca. 1925.

Another entertainer of blackface pedigree, Emmett Miller, fought more vigorously, though helplessly, against obscurity during much of a career on the receding fringes of almost-famousness.[8]

That career had flowered just in time to make Miller a defining artist within an Ecclesiastically doomed form of commercial artistry. To everything there is a season, all right—but sometimes a season runs short. Miller's struggles to resuscitate his chosen line of work in the face of diminished popular interest only deepened his predicament.

Miller outlived by almost a decade a fellow Southerner, the country-into-pop crossover artist Hank Williams. Williams is pertinent, here, because he had restored to prominence one of Miller's signature tunes of the 1920s, "Lovesick Blues"—recasting what had originated as a minstrel-show yodel in a more fashionable hillbilly-troubadour template. But Miller might as well not have bothered with the chore of surviving. Artistically and commercially speaking, Miller had become a dead man walking, cut-and-dried Southern-fried zombiefied, before the 1940s had given way to the '50s. *Move over, boys—I'm one of the gang of mummified minstrels, now.*

---

[1] Moreland's local-television appearances during the late 1960s and early '70s also included a pilot-program showcase as a starring prospect for himself, at Oakland. His routine commuting between Los Angeles and the Bay Area placed an inordinate strain upon his fragile health, as Marcella Young has recalled, adding: "But it was Daddy's way to push himself."

[2] *King of the Zombies* became an unlikely Oscar-bait contender during 1941–1942, for its musical score—the work of the Monogram-based composer Edward Kay.

[3] The Depression-era's Monogram Pictures Corporation was absorbed during the middle 1930s, along with other small-change independent studios, into Republic Pictures. The consolidation amounted to a forced merger initiated by Republic's founder, Herbert J. Yates, who held film-processing liens against the studios thus affected. A new Monogram came into being as the 1930s lapsed into the '40s. This reincorporated Monogram evolved during the post-WWII years into a more ambitious studio known as Allied Artists.

[4] The officiants-of-record at Mantan Moreland's funeral ceremonies—October 3, 1973, at Los Angeles' Victory Baptist Church—were Victory's resident pastor, the Rev. A.A. Peters and Mother Bernice Smith, of the Temple of Love & Christ.

[5] The insult-swapping practice known as *toasting*, whether in rhyme or in metered blank verse, also bears the name of *the dozens*, or *the dirty dozens*, and can be found preserved on phonograph records dating from the 1920s. A classic example of this evolved tradition occurs between the blues-into-rock artist Bo Diddley (Ellas Bates McDaniel) and accompanist Jerome Green on the hit recording of "Say Man" (Checker Records No. 931; 1959): "I was walkin' down the street with yo' girl...," declares Bo, laughing. "And the wind blew her hair into my face...The wind blew her hair into *her* face... [And then] the wind blew her hair in the street!" Green rebuts this slander with: "I was walkin' down the street with *yo'* girl...I took her home, for a drink, you know...But that chick looked so ugly, she had to sneak up on a glass to get her a drink of *water*!" Bo snaps back: "You've got the nerve to call somebody *ugly*! Why, *you* [are] so ugly 'til the stork that brought you in the *world* oughtta be ar*rest*ed!" All in good fun, of course. An open-ended, catch-all insult beginning with "Yo' mama..." also derives from this custom of backhanded toasting, which has prominent counterparts in the Yiddish and Scots-Irish cultures.

[6] The obvious Bowdlerization of this phrase is entirely a case of self-censorship on Moore's part; his raunchier show-business image notwithstanding, Moore has proved himself soft-spoken and

polite when away from the spotlight, and his wit and timing work, as well, on general-audience material. Which makes for a healthy distinction between Art and Life. But turn Moore loose on the right nightclub stage—and it's a case of Katy Bar the Door and Every Man for Himself.

[7] Lee "Lasses" White's nickname is a diminutive form of *molasses*. Much of White's stage-and-radio career was carried out as half of an *Amos 'n' Andy*-like team known as Honey & Lasses.

[8] Emmett Miller's story is the damnably elusive macguffin at the heart of Nick Tosches' brilliant and nightmarishly perplexing book *Where Dead Voices Gather*.

# 18
# Mingled, if Not Mangled, Ancestry

> Some colored people are envious
> of my position among white people.
> They follow me because they know
> I can get help from the white people,
> but they do not trust me. Someday, they will understand me.
> —Matthew "Bones" Hooks, pioneering black entrepreneur

My family-at-large never knew quite what to make of my childhood fascination with the funny business of Mantan Moreland. Or so I had believed at the time, and for a long time thereafter.

This was a convenient conclusion, in view of the self-evident truth that my proto-hipster uncle, Grady L. Wilson, was the sole partner in the acknowledged Scots-Welsh-Irish and American Indian lineage of Price-Wilson-King-Ralston *et cetera* to express any participatory interest in black-folks America. That is, beyond the household's matter-of-fact, safe-distance acceptance of *Amos 'n' Andy* as a radio-and-television staple and the occasional outburst of enthusiasm for this recording or that from Louis Armstrong or Fats Waller or the orchestra-and-chorus outpourings of Nat "King" Cole and Brook Benton.

"That Fats Waller, yeah, he sure could play a mean piano," as my father, John A. Price, often said, adding this: "Too bad he had to haul off and ruin it by tryin' to sing." I agreed as to the "mean piano" part but begged to differ as to the quality of Waller's singing-with-comedic-intent. This style suited me just fine and dandy: One good blues-belting baritone is worth any number of whispery crooners. Dad preferred Ralph Sutton's note-perfect reinterpretations of Waller—no singing, there, just a willingness to Get It Right on the keys. And Dad and I found many areas on which we could agree, without denying ourselves the occasional constructive argument.

For my purposes, it was Sutton's Columbia- and Harmony-label remakes of Waller's melodies—along with an article about Waller's brief and turbulent life in a manly magazine called *Saga*—that provoked an interest in the Genuine Article. Waller (1904–1943) is among the few long-defunct recording artists whose essential body of work has remained in print without interruption. It was a piece o' cake in 1960 to stroll into Amarillo, Texas' Cooper & Melin Records or its down-the-street rival, Go-Low Records, and score a 45-r.p.m. pressing of "Your Feet's Too Big" or the *Ain't Misbehavin'* album, over-the-counter, with a try-before-you-buy preview in either store's listening booth.[1]

The defiant humor implicit in the Waller canon—more of that laughin'-to-keep-from-cryin business, given his signature tactic of wrenching some overwrought lament-ballad inside-out with boisterous hilarity—had reminded me of Mantan Moreland from the moment I first plunked Waller's version of the "Your Feet's Too Big," a novelty composed by Ada Benson and Fred Fisher, onto a phonograph turntable.[2]

It took a couple of later discoveries, however, to cinch the affinity for Fats Waller, beyond his mastery of those 88 keys, as a comedian worthy of measurement alongside Moreland. One of these is Waller's introductory dialogue-in-dialect with his drummer, Harry Dial, on a 1934 waxing of a Mack Gordon–Harry Revel composition called "Don't Let It Bother You."

"*Boy*," barks Waller, "what's the *matter* with you?"

"Aw, man, *ever'*thin's wrong!" answers Dial. "Mah ol' lady done run off with the iceman… Yep! And mah daughter run off with the undertaker. And *I'm* about to *die*, an' I *ain't* got nobody to *bury* me!"

"Son," replies Waller, at once addressing Dial's mock-miseries and announcing the song, "*don't* let it bother you!" The lyric is conceptually bland and vapid—one of those grin-and-bear-it anthems that must have served to make the crappy-days-are-here-again Depression feel all the more depressing for any listener attuned to the more urgent realities. But Waller reads "Don't Let It Bother You" with a thoroughgoing unruly irony, in a voice as raspy and treacherous as the country's cratered economic system.

The other such discovery is Waller's 1939 recording of a Neal Lawrence–Slick Jones throwaway called "Abdullah" (1939)—a nonsense song from Back in the Day when Middle Eastern cultural stereotypes seemed somehow friendlier than the present day's popular conception. Seems that this Abdullah character "was the King of Amazullah" who "lived in a harem down in Boolah," but "took a trip to Honolullah" where he fell into the company of some chick named Lullah and promptly began two-timing his main wife, whose name was Zambullah. Pure poetry, of a variety that the great poet John Ciardi would have called "superfluous redundant overkill," relishing his own contrivance of redundancy.

Now, Fats Waller customarily resented RCA Victor's contractual insistence that he front-load each new session with the latest schmaltz-pop ditties from Tin Pan Alley, that commerce-over-art Mecca of Dominant Culture Mediocrity. Waller responded to this chronic insult—he was, after all, an inventive composer who sought to validate jazz as a born-American classical idiom—not by complaining, but rather by inverting and undermining the schmaltz and sappiness with nonsensical wit and concerted musicianship. When occasionally confronted with a none-too-serious trifle such as "Abdullah," Waller simply let the nonsense rip and allowed the musicianship to settle to its own level.

"Fats had good reason to stay impatient with Victor," as Orrin Keepnews explained to me during the 1970s, "even though the label, as much as radio and more so than the movies, helped to keep his name before the public."

And Keepnews should know: The pioneering producer and historian was a partner in the establishment of an aggressive jazz-reissue division at RCA Victor during the prior century. Keepnews unearthed, in the process, vast bodies of work both commercially issued and long misplaced or neglected, along with anecdotal and biographical insights as enlightening ballast.

"Fats found Victor entirely willing to exploit his crowd-pleasing abilities with the pop-ditty material, often at the sacrifice of his finer musicianship," said Keepnews. "And Fats found the company completely *un*-willing to give him a crack at the classical-piano market that he believed might be his truer realm.

"Fats *was* granted an opportunity, late in the 1930s, there at Victor's Camden [New Jersey] studios, to record perhaps an album's worth, maybe more, of the pyrotechnical piano classics. The objective was the prospect of his appearing on Victor's Red Seal classical label, with the only seeming obstacles being whether to bill him on Red Seal as 'Fats,' or by his more dignified-sounding name of Thomas Waller. That, along with the question of whether to put his portrait, that big, laughing face, on an oh-so-dignified Red Seal album jacket. I'm inclined to believe that the 'Fats' identity might have drawn a good many new converts into the classical sector."[3]

"And now, Fats was playing, here, with all the right classical purity and passion, I mean," continued Keepnews. "For such was Fats' academic background—some serious credentials, there.

"But when the Great Goda'mighty [Vladimir] Horowitz, who'd been recording for Victor since 1928, heard the evidence of this American *schwartzer* jazzman upstart, excelling at material that Horowitz regarded as his exclusive domain, he threatened to walk out on Victor and defect to some other label, just like that. And don't go thinking that Masterworks [Columbia Records' classical label] wouldn't've nabbed him right up!"

And almost needless to say, RCA Victor erred on the side of Vladimir Horowitz (1903–1989), who remained encamped at Victor Red Seal for the longer span. The anecdotal evidence might suggest that Horowitz found Waller intimidating in his command of Bach, Brahms, and Beethoven. (And certainly, Horowitz' grasp of jazz, assuming any interest at all, cannot have approached that which Waller commanded.) Whereupon RCA Victor retained not only Horowitz as a Euro-classical Genius-in-Residence at Red Seal, but also Waller as a workhorse jazz artist and mass-market commercial entertainer for its main-label Victor imprint and its RCA Bluebird subsidiary label—a regular RCA Victim.[4] Waller's only other record-company indulgence in the classically biased sector occurred in London, in 1939, where he committed six movements of his original *London Suite* to a set of disks for the HMV label—a Victor affiliate, though without domestic U.S. distribution.[5]

But I digress, and I will do so again, so bear with me. So yes, anyhow, in a time and a place where a movie-struck fan of Mantan Moreland could find few of his motion pictures in quest of a ready supplement of glee, such discoveries as Fats Waller's recordings proved a godsend.

My family, meanwhile, began proving itself more deeply entrenched in polyethnic interests than I could have suspected. There surfaced guarded hints, now and again, of a curious genealogical discovery made during the 1940s by my Great-Aunt Pelinah Price, who had come into a spot of unexpected wealth and commissioned a family-tree search. Reports, so the story goes, came in with great frequency of this or that Distinguished Ancestor, such as a West Virginia planter named Sterling Price and his service with the Confederate Army, and a Revolutionary War-era hero bearing the name of Michael Price. The family's truer name turned out to be the Welsh-origin *Rhys*, with its evolution to *Price* deriving from a prefix, *Ap*, meaning "son of." Ap Rhys. Son of Rhys-equals-Rice. *Well, I'll be a son-of-a-Rhys.*

By this time, during my schoolboy days of the 1950s and '60s, I already had gathered that we Prices must have some linkage with the likes of the Hollywood actor Vincent Price (who turned out to be a distant cousin); the *MAD* magazine essayist, publisher and television comedian Roger Price (likewise); the pulp-magazine horror-story specialist E. Hoffmann Price (and likewise); and the English jazz-into-rock singer and organist Alan Price (well, maybe), whose band had helped to touch off the so-called British Invasion of the American pop-music charts before the more show-offish but less accomplished Eric Burdon rechristened the bunch as the Animals and usurped top billing.

There seemed a more tantalizingly scandalous connection with the motion-picture cameraman and director Roland C. Price (1893-1966), who once had photographed, from hiding, a taboo crucifixion ritual of a Southwestern religious cult called the Penitentes and then incorporated that documentary footage into a notorious movie called *Lash of the Penitentes*, a.k.a. *The Penitente Murder Case* (1937). It turns out that Roland Price also had been the cinematographer-of-record on the 1939 installments of Herb Jeffries' Harlem-gone-West series of cowboy movies, in whose earlier stages Mantan Moreland had gained a foothold in Hollywood. I found this possibility of family ties particularly appealing—six, or maybe six-and-a-half, degrees of separation.

Any mention of my Great-Aunt Pelinah's genealogy project would trigger all manner of reminiscences and speculations at this or that family gathering, invariably climaxing with this anticlimax:

"But then, she quit writing altogether about what-all Important People she'd turned up within the family tree," my Dad would say. "Just clammed up on the topic."

"Well, then, how come?" asked one or another of us come-lately off-spring.

"Isn't it getting to be mighty near you-all kids' goodnight time?" interrupted my Uncle Horace Price, Dad's kid brother. His over-obvious point was an attempt to drop the family-tree discussion altogether.

"Aw, what's the harm in their knowin'?" insisted Dad, proceeding thusly:

"Well, it turns out that Aunt Pelinah found something she didn't particularly like, an embarrassment, in her ancestry." My uncle tensed, as if expecting an unwelcome giveaway that he already had learned by heart.

Dad continued: "Well, she wouldn't just come on out and *say* it, not outright—but it turns out that this family-tree surgeon turned up a couple or three Prices who had [*a suspenseful pause, here*] got themselves hanged for horse-thieves, 'way off in Ireland, or Welsh-land, or one of those ancestrable dominions."

And so much for revelations.

Forbidden insights awaited, however. An older cousin, Jimbo Price, took it upon himself, later and guardedly, to set the account right for my benefit.

"You wanta know what *really* happened with ol' Great-Aunt What's-'Er-Name's family-tree thing?" asked Jimbo, a model of eloquence. At 14, he sported a rockabilly-rebel haircut, suited to the mid-1950s setting, and an attitude of general defiance to match, along with the stereotypical redneck biases common to the time and the place.

"Well...," said I.

"She turned up some *coloreds*!"

"Say *what*?"

"Nigras—*you* know! ...*You* know, from the *plantation* days!"

"Yeah, well, my Dad said it was Irish horse thieves, from even farther back than that."

"Aw, *phooey*!" said Jimbo.

This was no time for an argument, though. I was keener upon absorbing my cousin's assertion in all its ill-intentioned spite. The notion of horse-napping Prices had seemed more fascinating than scandalous, as far as I was concerned—but a branch of Negro Prices sounded too iconoclastically good to be true.

"Horse-thieves, you *wish*!" Jimbo snapped back. "*My* Daddy said it was *nigras* that his aunt found out about—and better you not *tell* nobody, on account of it's a shame and a disgrace to the fam'ly name!"

"Yeah, well, then—so how come Uncle Horace told *you*?"

"On account of he said I needed to know, is how come. To help him keep it a *secret*."

"And so you're keeping the secret by telling *me*—?"

"Yeah, so we can all of us go to feelin' bad about it together," said Jimbo. "But don't you tell nobody *else*—or else I'll have to whup up on yuh!"

Quite the opposite effect, of course—no "feelin' bad about it," at all, on my part.

But thus sworn to secrecy—and my Cousin Jimbo could administer one righteous whuppin', whenever the urge struck—I honored the commitment for the long term.

No telling what our great-aunt had turned up, of course, in her *cul-de-sac* campaign of genealogical zealotry. Somewhere along the way, it must have dawned upon her that *our* more nearly direct ancestors were still crawling about on their all-fours in caves in the Welsh Highlands at a time when, say, the savants of China were inventing the art of printing and the tribes of Africa and the Americas-to-be were sustaining dynasties all their own. Some mysteries are more to be appreciated than solved.

But then my Uncle Horace, during his fading years of the 1990s, took it upon his worried soul to reveal to me precisely the information that his son Jimbo had passed along 40 years earlier. Fact? Fancy? *Quién sabé*, and so what of it? There is a careworn streak a mile wide running through most of the Southern families I have known, whether white or black or muckledy-dun, and I suspect it must have a great deal to do with an endemic inability to ignore superficial differences. A wise colleague, the jazz percussionist Ozell "Larry" Reynolds, has appraised the prevailing situation in these terms: "What happened to divide us all so bad as a society was that we got so all caught up in desegregating—that we forgot to *integrate*."

I had figured, in any event, that any overt display of boasting about even a hint of presumed black ancestry could only prove awkward, coming from a middle-class white kid who had never felt obligated to retreat to the rear-section seats of a 'cross-town bus or to drink from a Colored Only water fountain.

I reserved, nonetheless, the right to dig ever deeper in search of an understanding of black-rooted music and all its trans-cultural offshoots. By the time I had organized my first rock 'n' roll band during 1957–1958, I was in possession of a song-list that had nothing to do with Elvis Presley and little enough to do with Buddy Holly, and plenty in common with Bo Diddley, B.B. King, Ray Charles and the Coasters. Better if I could have integrated my band so early on—fat chance of that, in mid-century Texas, where one Remembered One's Place on either side of the tracks and where black schoolchildren were being conditioned to believe that the blues in its purer forms was a throwback to Jim Crow. I compensated for this social deficiency by commencing to steal away to the Flats, my town's black juke-joint district, at the soonest opportunity.

My father was hardly what one might call an integrationist, but he made an unobtrusive point of hiring white and black and American Indian and Latinate employees, and probably combinations thereof, for his industrial-supply company's warehouses and sales departments around Texas and New Mexico. And Dad made job-promotion decisions on grounds of ability, irrespective of ethnic pedigree. Any favoritism he might have shown was a bias on behalf of plain competence and the willingness to produce. The shipping docks and City Order Desks at Clowe & Cowan, Inc., in the Texas Plains towns of Amarillo and Lubbock, the Mexican-border city of El Paso, Texas and Roswell, New Mexico, were prototypes for the since-fashionable concept of Ethnic Diversity, with camaraderie and horseplay to match. Good marketplace sense can pack more progressive weight, in any case, than any attempts to meet some bureaucratized quota. Dad was many years ahead of the curve, with no agenda other than commercial productivity, in anticipation of federal Equal Opportunity policy.

Dad also spoke fondly of a black man who "saved my life, he did, once, when I was just a little ol' sprout." The story—told on many occasions, down through the years—had to do with a runaway horse, harnessed to a buckboard in which my father-to-be was a hapless passenger. The time was the late 1910s or perhaps 1920, when Dad would have been, indeed, "just a little ol' sprout," of age six or thereabouts.

Dad's father, a dairyman named Absolom A. Price, had parked the wagon to make a delivery, leaving his son seated aboard. Something spooked the horse, and it bolted.

"I was all set to either crash or be thrown off," as Dad recalled. "Looked like certain doom, y'know. But then, all of a sudden, this ol' colored guy, he runs right up, just as fast as that horse is travelin'—leaps onto its back—leans forward onto its neck—and *sinks his teeth smack-dab into that horse's lip*!

"And that's the one certain way to stop a horse—no pullin' back on any reins, no '*Whoa*!' about it. Just bite down on its lip, and don't let go! Brought that horse to a dead stop, he did. Saved my life, sure enough!"

And did my father recall the identity of this heroic "ol' colored guy"—?

"Yeah, well, he was a kind of a local-character figure, here in Amarillo," Dad said. "Well known around town, he was."

Yes, okay—but his *name*?

"Never *knew* his right name," Dad said. "Ever'body just called him 'Nigger Jerry.'"[6]

It turns out that the name—perhaps condescendingly affectionate, certainly dismissive—had been bestowed by what passed locally for the Ruling Class. An Amarillo-based historian named Bruce G. Todd has solved that mystery in recent years in a volume called *Bones Hooks: Pioneer Negro Cowboy*.

Todd's account, ragged in the presentation but diligently researched, centers upon Matthew "Bones" Hooks (1867–1951) as an entrepreneurial black frontiersman who developed strategic alliances with white-folks in Amarillo early in the prior century; these connections Hooks used to help develop churches and schools and an entire neighborhood where black residents could become property owners. Hooks emerges in this groundbreaking study as something of a Booker T. Washington of the Southwestern borderlands, with independent-businessman traits in common with Mantan Moreland's father-in-law from Louisiana, Will "Chip" Henry—though lacking in the rebellious arrogance that seems to have prevented Henry from forming cross-cultural partnerships to mutual benefit.

And Hooks' tactics included a business arrangement with a progressive-minded white developer named Angus McSwain, who became Amarillo's first citizen to make real estate available for sale to black residents. Together, and in alliance with an early-day mayor of Amarillo named Lee Bivins, Hooks and McSwain established a middle-class black neighborhood known as North Heights—the upwardly mobilized Heights, as opposed to the low-down Flats—from which sprang a monied-class black enclave known as Hampton Heights, during the 1950s.

The mysterious "Nigger Jerry"[7] proves to have been "the first black resident of Amarillo, since around 1895," as my brother, Kerry Price, reported upon first digesting Bruce Todd's book. My brother adds: "[Jerry] was a big bad-ass who escorted the black women home to the Flats [in Northwest Amarillo] from their jobs at the hotels, carrying a bullwhip to deter the white boys who liked to bother the women. He was known to the blacks as Brother Jerry Calloway."

And finally: A name to flesh out our father's reminiscence. Now, whether Calloway had been a working cowboy, like Bones Hooks, remains undocumented, for Calloway had settled into Amarillo as a servant-in-residence. But the knowledge to use the lip-biting ploy as a means of halting a horse suggests a sure-enough cowhand background.

The most immediate suggestion of a black presence within my extended family seems to have come in the person of an uncle-by-marriage—not that anyone seems to have remarked any particularly non-Caucasian aspect about the fellow during his mortal span.

Now, Woodrow Carter was fondly regarded among the Prices-as-a-class as the overdue Mr. Right who had rescued my Aunt Nola Mae, Dad's wild-at-heart younger sister, from a tendency to hook up with one volatile honky-tonking redneck after another. Woodrow and Nola sustained a viable marriage-with-offspring from the 1940s until his death during the waning '60s. Uncle Woodrow was a thoroughly well-assimilated Good Citizen of down-home honkified Dumas, Texas. There, he operated a retail-appliance store and repair shop in those days prior to the Wal-Martification of American commerce and the resulting weakening of small-town mom-and-pop entrepreneurialism.

On this occasion or that, and apropos of nothing in particular, Uncle Woodrow would bring up a reference to what he called "Indian blood" within his family, as if pretending to answer a question that nobody had asked. Preemptive explanation, maybe. And sure-enough, he presented a profile unlike any within my blood-kin circle, with outthrust cheekbones and flared nostrils, though nonetheless fair-to-ruddy in the complexion department. If Woodrow Carter might have been "passing for white," as the saying goes—a questionable tactic, however comprehensible in light of the separate-and-unequal social construction of those times—then certainly he pulled off the masquerade with skill and confidence and benevolent grace. Everybody liked the guy, as much for his easygoing wit and pleasant nature as for the self-evident truth that he had introduced Dad's kid sister to a life of stability and security.

I had not thought in years about our long-gone kinsman-by-marriage until my brother inquired—quite recently, and straight-out-of-left-field—whether I ever had noticed "how much ol' Uncle Woodrow looked like a Negro." Well, now, I cannot say that I had done so, but then I cannot say that I *had not* done so, either. Familiarity breeds acceptance, y'know. My brother and I pondered the notion straight into a dead-end non-conclusion until some topic more interesting weaseled its way into the conversation.

Later on, but not much later on, I went sorting through a drawer of Price-family photographs in search of nothing in particular. There, I turned up a snapshot from around 1950, portraying my Aunt Nola and Uncle Woodrow Carter and their family-to-date. He is, in aspect, a lighter-complexioned Tim Moore—the Kingfish, from *Amos 'n' Andy*—with a suggestion of the hatchet-faced aspect shared in common by T-Bone Walker and Huddie "Leadbelly" Ledbetter. And what was that I was saying about how some mysteries are more to be appreciated than solved?

"Indian blood," indeed. Mantan Moreland, in his later years as a nightclub comedian, often told a story about a black athlete who finagles a tryout with an entirely white baseball team—on condition that the player must prevail at bat over three dedicated basemen. The black guy socks the ball into the stratosphere and goes zooming toward home plate before anyone knows what has happened. The manager shouts: "Look at that Cuban *run!*"

And so what's the big deal, anyway? We all come from Africa at one point or another in prehistory.

## II

If Mantan Moreland had sprung from a somewhat complicated family history—would he be a Brodnax, or a Bordeneaux, or a Moreland, denied the certification of that paternal birthright?—then certainly the lineage that followed him can be simply traced.

Mantan and Hazel Moreland begat a daughter, of course, Marcella Moreland. Marcella married in 1961 to become Marcella Moreland Young, or Mrs. Gilbert Young. Gilbert Young had offspring from a prior marriage. And on May 19, 1968, a daughter was born to Gilbert and Marcella. They named her Tana, in subtle homage to her Grandfather Mantan.

"Daddy loved the idea of my being married and raising a family," Marcella said. "He and Gilbert were good friends, and Gilbert's kids were just as much grandkids to Daddy as Tana was, herself, as Gilbert's and my only child together. But sometimes, things just can't be counted on to last."

The Youngs' divorce in 1978 left Marcella in charge of the raising of not only Tana but also the four stepchildren: Gilbert "Punch" Young, Jr., Mark Young, Yolanda Young and Ramona Young.

"I was still being a mother—for the long term," explained Marcella. "Then, I became a mother all over again, I guess you could say, when I wound up caring for my Daddy, and then, later, for Mom, during their final years."

Hazel Moreland, despite her having walked out on Mantan during a time of generalized trouble for his health and his career, seems never to have ceased to consider herself "the one-and-only Mrs. Moreland," to use Marcella's terminology. Hazel Henry Moreland and her mother, Estella (Mrs. Will "Chip" Henry), lived on into the new century; both died in 2001.

Hazel was maintaining a residence in Oakland, California, during the early 1980s, when the Oakland-based Black Filmmakers Hall of Fame arranged a memorial induction for Mantan Moreland.

"That ceremony, now—that one was an awkward occasion, believe you me!" said Marcella. "There was a lot of irony in that, in that it was a black honor bestowed by black artists, and here, my Daddy had experienced a blacklisting from within the black community on account of his supposed stereotyping. But I reasoned it better to let bygones be bygones, and to accept the honor at its face value.

"Daddy and my Mom had divorced, of course, a long time before he had died, but through it all neither one of them ever lost any of their love for one another, however lopsided a love it might've been. With her living right there in Oakland, it seemed to me it'd be a shame to not let her know about this ceremonial recognition.

"The Hall of Fame invitation had come to me, and they wanted me and my daughter, Tana, to attend the festivities. I debated with myself as to whether I should let Mom know, or not.

"Now, really, I didn't want Mom to be left out, since she and Daddy had been together when his career had really begun taking off. But I also didn't want to be bothered with her and her pushy ways, just being her same old nuisance self. But I erred on the side of including her, and of course she immediately began picturing herself as the recipient of this posthumous award for Daddy. Made a regular spectacle of herself, she did! But better to include her than to exclude her. And *I* knew it was Daddy, anyhow, who was the point of the recognition, and not any of us who had lived on after him."

And for all that, Marcella Moreland Young seems never to have felt entitled to any reflected glory: "I was my Daddy's helper, that's all, and a helper sticks—through the good times, and through the bad times."

Diane Disney Miller—yes, *that* Disney—has recalled a household conversation that took place when she was about six years of age, around 1940. Her father had long since become an iconic figure in light of his studio's animated cartoons, but to Diane Disney he seemed too homebody-familiar to be particularly famous. A neighborhood friend had hipped her to the celebrity angle.

Diane approached her father and asked, "Who are you?"

"You know who I am," he answered.

"Are you Walt Disney? *The* Walt Disney?"

"Yes," he answered.

Whereupon she replied: "May I have your autograph?"

And so it went, more or less, within the Moreland home: "It never quite clicked with me that my Daddy was who the rest of the world knew him to be, although I respected him as an artist and as an entertainer," said Marcella. "He was just Daddy, to me—that was his job, as far as I saw it, just being my Daddy, and that was all that he ever wanted to be, anyhow.

"Still," she continued, "I was 'raised in a suitcase,' as the show-folks' saying goes, and I knew that world just like I knew my own household.

"I knew all of Daddy's comedy routines, and I knew whether a performance was working or not. I was his critic, and he accepted my criticisms with great joy and appreciation. 'Honey, you've got a sharp eye,' he'd say.

"I'd let him know if I thought he was laying on the dialect business a little too thickly—and we went 'round and 'round, arguing about the heavy dialect he used on that *Green Pastures* record album," she said, alluding to Moreland's recitations from Roark Bradford's *Ol' Man Adam* Bible stories for Caedmon Records. "To this *day*, I think he overdid it on that record.

"Now, his later party-record albums, those dirty-joke routines that he did for that Laff Records outfit about three years before his death—well, I thought they were beneath Daddy's dignity, and kind of at odds with the good, respectable work he was getting on network television, there, during his last years. But those party records were *funny*. I couldn't deny that. And the live-audience reactions, there on those recordings, are honest laughter.[8]

"Whatever his circumstances, Daddy liked for me to gauge an audience's reaction to what he was doing—because although he had a set of fixed, established routines to anchor any performance, he liked to ad-lib a lot. I could tell whether the laughter he was getting was genuine or just polite laughter, and

such observations as that seemed to help Daddy to determine whether his stuff was going over the way he had intended it to do.

"My Daddy put up with a lot of heartache and misery, and he never backed down from the responsibility that he felt to give people some reason to laugh," said Marcella. "He wound up fighting his way back, time and again, from thirteen different physical ailments—the diabetes and the high blood pressure were the worst, I suppose—and on top of all that, the heartbreak of loving my Mom altogether more than she might have deserved. That was *his* choice, and his devotion to her was steadfast and genuine, no matter how strenuously she tested and taxed him.

"But Daddy chose to keep laughing, and to keep seeking ways to share that sense of humor that sustained him.

"To be quite honest with you," Marcella added after a thoughtful pause, "when Daddy died, I just sort of died along with him. That withdrawal lasted a good many years, on my part. But once in a while, I'd find a reminder that Daddy was bound to live on through all the work he had accomplished.

"Sometimes, the reminder turns out not to be all that positive—like that Spike Lee movie [*Bamboozled*, that is] where the name *Mantan* is trotted out to derogatory effect, all over again. Maybe I shouldn't take it all that personally, but that Spike Lee fellow, now, he just kind of blindsided the family with that one.

"But then, I see how many people are discovering my Daddy for the first time, through all the pictures of his that have resurfaced on videotapes and videodisks. And I hear about how people who had never heard of my Daddy before are beginning to relish his generosity with the funny business.

"And I realize just how lasting a body of work he had built, and how great a responsibility it is that I've inherited, to help preserve his memory—beyond just the images of him that appear on the movie screen," said Marcella Moreland Young.

[1] Both Cooper & Melin Records and Go-Low Records championed indigenous American music in all its many forms. Cooper & Melin leaned more toward a preference in jazz and folk-ballad traditions. Go-Low exerted a blues/R&B bias, giving even the black-neighborhood record stores a run for their money. Go-Low, which sat just across the street from my Uncle Grady Wilson's State Theatre, boasted the more adventurous inventory, overall. A factor here was the willingness of owner Jim Biard to buy up 78–r.p.m. warehouse lots after that medium had been driven into near-oblivion by the 45–r.p.m. vinyl platter. Most of my permanent collection of T-Bone Walker's 78s owes its origins to Go-Low.

[2] Yes, well, and what *doesn't* remind me of Mantan Moreland? The comedian had impressed me early and effectively as a standard by which any and all attempts at humor might bear judgment. Groucho Marx and Milton Berle, in their declining heyday as television personalities, had seemed a great deal funnier before I discovered the sainted Mantan. The work of Laurel & Hardy and Abbott & Costello and Red Skelton became all the more impressive with Moreland's artistry as a yardstick. And as to "Your Feet's Too Big": The Ink Spots, a fine harmonizing ensemble whose work foreshadowed the doo-wop movement of early-day rock 'n' roll, also performed that song well—but nowhere near so ebulliently as Fats Waller.

[3] During the 1940s and '50s, Trinidad-born Winifred Atwell (1914–1983) would become a rare model for such crossover appeal as Fats Waller had envisioned. Miss Atwell pursued parallel careers in classical piano and a more commercialized combination of ragtime and boogie-woogie.

[4] The notion of a "hit record," relatively speaking, was unheard of in the classical realm until 1958, when Van Cliburn's RCA Red Seal recording of the Tchaikovsky *Piano Concerto No. 1 in B flat minor* broke the million-seller mark, probably owing as much to Cliburn's youth-market appeal (the illusion of classicist-as-rock-star) as to his artistic proficiency and fidelity to the Old Masters. Vladimir Horowitz, who had practically owned this composition as a concert-hall staple, is known to have harbored some insecurities about Cliburn's ascent, as well.

[5] The HMV Records label of Great Britain derived its name from the dog-at-the-phonograph slogan ("His Master's Voice") of the Victor Talking Machine Company, which of course became RCA Victor.

[6] That end-note term pops up like a red flag. And of course: I have gone the length of this book-so-far without invoking such verbal artillery, so why begin at so late a stage? Well, for one thing, because any censorship on my part would render inaccurate the speech thus quoted. For another, I consider the use of such transparent, prissy Bowdlerisms as "the *N*-word" and its kindred alphabet-soup Anglo-Saxonisms to be at best disingenuous and, at the worst, schoolmarmish and passive-aggressively dirty-minded. And as I have maintained in my historical survey of Texas-bred musical forms, *Daynce of the Peckerwoods* (Music Mentor Books; 2006), one can scarcely relate the story of the Southland—or the story of America, for that matter—without the use of certain ingrained objectionable terms.

[7] Like I said... (above).

[8] The Laff Records albums, dating from 1969–1970, are *That Ain't My Finger!* and *Elsie's Sportin' House*. Many of the routines preserved here team Moreland with two lesser comedians, Roosevelt "Livinggood" Myles and Janet Taylor.

# Mantan and Chan

Charlie Chan, novelist Earl Derr Biggers' genial and relentless homicide detective, had served long and well as a ticket-selling personality at 20th Century-Fox, but all good things must come to an end. The *Charlie Chan* series lapsed, belatedly, from Fox to Monogram with 1944's *Charlie Chan in the Secret Service*, which—despite the continuing presence of Sidney Toler in the title role—represents a steep drop in quality as well as in continuity. Production values are scarcely everything, but Fox's high-gloss budget-picture unit had so accustomed the customers to a finely wrought, atmospheric treatment that the shift to Monogram's rawboned style can only have come as a disappointment. Where Fox *had* a B outfit, Monogram *was* its own B outfit.

For us unapologetic fans, however, the only bad *Charlie Chan* is no *Charlie Chan*, and *Charlie Chan in the Secret Service* demonstrates that Monogram and veteran suspense director Phil Rosen came prepared to compensate in other ways. The story is classically weird, even science-fictional, having to do with government agent Chan's investigation of the murder of an inventor, and his search for a stolen cache of documents. Benson Fong makes a suitably overeager son to the great detective, and—in what many followers consider the saving grace of the Monogram *Chans*—Mantan Moreland brings wit and energy to the recurring role of Chan's wisecracking cohort, Birmingham Brown. Toler resumes his stride gracefully from Fox's *Castle in the Desert* (1942).

As the treadmill turns, there comes a significant lapse of time between Toler's death and the arrival of Roland Winters. Although Winters makes a perfectly okay Chan, the series grows to feel ever more desultory until it rallies for the rousing penultimate adventures of *The Golden Eye* and *The Feathered Serpent*—only to stumble again with *The Sky Dragon*.

A Cine McNuggets rundown on the Monogram *Chans* follows herewith, spanning 1944-49:

***Charlie Chan in the Secret Service* (1944):** The *Chan* series was a life sentence—gratefully accepted—for, first, Warner Oland and, then, Sidney Toler. Toler, who had assumed the role

Mantan as Birmingham Brown in *Charlie Chan in the Secret Service*

upon Oland's death in 1938, at length purchased the movie rights from the Biggers estate, thus seeing to it that he would continue to star as Charlie Chan; the strategy was halted only by Toler's own death in 1947. This creaky but earnest new beginning involves the murder of an inventor and the theft of a device designed to combat U-boats. Phil Rosen directs with more of an ear for dialogue than an eye for action, and the story unfolds for the most part inside the mansion of the victim, lending a claustrophobic quality that places *Secret Service* squarely in the old-dark-house tradition.

***The Chinese Cat* (1944):** An epidemic lust for diamonds provokes an outbreak of murder in this law-baffling locked-room mystery. Extensive on-location shooting in an authentic carnival-midway fun house lends an intriguing subtext and enhances the excitement, which frankly needs all the help it can get. The atmosphere and the spoken word again prevail over any acts of violence or heroism, thanks to an immersion in character by both Sidney Toler and Mantan Moreland. As Chan might phrase it: Owner of monogrammed dagger, carelessly deployed, is murderer.

***Black Magic* a.k.a.: *Meeting at Midnight* (1944):** A more impressively entertaining entry pivots upon a reassuring element of friendship between Moreland's Birmingham Brown and Frances Chan, as Charlie's daughter. Plotwise, it's

just a matter of the old-standby fake-seance scam, dusted off for another overworking. The murder weapon is a grisly bullet, fashioned from frozen blood. (One foreign-market alternate title is *La Bala de Sangre*, which translates as *The Bullet of Blood*.) The reissue title, *Meeting at Midnight*, represented an attempt to avoid confusion with Gregory Ratoff's *Black Magic* (1949), starring Orson Welles.

***The Jade Mask* (1945):** Edwin Luke, kid brother of Keye "Number One Son" Luke from the earlier Fox *Chan*s, weighs in as Number Four Son, egghead brat Eddie Chan. A gas chamber, poisonous darts and a scam to impersonate murder victims keep the thin plot vigorously stirred. The body count is remarkable, at five. Frank Reicher plays the first casualty as a thoroughly well-despised scientist, automatically padding the suspect roster.

Mantan and Edwin Luke in *The Jade Mask*

Notably weird, however cumbersome, is the ploy of causing a dead man to walk by means of a marionette-strings rigging.

***The Scarlet Clue* (1945)**: Federal agent Chan trails a spy ring bent on stealing radar secrets. The lethal weapon of preference is a deadly gas, activated by tobacco smoke. Mantan Moreland's famous anticipation-and-interruption routine with Ben Carter, a Vaudeville staple in which each finishes the other's sentences with mind-boggling results, receives a generous showcase. Much of the action takes place in the then-exotic setting of a television studio.

***The Shanghai Cobra*** **(1945)**: Deformed villain Addison Richards has a reputation for dispatching victims with cobra venom. The real murderer proves to be a Shanghai police official, disguised as a banker. Benson Fong, who plays Tommy Chan, later developed the popular Ah Fong restaurant chain. This most stark and foreboding of the Monogram *Chan*s boasts a *bona fide* film noir sensibility. Director Phil Karlson later delivered the tough-guy extravaganza *Kansas City Confidential* (1952), with John Payne, Preston Foster, Neville Brand, Lee Van Cleef and Jack Elam.

***Dark Alibi*** **(1946)**: The film is not to be confused

**Benson Fong and Mantan in *Dark Alibi***

with the Cornell Woolrich novel *Black Alibi*, which supplied the basis for a Val Lewton picture, *The Leopard Man*. Here, forged fingerprints implicate innocent persons. Chan places himself in mortal peril by staking out a creepy warehouse where the incriminating equipment has been stashed. *Dark Alibi* is not among Phil Karlson's better work, though the return of the Mantan Moreland–Ben Carter team enlivens things considerably.

***Shadows over Chinatown* (1946):** A victim is found bereft of head and limbs. A mass attack of pickpocketing follows, aboard a long-distance bus bearing Charlie Chan to the crime scene. The thief (Jack Norton) proves so grateful to Chan for allowing him a second chance that he winds up using his lightfinger skills to save the detective from a late-in-the-game attack. Mantan Moreland renders the picture better than its script. The routine insurance-scam plot fails to honor the horrific promise of the premise.

*Shadows over Chinatown*

***The Trap* (1946):** Sidney Toler delivered an unwitting farewell with this picture,

which generally is conceded the least of the Monogram *Chan*s. A series of beachfront murders within a show-business community recalls a finer-by-far Fox *Chan*, 1931's *The Black Camel*. There is an unusually great deal of outdoor location shooting. Toler died in February of 1947, at age 72. Production on the series resumed the following August, with *The Chinese Ring*.

**The Chinese Ring (1947):** The series regathers self, with Roland Winters as Chan. The historian David Zinman related the transition thusly in a splendid, deep-perspective book called *Saturday Afternoon at the Bijou*: "[Winters'] blond hair and prominent nose made him an unlikely Oriental, but he won the part with a little ingenuity."

"They had never seen me when I was invited... for a screen test," Winters told Zinman. "I'd sent them a picture, of course. But it didn't bear the slightest resemblance to me. I wore a hat and a moustache in it and squinted my eyes because...I assumed this made me look inscrutable."

As to the problem of the honker, Winters added: "I always

looked straight into the camera. And when I was talking to someone at the side, I just moved my eyes. I never saw half the people I was supposed to be talking to. But at least my nose didn't give me away."

The forced squint of his tryout portrait proved workable, as well, on-screen: "They tried makeup... [and] fiddled around with wax for the eyes, putty and stuff...So I did it myself," said Winters. "Before every shot, the director would say, 'Remember the eyes.'"

The two-weeks-or-less pace of shooting on each late-in-the-game *Chan* has struck some buffs as a marvel of efficiency. Winters held otherwise: "It wasn't amazing," he told Zinman. "It was horrible."

*The Chinese Ring* is a remake of Monogram's *Mr. Wong in Chinatown* (1939), part of a shorter-lived but overall more satisfying series starring Boris Karloff. *Ring*'s promising first reel finds a doomed Chinese princess (Jean Wong) entrusting the sacred title object to Birmingham Brown (Mantan Moreland). Louise Curry, as an impulsive, interfering news reporter, provokes Winters' Chan to observe that women are incapable of rational conduct—a sentiment guaranteed to drive even most moderate feminists to a dithering rage, as witnessed at screenings in our own homes. These responses invariably proved more entertaining than the movie.

**Docks of New Orleans (1948):** An ill-advised business deal, involving a shipment of a secret chemical formula from Louisiana's Crescent City to South

America, finds Chan and his friends theatened by poisonous gas attacks. The score gets a boost from the use of New Orleans jazz, but there is little in way of suspense, shock value or even local color. The film is a remake of Monogram's *Mr. Wong, Detective* (1938).

***The Shanghai Chest*** **(1948):** An intruder stabs a judge (Pierre Watkin) to death within hizzonner's private chambers. An executed killer appears to have been brought back to life, if fresh fingerprints can be credited. The chilling notion receives a lukewarm treatment. Mantan Moreland has the distinction of nabbing the fleeing perpetrator, if only by accident.

***The Golden Eye*** **(1948):** Chan sojourns out West, investigating murders centering upon a played-out mine that unexpectedly yields a new gold strike. Creepy nun Evelyn Brent proves to be a pistol-packing menace. The picture allows a nice reassertion of eerie ferocity for the flagging series.

***The Feathered Serpent*** **(1948):** Oliver Drake rewrites his collaborative screenplay for the 1936

*The Golden Eye*

Western creepshow, *Riders of the Whistling Skull*. Keye Luke makes an overdue return. The search for a lost Aztec temple turns up a scam to smuggle priceless Mexican Indian artifacts. Bob Livingston, the key hero of *Whistling Skull*, serves this remake in a clever bit of self-referential turnabout casting as a villain.

***The Sky Dragon* (1949):** A claustrophobic airliner setting helps to suffocate this final entry. Not even a larger-than-usual body count can raise the ante sufficiently to yield the required suspense. There is a helpful climactic struggle between villains Paul Maxey and John Eldredge. Unlike Sidney Toler and Warner Oland, Winters still had plenty of his career ahead of him following the *Chan*s.

***Charlie Chan in the Secret Service* (1944):**
CREDITS: Producers: Phillip N. Krasne and James S. Burkett; Director: Phil Rosen; Story: George Callahan; Photographed by: Ira Morgan; Editor: Marty Cohen; Assistant Director: George Moskov; Running Time: 65 Minutes; Released: February 14, 1944

CAST: Sidney Toler (Charlie Chan); Gwen Kenyon (Inez); Mantan Moreland (Birmingham Brown); Marianne Quon (Iris); Arthur Loft (Jones); Lelah Tyler (Mrs. Winters); Benson Fong (Tommy Chan); Gene Stutenroth (Vega); Eddie Chandler (Lewis); George Lessey (Slade); George Lewis (Paul); Muni Seroff (Peter)

***The Chinese Cat*** **(1944):**
CREDITS: Producers: Philip N. Krasne and James S. Burkett; Director: Phil Rosen; Screenplay: George Callahan; Photographed by: Ira Morgan; Assistant Director: Bobby Ray; Art Director: Dave Milton; Editors: Fred Allen and Martin Cohn; Décor: Tommy Thompson; Musical Supervisor: David Chudnow; Musical Score: Alexander Laszlo; Sound: Tom Lambert; Production Manager: Dick L'Estrange; Running Time: 65 Minutes; Released: May 20, 1944

CAST: Sidney Toler (Charlie Chan); Mantan Moreland (Birmingham Brown); Joan Woodbury (Leah Manning); Benson Fong (Tommy Chan); Cy Kendall (Webster Deacon); Weldon Heyburn (Harvey Dennis); Anthony Ward (Catlen); John Davidson (Carl Kazdas and Kurt Kazdas); Dewey Robinson (Salos); Betty Blythe (Mrs. Manning)

***Black Magic*** **a.k.a.:** ***Meeting at Midnight*** **(1944):**
CREDITS: Producers: Philip N. Krasne and James S. Burkett; Director: Phil Rosen; Screenplay: George Callahan; Photographed by: Arthur Martinelli; Assistant Director: Bobby Ray; Operative Cameraman: Dave Smith; Assistant Camera Operator: Monty Steadman; Gaffer: Joseph Wharton; Stills: Earl Crowley; Special Effects: M.B. Kinne; Art Director: Dave Milton; Editor: John Link; Décor: Al Greenwood; Props: Samuel Gordon and Ralph Martin; Wardrobe: Harry Bourne; Musical Director: David Chudnow; Musical Score: Alexander Laszlo; Sound: Max Hutchinson; Production Manager: Dick L'Estrange; Script Clerk: Marie Messinger; Grips: Lew Dow and George Booker; Running Time: 67 Minutes; Released: September 9, 1944

CAST: Sidney Toler (Charlie Chan); Mantan Moreland (Birmingham Brown); Frances Chan (Frances Chan); Joseph Crehan (Inspector Matthews); Helen Beverly (Norma Duncan); Jacqueline de Wit (Justine Bonner); Geraldine Wall (Harriett Green); Ralph Peters (Rafferty); Frank Jacquet (Paul "Chardo" Hamlin); Claudia Dell (Vera Starkey); Charles Jordan (Tom Starkey); Byron Foulger (Charles Edwards); Joe Whitehead (Dawson); Crane Whitley (Bonner); Darby Jones (Johnson); and Richard Gordon, Harry Depp

*The Jade Mask* (1945):
CREDITS: Producer: James S. Burkett; Director: Phil Rosen; Screenplay: George Callahan; Photographed by: Harry Neumann; Assistant Director: Eddie Davis; Second Camera: William Margulies; Technical Director: Dave Milton; Editors: John C. Fuller and Dick Currier; Décor: Vin Taylor; Musical Director: Edward J. Kay; Musical Score: Dave Torbett; Sound: Tom Lambert; Production Manager: William Strobach; Running Time: 66 Minutes; Released: January 26, 1945

CAST: Sidney Toler (Charlie Chan); Mantan Moreland (Birmingham Brown); Edwin Luke (Eddie Chan); Janet Warren (Jean Kent); Hardie Albright (Walter Meeker); Frank Reicher (Harper); Cyril Delevanti (Roth); Alan Bridge (Sheriff Mack); Ralph Lewis (Jim Kimball); Dorothy Granger (Stella Graham); Edith Evanson (Louise Harper); Joe Whitehead (Dr. Samuel R. Peabody); Henry Hall (Inspector Godfrey); Jack Ingram (Lloyd Archer); Lester Dorr (Michael Strong); and Danny Desmond

*The Scarlet Clue* (1945):
CREDITS: Producer: James S. Burkett; Director: Phil Rosen; Screenplay: George Callahan; Photographed by: William Sickner; Assistant Director: Eddie Davis; Second Camera: Vincent Farrar; Technical Director: Dave Milton; Editor: Richard Currier; Music: Edward J. Kay; Sound: Tom Lambert; Re-Recording and Effects Mixer: Joseph I. Kane; Music Mixer: William H. Wilmarth; Production Manager: William Strobach; Running Time: 65 Minutes; Released: May 11, 1945

CAST: Sidney Toler (Charlie Chan); Mantan Moreland (Birmingham Brown); Benson Fong (Tommy Chan); Ben Carter (Himself); Virgina Brissac (Mrs. Marsh); Robert E. Homans (Capt. Flynn); Jack Norton (Willie Rand); Janet Shaw (Gloria Bayne); Helen Devereaux (Diane Hall); Victoria Faust (Hilda Swenson); Milt Kibbee (Herbert Sinclair); I. Stanford Jolley (Ralph Brett); Reid Kilpatrick (Wilbur Chester); Charles Sherlock (Sgt. McGraw); Leonard Mudie (Horace Carlos)

*The Shanghai Cobra* (1945):
CREDITS: Producer: James S. Burkett; Director: Phil Karlson; Screenplay: George Callahan, from His Story, and George Wallace Sayre; Photographed by: Vincent Farrar; Assistant Director: Eddie Davis; Second Camera: Al Nicklin; Special Effects: Ray Mercer; Transparency Projection Shots: Mario Castegnaro; Art Directors: Vin Taylor and Dave Milton; Editor: Ace Herman; Music: Edward Kay; Sound: Tom Lambert; Re-Recording and Effects Mixer: Jack Noyes; Music Mixer: William H. Wilmarth; Production Manager: Glen Cook; Technical Director: Ormond McGill; Running Time: 64 Minutes; Released: September 29, 1945

CAST: Sidney Toler (Charlie Chan); Mantan Moreland (Birmingham Brown); Benson Fong (Tommy Chan); James Cardwell (Ned Stewart); Joan Barclay (Paula Webb); Addison Richards (John Adams); Arthur Loft (Bradford Harris); Janet Warren (Lorraine); Gene Stutenroth (Morgan); Joe Devlin (Taylor); James Flavin (H.R. Jarvis); Roy Gordon (Walter Fletcher); Walter Fenner (Inspector Davis); George Chandler (Joe Nelson); Mary Moore (Rita)

*Dark Alibi* (1946):
CREDITS: Producer: James S. Burkett; Director: Phil Karlson; Screenplay: George Callahan; Photographed by: William Sickner; Assistant Director: Theodore Joos; Second Camera: Al Nicklin; Special Effects: Larry Glickman and Mario Castegnaro; Technical Director: Dave Milton; Supervising Editor: Richard Currier; Editor: Ace Herman; Set Dresser: Max Pittman; Music: Edward J. Kay; Sound: Tom Lambert; Re-Recording and Effects Mixer: Joseph I. Kane; Music Mixer: William H. Wilmarth; Production Manager: Glenn Cook; Running Time: 61 Minutes; Released: May 25, 1946

CAST: Sidney Toler (Charlie Chan); Mantan Moreland (Birmingham Brown); Ben Carter (Himself); Benson Fong (Tommy Chan); Teala Loring (June Harley); George Holmes (Hugh Kensey); Joyce Compton (Emily Evans); John Eldredge (Morgan); Russell Hicks (Warden); Tim Ryan (Foggy); Janet Shaw (Miss Petrie); Edward Earle (Thomas Harley); Ray Walker (Danvers); Milton Parsons (Johnson); Edna Holland (Mrs. Foss); Anthony Warde (Jimmy Slade)

*Shadows over Chinatown* (1946):
CREDITS: Producer: James S. Burkett; Director: Terry Morse; Screenplay: Raymond Schrock; Photographed by: William Sickner; Technical Director: Dave Milton; Assistant Director: William Callahan, Jr.; Supervising Editor: Richard Currier; Editor: Ralph Dixon; Music: Edward J. Kay; Sound: Tom Lambert; Makeup: Harry Ross; Production Manager: Glenn Cook; Running Time: 61 Minutes; Released: July 27, 1946

CAST: Sidney Toler (Charlie Chan); Mantan Moreland (Birmingham Brown); Victor Sen Yung (Jimmy Chan); Tanis Chandler (Mary Conover); John Gallaudet (Jeff Hay); Paul Bryar (Mike Rogan); Bruce Kellogg (Jack Tilford); Alan Bridge (Capt. Allen); Mary Gordon (Mrs. Conover)

*The Trap* (1946):
CREDITS: Producer: James S. Burkett; Director: Howard Bretherton; Screenplay: Miriam Kissinger; Photographed by: James Brown; Assistant Director: Harold Knox; Technical Director: Dave Milton; Supervising Editor: Richard Currier; Editor: Ace Herman; Décor: Raymond Boltz, Jr.; Music: Edward J. Kay; Sound: Tom Lambert; Makeup: Harry Rose; Production Manager: William Calihan, Jr.; Running Time: 68 Minutes; Released: November 30, 1946

CAST: Sidney Toler (Charlie Chan); Victor Sen Yung (Jimmy Chan); Mantan Moreland (Birmingham Brown); Tanis Chandler (Adelaide); Larry Blake (Rick Daniels); Kirk Alyn (Sgt. Reynolds); Rita Quigley (Clementine); Anne Nagel (Marcia); Helen Gerald (Ruby); Howard Negley (Cole King)

*The Chinese Ring* (1947):
CREDITS: Producer: James S. Burkett; Director: William Beaudine; Screenplay: W. Scott Darling; Photographed by: William Sickner; Assistant Director: William Calihan; Technical Director: Dave Milton; Editor: Richard Heermance; Set Dresser: Ray Boltz, Jr.; Music; Edward J. Kay; Sound: W.C. Smith; Production Supervisor: Glenn Cook; Running Time: 68 Minutes; Released: December 6, 1947

CAST: Roland Winters (Charlie Chan); Warren Young (Sgt. Bill Davidson); Victor Sen Yung (Tommy Chan); Mantan Moreland (Birmingham Brown); Louise Currie (Peggy Cartwright); Philip Ahn (Capt. Kong); Byron Foulger (Armstrong); Thayer Roberts (Capt. Kelso); Jean Wong (Princess Mei Ling); Chabing (Lily Mae); George L. Spaulding (Dr. Hickey)

*Docks of New Orleans* (1948):
CREDITS: Producer: James S. Burkett; Director: Derwin Abrahams; Adapted Screenplay: W. Scott Darling; From a Screenplay by: Houston Branch; Photo-

graphed by: William Sickner; Assistant Director: Theodore Joos; Camera Operator: John Martin; Running Time: 64 Minutes; Released: March 24, 1948

CAST: Roland Winters (Charlie Chan); Virginia Dale (René); Victor Sen Yung (Tommy Chan); Mantan Moreland (Birmingham Brown); John Gallaudet (Capt. Pete McNally); Carol Forman (Nita Aguirre); Douglas Fowley (Grock)

*The Shanghai Chest* **(1948):**
CREDITS: Producer: James S. Burkett; Director: William Beaudine; Screenplay: W. Scott Darling and Sam Newman, from His Story; Additional Dialogue: Tim Ryan; Photographed by: William Sickner; Assistant Director: Wesley Barry; Running Time: 56 Minutes; Released: July 11, 1948

CAST: Roland Winters (Charlie Chan); Victor Sen Yung (Tommy Chan); Mantan Moreland (Birmingham Brown); Tim Ryan (Lt. Michael Ruark); Deannie Best (Phyllis Powers); Tristram Coffin (Ed Seward); and Willie Best

*The Golden Eye* **(1948)**
CREDITS: Producer: James S. Burkett; Director: William Beaudine; Screenplay: W. Scott Darling; Photographed by: William Sickner; Assistant Director: Wesley Barry; Operative Cameraman: John Martin; Stills: Al St. Hilaire; Art Director: Dave Milton; Supervising Editor: Otho Lovering; Editor: Ace Herman; Running Time: 69 Minutes; Released: August 29, 1948

CAST: Roland Winters (Charlie Chan); Wanda McKay (Evelyn Manning); Mantan Moreland (Birmingham Brown); Victor Sen Yung (Tommy Chan); Bruce Kellogg (Talbot Bartlett); Tim Ryan (Lt. Mike Ruark); Evelyn Brent (Sister Teresa); Ralph Dunn (Driscoll); Lois Austin (Margaret Driscoll)

*The Feathered Serpent* **(1948)**
CREDITS: Producer: James S. Burkett; Director: William Beaudine; Story and Screenplay: Oliver Drake; Additional Dialogue: Hal Collins; Photographed by: William Sickner; Assistant Director: William Calihan; Operative Cameraman:

John Martin; Stills: Eddie Jones; Gaffer: Lloyd Garnell; Special Effects: Ray Mercer; Technical Director: David Milton; Supervising Editor: Otho Lovering; Editor: Ace Herman; Décor: Ray Boltz; Music: Edward J. Kay; Running Time: 68 Minutes; Released: December 19, 1948

CAST: Roland Winters (Charlie Chan); Keye Luke (Lee Chan); Victor Sen Yung (Tommy Chan); Mantan Moreland (Birmingham Brown); Carol Forman (Sonia Cabot); Robert Livingston (John Stanley); Nils Asther (Prof. Paul Evans); Beverly Jons (Joan Farnsworth); Martin Garralaga (Pedro); George J. Lewis (Capt. Juan)

### *The Sky Dragon* (1949)

CREDITS: Producer: James S. Burkett; Director: Leslie Selander; Screenplay: Oliver Drake and Clint Johnson, from His Story; Photographed by: William Sickner; Assistant Directors: Wesley Barry and Ed Morey, Jr.; Operative Cameraman: John Martin; Gaffer: Robert J. Campbell; Stills: Bud Graybill; Special Effects: Ray Mercer; Technical Director: David Milton; Editors: Roy Livingston and Ace Herman; Running Time: 64 Minutes; Released: Following Los Angeles Premiere on April 27, 1949

CAST: Roland Winters (Charlie Chan); Keye Luke (Lee Chan); Mantan Moreland (Birmingham Brown); Noel Neill (Jane Marshall); Tim Ryan (Lt. Mike Ruark); Iris Adrian (Wanda LaFern); Elena Verdugo (Marie Burke); Milburn Stone (Tim Norton); Lyle Talbot (Andy Barrett); Paul Maxey (John Anderson); Joel Marston (Don Blake); John Eldredge (William E. French)

# Appendix
# Mantan Moreland:
# A Representative
# Stage- and-Screenography

Depending upon what know-it-all sources one consults in this age of instant-authority Internet blather, Mantan Moreland is popularly supposed to have cracked the Hollywood system with either a small role in a big-studio production of 1936 (Warners' *The Green Pastures*) or a bigger role in a small-studio production of 1938 (*Spirit of Youth*).

Neither citation nails the reality, as it turns out. One is way off base, and the other is a few years past the mark. For Moreland's earliest documented movie assignment, a direct segue from his heyday on Broadway, proves to have been a big role in a tiny film from an off-Hollywood subsidiary of the Warner Bros. Studios.

This appearance occurs alongside Moreland's Vaudeville-to-Broadway cohort Flournoy E. Miller in a musical short subject called "That's the Spirit." The entry is something of a case of Too Much, Too Soon, in the greater perspective of Moreland's movie career: Four years would elapse before Moreland was to see a feature-film breakthrough, such as it was. That would be the black-ensemble Western *Harlem on the Prairie*, which provided Moreland with a comic-relief prelude to a dramatically essential supporting role in *Spirit of Youth*.

An annotated filmography, interleaved with stage appearances, follows herewith, including the screen work of Moreland's daughter, Marcella.

**Blackbirds of 1928**
(Broadway's Liberty Theatre; 1928)

The music-and-comedy revue billed itself as "a distinctive and unique entertainment." The *New York Times'* Brooks Atkinson appraised the production in these terms: "... an amusing spectacle of rolling, mischievous eyes and gleaming

teeth—some of which are heavily inlaid with gold… When performers enjoy themselves so immediately, audiences are like to find themselves amused."

Atkinson reported further: "Even in what is supposedly an authentic Negro entertainment, the comedians appear in blackface [*a holdover tactic, actually, from black-artist minstrelsy*]. Tim Moore, whose wild talk and wild lunges supply most of the fun, puts on his makeup according to form, and his enormous mouth opens capaciously between streaks of light tan color. As a blustering uptown bully, [Moore] puts a good deal of fun into a burlesque boxing match. With three other players, none of them slaves to card etiquette, he feels his way cautiously through a Harlem poker game. When he sees a dancing skeleton in a graveyard, the look of horror in his eyes, gradually turning to terror, makes for eloquent Negro comedy. Such humor as *Blackbirds of 1928* affords comes chiefly from Tim Moore's threatening personality and robust physiognomy, and Manton [sic] Moreland's nervous card-concealing act in the poker game." Quote/unquote.

**CREDITS:** Producer and Director: Lew Leslie; Music: Jimmy McHugh; Lyrics: Dorothy Fields; 518 Performances, Beginning May 9, 1928

**OPENING-NIGHT CAST:** Baby Banks, George Cooper, Billie Cortez, Adelaide Hall, Marjorie Hubbard, Crawford Jackson, Ruth Johnson, Blue McAllister, Lloyd Mitchell, Tim Moore, Mantan Moreland, Philip Patterson, Bill Robinson, Mamie Savoy, Eloise Uggams, Aida Ward, and Elizabeth Welch

### Lew Leslie's Blackbirds
(Broadway's Royale Theatre; 1930)

Producer-director Lew Leslie touted this sequel to *Blackbirds of 1928* as "the world's funniest and fastest revue glorifying the American Negro." Brooks Atkinson's review in the *New York Times* mentions the teamwork of Flournoy Miller & Mantan Moreland: "Flourney [sic] Miller, tall and brutal, and Manton [sic] Moreland, his frisky satellite, are the comedians here, and their appearance is suitably raffish. But the skits they have to perform have little racial humor to enliven them, nor humor or any color."

**CREDITS:** Producer and Director: Lew Leslie; Music: Eubie Blake; Book: Flournoy E. Miller; Lyrics: Andy Razaf; 57 Performances, Beginning October 22, 1930

**OPENING-NIGHT CAST:** The Berry Bros., Buck & Bubbles, Minto Cato, Broadway Jones, Cecil Mack's

Choir, Mercer Marquise, Blue McAllister, Flournoy E. Miller, Mantan Moreland, Jazzlips Richardson, Neeka Shaw, and Ethel Waters

### Singin' the Blues
(Broadway's Liberty Theatre; 1931)

**CREDITS:** Producers: Alex A. Aarons and Vinton Freedley; Written by: John McGowan; Choreographed by: Sammy Lee; 45 Performances, Beginning September 16, 1931

**OPENING-NIGHT CAST:** Estelle Bernier, Joe Byrd, Jack Carter, Ashley Cooper, C.C. Gill, Shirley Jordon, Millard Mitchell, Mantan Moreland, Johnny Reid, Jennie Sammons, John Sims, Ralph Theodore, Percy Wade, S.W. Warren, Isabell Washington, Frank Wilson, and James Young

### Blackberries of 1932
(Broadway's Liberty Theatre; 1932)

**CREDITS:** Producers: Max Rudnick and Ben Bernard; Director: Ben Bernard; Music: Donald Heywood and Tom Peluso; Book: Lee Posner and Eddie Green; Lyrics: Donald Heywood and Tom Peluso; 24 Performances, Beginning April 4, 1932

**OPENING-NIGHT CAST:** Susaye Brown, John Dickens, Eddie Green, Alice Harris, Johnny Long, Jackie "Moms" Mabley; Dewey "Pigmeat" (a.k.a. "Alamo") Markham, Thelma Meers, Tim Moore, Mantan Moreland, Harold Norton, Samuel "Sammy" Paige, and Gertrude Saunders

### Yeah, Man
(Broadway's Park Lane Theatre; 1932)

**CREDITS:** Producers: Walter Campbell and Jesse Wank; Director: Walter Campbell; Music: Al Wilson, Charles Weinberg and Ken Macomber; Book: Leigh Whipper and Billy Mills; Lyrics: Al Wilson, Charles Weinberg and Ken Macomber; Four Performances, Beginning May 26, 1932

**OPENING-NIGHT CAST:** Walter Brogsdale, Harry Fiddler, Russell Graves, Adele Hargraves, Rose Henderson, Jarahal, the Melodee Four, Billy Mills,

Mantan Moreland, Hilda Perleno, Peggy Phillips, Eddie Rector, Marcus Slayter, Leigh Whipper, and Lily Yuen

**Shuffle Along (Revival)**
(Broadway's Mansfield Theatre; 1932-33)

**CREDITS:** Produced by: Mawin Productions, Inc.; Music: Eubie Blake; Book: Flournoy E. Miller; Lyrics: Noble Sissle; Choreographed by: Carey & Davis; Scenic Design: Karl Amend; 34 Performances, Beginning December 26, 1932

**OPENING-NIGHT CAST:** James Arnold, Vivian Baber (Given Elsewhere as Barber), Catherine Brooks, Lavada Carter, Howard Hill, George McClennon, Flournoy E. Miller, Taps Miller, Mantan Moreland, Herman Reed, Clarence Robinson, Marshall Rodgers, Noble Sissle, Louise Williams, Joe Willis, and Edith Wilson

**That's the Spirit**
(Vitaphone; 1933)

Warner Bros.' East Coast Vitaphone unit served primarily to provide short-subject comedies, musical selections and melodramas as added big-screen attractions in support of the big studio's feature-length pictures. Vitaphone seized opportunistically upon the Broadway teaming of Mantan Moreland and Flournoy E. (or F.E.) Miller with bandleader Noble Sissle to patch together "That's the Spirit."

The film provided Moreland with a premature, semi-starring role and a false start overall. As a rare filmed document of the work of some primary artists of the self-consciously progressive Harlem Renaissance, "That's the Spirit" plays out more as a throwback to minstrel-show comedy. Miller and Sissle had been among the creators of Broadway's first all-black musical, 1921's *Shuffle Along*, which had experienced a revival (see above) at the close of 1932.

Moreland and Miller—wearing exaggerated blackface makeup—launch "That's the Spirit" as night watchmen, reporting for duty at a pawnshop that turns out to be haunted by music-making ghosts. The gents register all the expected reactions, including a hasty exit at the end. But the film devotes its greater attention to a selection of tunes, with generous showcase segments for Sissle & His Orchestra. Director Roy Mack specialized in such short-form musical comedies. "That's the Spirit" has reappeared in recent times as incidental, between-the-features programming on cable-television's Turner Classic Movies network.

**CREDITS:** Director: Roy Mack; Photographed by: Edwin B. DuPark; Composers Including: Jack Little, John Siras and Joe Young; Running Time: 11 Minutes

**CAST:** Noble Sissle (Himself); Buster Bailey (Bandsman); Clarence Brereton (Bandsman); Edward "Jelly" Coles (Bandsman); Wendell Culley (Bandsman); Wilbur De Paris (Bandsman); Cora La Redd (Vocalist and Dancer); Flournoy E. Miller and Mantan Moreland (Watchmen); and the Washboard Serenaders

### Harlem on the Prairie
a.k.a.: BAD MAN OF HARLEM
(Merit Pictures, Inc./Sack Amusements Enterprises; 1937)

Modern-day sources often cite Mantan Moreland as an uncredited player in *The Green Pastures* (1936), Warner Bros.' filming of a Pulitzer-anointed stage production derived from the *Ol' Man Adam* tales of Roark Bradford; and in RKO–Radio's *Shall We Dance* (1937), a teaming of Fred Astaire and Ginger Rogers with the music of George and Ira Gershwin. Our crew of face-in-the-crowd spotters hasn't found Moreland in either of those big-deal pictures, however, and neither has the American Film Institute, with its matched compulsions for minutiae and accuracy. So maybe we're missing something, and demonstrable proof to the contrary is always welcome. The truer feature-film starting point for Moreland is *Harlem on the Prairie*, first in a string of Negro-ensemble Westerns starring Herb Jeffries.

In May of 2003, Jeffries—well into his 90s and as vigorous as ever—attended a screening of *The Bronze Buckaroo*, *Harlem Rides the Range* and *Two-Gun Man from Harlem* at Texas' Cowboys of Color Museum in Fort Worth. The occasion was Jeffries' induction into the museum's Hall of Fame. He prefaced each selection with anecdotes that a packed house found as spellbinding as the films themselves. A tall, imposing presence of genial good humor and quiet authority, Jeffries seemed to recall the moviemaking experience with fond immediacy.

"And why not?" Jeffries asked, fielding a question as to why he should regard such a tiny pocket of his career with such reflective clarity. "We were breaking some ground, here, blazing some trails—first black-cowboy hero in the talking pictures, don't you know? Not to say the first black-cowboy heroic business in the movies, 'cause there'd been some little ol' black-ensemble Westerns in the silent-screen days. But we were the first in the talkies. And I suspect these pictures proved as proportionately influential, in their small way, as the more extensive output of the bigger-name Westerns starring Gene Autry and Roy Rogers, to name some contemporaries within the so-called Dominant Culture. Certainly, we were all cut from the same template of Western-movie formula. And I count it 'specially a coup that my pal Mantan Moreland played backup in my Western series, and alongside Tex Ritter in *his* series, at around the same time in history." (Moreland would receive a Cowboys of Color Hall of Fame memorial the following year.)

Jeffries wouldn't trade for his tenure as low-rent Hollywood's Bronze Buckaroo, the original Two-Gun Man from Harlem and proud of it. Here was a hero-on-horseback who rode as tall in the saddle as Gene Autry and John Wayne, and who (in the process of fostering a singing-cowboy fantasy) also served crucial notice about some greater truths of frontier life that had faded from popular awareness.

The Anglo-Saxons were hardly the only settlers of the Western frontier, and the cowboys of color—to coin a phrase—played crucial roles in the range-busting business, outmoded stereotypes notwithstanding. As far as pre-fashionable diversity goes, Jeffries' brand of heroism proved consistent with the early-day renown of the Jewish Broncho Billy Anderson (Arkansas-born Max Aaronson; 1880–1971), the movies' first cowboy star, and of the Cisco Kid, a Mexican Robin Hood impersonated by both Anglicized and Latinate actors.

The work itself was the reward, as Jeffries often has said. But there also were the beneficial after-effects of watching his films cross over, as early as 1937, from their intended showplaces in black-neighborhood theaters to the uptown picture palaces; of on-the-spot praise from Gene Autry, who had helped to invent the cowboy-crooner subgenre that revolutionized the Hollywood Western; and of the realization that these few films had given black kids a cowboy hero of a decisive ethnic identification. If the advertising campaigns occasionally got his name wrong—and some posters identify him as "Herbert Jeffrey"—then the prominence compensated.

Jeffries was born Umberto Balentino—of mingled Ethiopian, French-Canadian, Irish and Italian ancestry—on September 24, 1911, in Detroit. He became an accomplished horseman, in inadvertent preparation for the movies, while spending summers at a grandfather's farm. He discovered his singing voice in church.

While touring the Southern states during the 1930s with the pianist-bandleader Earl "Fatha" Hines, Jeffries came up with an idea for a movie.

"I had seen how blacks could see only white cowboys in segregated movie theaters," Jeffries said. "So I thought, 'Why not put movies about black cowboys in those theaters?' It could be good for business, and good for the kids."

An approach to the low-rent producer Jed Buell, who tended to prize ticket-selling gimmickry over Big Ideas or substantial production values, clicked for both men: "I wasn't there 15 minutes before Mr. Buell fired off a call to Alfred Sack, his film distributor in Dallas," Jeffries told me. "And Al Sack said, 'I'll take all of 'em you can send me.'"

Jeffries had not intended to present himself as the star player—just to sell the conceptual pitch and take a hand in production. His mixed ethnicity, with a fair complexion and blue eyes and naturally straight hair, might have seemed a disqualification. So what happened?

"I won the lead by default, you might say," Jeffries explained. "Of supporting players, we had found plenty. But a leading man who could ride, and sing and act—that wasn't easy. One guy might sing, but he'd be afraid of horses. One might ride all right, but he couldn't handle the other requirements. It went on and on like that.

"So Mr. Buell said to me, 'What are we going to do?' And I said, 'Well, now, nobody can tell whether my eyes are blue in a black-and-white movie. Just brown me up, and I'll tie my hat on so that nobody can see my hair.' And as for the riding ability—well, I'd been riding since I was 8. So that pretty well settled it."

His makeup, he said, "wasn't done in any exaggerated way. They bronzed me up just enough. We weren't going for caricature, here."

The short-term result was a self-contained series. But the films would have a greater long-term effect, specifically influencing Mario Van Peebles' black-ensemble Western of 1993, *Posse*, and overall suggesting possibilities for star-casting without heed for any stifling color bars. "Today, we have actors, such as Denzel Washington, who can take on any role that suits them," said Jeffries, "regardless of whether a role requires a particular ethnicity."

Jeffries' cowboy-movies ensemble over the longer term included such talents as the comedy team of Flournoy Miller & Mantan Moreland, along with Matthew "Stymie" Beard, an *alumnus* of the *Our Gang* comedies, and Spencer Williams, Jr. (Williams would spend the 1940s in Dallas and Fort Worth as a writer-director with Al Sack's movie company before landing the role of Andy Brown on the network teleseries *Amos 'n' Andy*.) Jeffries' pictures—*Harlem on the Prairie*, *Two-Gun Man from Harlem*, *The Bronze Buckaroo* and *Harlem Rides the Range*—pointed toward a longer-running series, but a fifth such picture was left in conceptual limbo as Jeffries' singing ambitions claimed priority.

In 1939, Jeffries visited a Detroit nightclub as a paying customer to hear Duke Ellington & His Orchestra.

"I was standing in front of the bandstand, in that full Western get-up," Jeffries recalled. "Duke spotted me and suddenly said to the audience, 'Well, looky here: If it isn't the Bronze Buckaroo, in the flesh!' Then, to me, he called, 'Why don't you come up and sing a few songs, Herbert?'

"That was surprise enough, but then Duke called me backstage and asked, 'What are your plans?' I said I guessed I'd go back to Hollywood and make some more movies. He said, 'That's too bad. I was going to offer you a job.' I said, well, then, I guessed it was time for me to change my plans."

Jeffries joined Ellington's orchestra at the peak of its game, scoring a hit with "You, You, Darlin'" and following through with "Flamingo," which would rack up sales of more than 14 million copies over the long term. Jeffries left Ellington in 1942 to join the Armed Forces Radio Services, recording programs expressly for the wartime troops and touring military installations. Jeffries' postwar career ranged from record-label management to acting assignments and nightclub work and a lengthy stint as a nightclub owner in Paris.

**CREDITS:** Producer: Jed Buell; Directors: Sam Newfield and Jed Buell; Screenplay: Fred Myton and F.E. Miller; Musical Score: Lew Porter; Photographed by: William Hyer; Editor: Robert Jahns; Running Time: 57 Minutes; Released: December 9, 1937

**CAST:** Herb Jeffries (Jeff Kincaid); F.E. Miller (Crawfish); Mantan Moreland (Mistletoe); Connie Harris (Carolina Clayburn); Maceo Bruce Scheffield (Wolf Cain); Spencer Williams, Jr. (Doc Clayburn); George Randol (Sheriff); Nathan Curry (Henchman); the Four Tones (Lucius Brooks, Rudolph Hunter, Ira Hardin, and Leon Buck, as Themselves); the Four Blackbirds (James Davis, Edward Brandon, Reg Anderson, and Edward Brandon, as Themselves)

Mantan Moreland, Joe Louis in *Spirit of Youth* (Photofest)

## Spirit of Youth
(Globe/Grand National; 1938)

The prizefighter Joe Louis signed with Globe/Grand National Pictures in 1937 to appear in a string of feature-film productions, all co-starring Clarence Muse. The plan went as far as this film, which proved to be Louis' only star vehicle, such as it is, and Globe Pictures Corp.'s only release. Globe was a partnership of Edward Shanberg and Martin Finkelstein, an *ad hoc* company organized for the sake of exploiting Louis' burgeoning popularity. Grand National was a general-purpose studio within Hollywood's Poverty Row sector.

The story is a vaguely fictionalized account of Joe Louis' career, starting around the time that Joe Thomas (played by Louis) decides to leave Alabama and seek his fortune in Detroit. The burly Thomas develops a friendship with a fellow wage-slave named Creighton Fitzgibbons (Mantan Moreland), who encourages Thomas to try a Golden Gloves bout. The rest is history, or at least histrionics.

In the Real World, Louis had won the World Heavyweight title in 1937. Before the year had run out, Shanberg and Finkelstein had enlisted Louis' cooperation and commissioned a script that went before the Production Code Administration's censorship that winter. Joseph Breen, the chief censor, challenged the script in light of its depiction of "several scenes of a black man victorious in a number of fistic encounters with white men." Breen also warned of "serious difficulty in the distribution of this film..especially in a number of states in the South."

The fight scenes were staged at the Old Hollywood Legion Stadium. Sports journalist Noble Chissell, who appears in a small role, once recalled that a New Jersey prizefighter named Willie Callahan, hired to portray an opponent, used the assignment as leverage intended to advance his own career.

"Callahan thought he could boost his reputation, maybe get himself a title bout for real, by actually knocking out Joe Louis while the movie was in production," Chissell told *The American Cinematographer* magazine's George E. Turner. "So he pulled a sneak attack—y'know, an unexpected blow from out of nowhere—before their make-believe bout was supposed to start for the movie. Staggered Joe a good one, he did. But Joe rallied and knocked the yutz out. You just didn't want to mess with Joe Louis."

Nor should Joe Louis have wanted to mess with an acting assignment. The champ fares well in the fight scenes, and he seems personable and pleasant in civilian guise. But he also appears thoroughly intimidated by the cameras and comes off as too timid to re-enact his own bold story. The supporting cast is distinguished chiefly by Mantan Moreland, as the agent of Louis' discovery, and Clarence Muse, who plays Louis' nurturing manager. The fight-ring sequences, staged expressly for the film, convey a smart combination of dramatic timing and documentary realism.

Moreland and Muse heft most of the dramatic weight, and Muse's operatic baritone receives a workout in a number of musical segments.

**CREDITS:** Producer: Lew Golder; Associate Producer: Edward Shanberg; Production Supervisor: Clarence Muse; Director: Harry Fraser; Assistant Director: Gordon Griffith; Screenplay: Arthur Hoerl; Photographed by: Robert Cline; Art Director: F. Paul Sylos; Film Editor: Carl Pierson; Musical Score Conducted by: Lee Zahler; Music Composed by: Clarence Muse and Elliott Carpenter; Songs, "Blue, What For?" "Little Things You Do," "No More Sleepy Time," "Magic Lover," and "Spirit of Youth," Composed by: Clarence Muse & Elliott Carpenter; Released: April 1, 1938, Following Washington, D.C., Premiere on January 20, 1938

**CAST:** Joe Louis (Joe Thomas); Clarence Muse (Frankie Walburn); Edna Mae Harris (Mary Bowdin); Mae Turner (Flora Bailey); Cleo Desmond (Nora Thomas); Mantan Moreland (Creighton "Crickie" Gibbons); Clarence Brooks (Speedy); Noble Chissell (Reporter); Willie Callahan (Challenger); Seal Harris (Sparring Partner); and Jewel Smith, Tom Southern, Jesse Lee Brooks, Margaret Whitten, Anthony Scott, Janette O'Dell, the Plantation Choir, the Creole Chorus, the Big Apple Dancers

### Two-Gun Man from Harlem
(Merit Pictures/Sack Amusement Enterprises; 1938)

This second entry in Herb Jeffries" Western series features Mantan Moreland in a prominent comic-relief role. The story has to do with Jeffries' impersonation of a notorious preacher-turned-gunslinger. See *Harlem on the Prairie*, above.

**CREDITS:** Producer: Jed Buell; Director and Screenwriter: Richard C. Kahn; Photographed by: Marcel LePicard and Harvey Gould; Art Director: Vin Taylor; Film Editor: WilliamFaris; Musical Selections Composed and Performed by: Herbert Jeffries and the Four Tones; Sound Engineer; Cliff Ruberg; Production Manager: Al Lane; Running Time: 65 Minutes; Released: May 1, 1938

**CAST:** Herbert Jeffries (Bob Blake); Marguerite [a.k.a. Margaret] Whitten (Sally Thompson); Clarence Brooks (John Barker); Mantan Moreland (Bill Blake); Tom Southern (John Steel); Mae Turner (Ruth Steel); Spencer Williams, Jr. (Butch Carter); Jess Lee Brooks (Sheriff); Matthew "Stymie" Beard (Jimmy Thompson); Rosalie Lincoln (Dolores); Paul Blackman (Paul); Faithful Mary (Mary); the Four Tones (Themselves); the Cats & the Fiddle (Musical Act)

### Frontier Scout
(Fine Arts/Grand National; 1938)

This one is a mildly ambitious combination of Civil War-era historical drama and hackneyed cattle-rustling tomfoolery—and strictly a case of marking time, as far as Moreland's career strategies might have been concerned: Work is work.

**CREDITS:** Producer: Franklyn Warner; Associate Producer: Maurice Conn; Director: Sam Newfield; Story and Screenplay: Frances Guihan; Photographed by: Jack Greenhalgh; Musical Score: Joseph Nussbaum; Editor: Richard G. Wray; Set Designer: Harri Reif; Sound: Hans Weeren; Special Effects: Howard A. Anderson; Stunts: Carl Mathews and Bob Woodward; Production Manager: J. Samuel Berkowitz; Montages: Howard A. Anderson; Running Time: 61 Minutes: Released: October 21, 1938

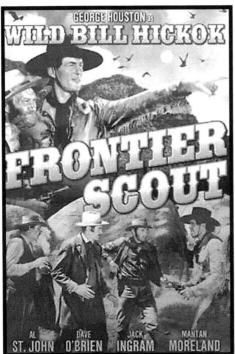

**CAST:** George Houston (Wild Bill Hickok); A. St. John (Whiney Roberts); Beth Marion (Mary Ann Norris); Dave O'Brien (Steve Norris); Alden Chase (Mort Bennett); Jack C. Smith (U.S. Grant); Jack Ingram (One-Shot Folsom); Dorothy Fay (Julie); Slim Whitaker (Davis); Kenneth [Kenne] Duncan (Crandall); Carl Mathews (Elliott); Kit Guard (King); Bob Woodward (Shorty); Walter Byron (Adams); Budd Buster (Jones); Frank LaRue (Norris); Minerva Urecal (Helen); Mantan Moreland (Butler)

### Next Time I Marry
(RKO–Radio; 1938)

The film is of modest interest within the Moreland canon (the customary servant role, albeit fairly prominent), serving primarily as a proving ground for Lucille Ball's leading-lady prospects. Miss Ball plays an heiress torn between upper-crust and working-class prospects of marriage.

**CREDITS:** Producer: Cliff Reid; Director: Garson Kanin; Assistant Director: Edward Donahue; Story and Screenplay: John Twist, Helen Meinardi, Dudley Nichols, and Thames Williamson; Photographed by: Russell Metty; Musical Score: Robert Russell Bennett and Roy Webb, incorporating Themes by Felix Mendelssohn-Bartholdy; Editors: Jack Hively and Harry Marker; Art Director: Van Nest Polglase; Running Time: 65 Minutes; Released: December 9, 1938

**CAST:** Lucille Ball (Nancy Crocker Fleming); James Ellison (Tony Anthony); Lee Bowman (Count Georgi); Granville Bates (H.E. Crocker); Mantan Moreland (Tilby); Elliott Sullivan (Red); Murray Alper (Joe); Jack Albertson, Grace Hayle, Ivan Miller, Bert Moorhouse, Frank O'Connor, Steve Pendleton

### There's That Woman Again
(Columbia; 1938)

Another step in Mantan Moreland's dues-paying phase with the major studios, this screwball comedy features him in a slight role as a porter. Moreland manages a spot of scene-stealing, nonetheless—what with his instinctive talent for quietly upstaging everybody else within shouting distance.

**CREDITS:** Producer: B.B. Kahane; Director: Alexander Hall; Screenwriters: Ken Englund, Philip G. Epstein, and James Edward Grant, from the Play by Wilson Collison and Gladys Lehman; Photographed by: Joseph Walker; Musical Score: Leigh Harline; Musical Director: Morris Stoloff; Editor: Viola Lawrence; Art Director: Lionel Banks; Décor: Babs Johnstone; Running Time: 72 Minutes; Released: December 24, 1938

**CAST:** Virginia Bruce (Sally Reardon); Melvyn Douglas (Bill Reardon); Margaret Lindsay (Mrs. Nacelle); Stanley Ridges (Tony Croy); Gordon Oliver (Charles Crenshaw); Tom Dugan (Flannigan); Don Beddoe (Johnson); Jonathan Hale (Rolfe Davis); Paul Harvey (Stone); Marc Lawrence (Stevens); Mantan Moreland (Porter); Lee Shumway (Policeman); Pierre Watkin (Mr. Nacelle)

### Gang Smashers
a.k.a.: GUN MOLL
(Million Dollar Productions; 1938)

Moreland plays a henchman in the service of a Harlem-based protection racket. The film is more a tale of conflicted romance and mistaken identity than an out-and-out crime melodrama, with a pleasingly jazzy musical score.

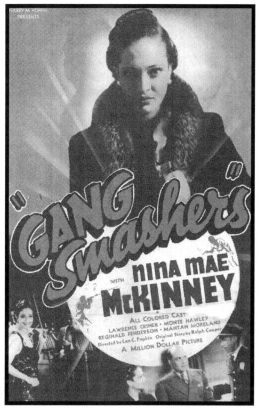

**CREDITS:** Producer: Harry M. Popkin; Director: Leo C. Popkin; Screenwriters: Hazel Barsworth and Phil Dunham, from a Story by Ralph Cooper; Musical Director: Phil Moore; Running Time: Approx. 60 Minutes; Released: January 1, 1939

**CAST:** Nina Mae McKinney (Laura Jackson); Monte Hawley (Lefty); Reginald Fenderson (Nick); Mantan Moreland (Gloomy); Edward Thompson

(Doyle); Vernon McCalla (Police Captain); Charles Hawkins (Gopher); Everett Brown (Police Lieutenant); Lester Wilkins (Police Officer)

## Tell No Tales
(MGM; 1939)

Actor-turned-director Leslie Fenton's crime melodrama veers into black underworld life in its tale of a reform-minded journalist (Melvyn Douglas) who clashes with his newspaper's crooked owner (Douglas Dumbrille). Mantan Moreland, as a flashy gambler-type, is in the good company of Ben Carter (soon to succeed Flournoy E. Miller as Mantan's comedy-team partner) and Mme. Sul-Te-Wan, who of course would become one of Moreland's make-believe tormenters in 1941's *King of the Zombies*.

**CREDITS:** Producer: Edward Chodorov; Directed by Leslie Fenton; Assistant Director: Tom Andre; Story and Screenplay: Edward Chodorov, Lionel Houser, Pauline London, and Alfred Taylor; Photographed by Joseph Ruttenberg; Musical Score: William Axt; Editor: W. Donn Hayes; Art Director: Cedric Gibbons; Associate Art Director: Daniel B. Cathcart; Sound: Douglas Shearer; Running Time: 69 Minutes; Released: May 12, 1939

**CAST:** Melvyn Douglas (Michael Cassidy); Louise Platt (Ellen Frazier); Gene Lockhart (Arno); Douglass Dumbrille (Matthew 'Matt' Cooper); Florence George (Lorna Travers); Halliwell Hobbes (Dr. D.A. Lovelake); Zeffie Tilbury (Miss Mary Anderson); Harlan Briggs (Davie Bryant); Sara Haden (Miss Brendon); Hobart Cavanaugh (Charles Daggett); Oscar O'Shea (Sam O'Neil); Theresa Harris (Ruby Alley); Jean Fenwick (Lydia Lovelake); ; Mantan Moreland (Mourner)

## Irish Luck
a.k.a. AMATEUR DETECTIVE
(Monogram; 1939)

Actor-turned-producer Grant Withers supervised the making of this initial entry in a buddy-picture series featuring Frankie Darro and Mantan Moreland. The dilettante-crimebuster angle would dominate this string of programmers. Monogram remade, or re-treaded, *Irish Luck* in 1944 as *The Adventures of Kitty O'Day*.

**CREDITS:** In Charge of Production: Scott. R. Dunlap; Associate Producer: Grant Withers; Director: Howard Bretherton; Assistant Director: W.B. Eason; Story and Screenplay: Charles M. Brown (story, "Death Hops the Bells") and

Mary McCarthy; Photographed by: Harry Meumann; Musical Score: Edward J. Kay; Editor: Russell F. Schoengarth; Production Manager: Charles J. Bigelow; Sound: Karl Zint; Wardrobe: Louis Brown; Running Time: 58 Minutes; Released: August 9, 1939

**CAST:** Frankie Darro (Buzzy O'Brien); Dick Purcell (Steve Lanahan); Lillian Elliott (Mrs. O'Brien); Dennis Moore (Jim Monahan); James Flavin (Fluger); Sheila Darcy (Kitty Monahan); Mantan Moreland (Jefferson); Ralph Peters (Jenkins); Tristram Coffin (Mace)

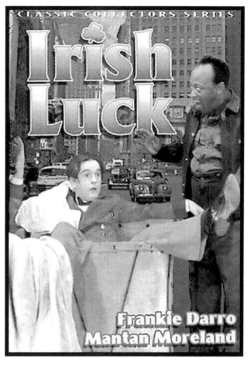

**Riders of the Frontier**
a.k.a. RIDIN' THE FRONTIER
(Boots & Saddles/Monogram; 1939)

As a chuckwagon cook named Chappie, Mantan Moreland lends witty support to Tex Ritter in this yarn about a scam to steal a spread of ranchland. Ritter and Moreland share a bit of philosophical repartee about the fallacies of prejudice before tackling a musical set piece, a comical duet on the traditional "Boll Weevil Song."

**CREDITS:** Producer: Edward Finney; Director: Spencer Gordon Bennet; Assistant Director: Jack Corrick; Story and Screenplay: Jesse Duffy and Joseph Levering; Photographed by: Marcel Le Picard; Editor: Frederick Bain; Production Manager: William L. Nolte; Stunts: Wally West; Musical Director: Frank Sanucci; Songs: "Rose of My Dreams" and "Ridin' Down To Texas," by Frank Harford, and the traditional "Boll Weevil Song"; Running Time: 60 Minutes; Released: August 16, 1939

**CAST:** Tex Ritter (Tex Lowery); White Flash (Tex's Horse); Jack Rutherford (Bart Lane); Jean Joyce (Martha Williams); Wally Wales [a.k.a. Hal Taliaferro] (Buck); Mantan Moreland (Chappie); Marin Sais (Sarah Burton); Olin Francis (Sam); Edward Cecil (Dr. Dolson); Nolan Willis (Gus); Roy Barcroft (Ed Carter)

## One Dark Night
### a.k.a. NIGHT CLUB GIRL
(Million Dollar/Sack; 1939)

This top-billed starring début for Mantan Moreland finds him in the W.C. Fields-like situation of a householder waiting for a business deal to come through while living in the midst of a family that can only ridicule and abuse him. Intended as the launcher of a *Brown Family* series—the trade paper *Variety* announced it as "a colored counterpart of the *Hardy*s, *Jones*es and other film-family groups"—the film spawned no sequels, after all.

**CREDITS:** Presented by: Alfred N. Sack; Producer: Harry M. Popkin; Director: Leo C. Popkin; Assistant Director: Eddie Saeta; Screenplay: Billie Myers; Songs: Johnny Lange and Lew Porter; Production Manager: Clifford Sanforth; Running Time: 81 Minutes; Released: Following New York opening on November 24, 1939

**CAST:** Mantan Moreland (Samson Brown); Betty Treadville (Hannah Brown); Josephine Pearson (Barbara Brown); Arthur Ray (Pop); Bobby Simmons (Jimmy); Laurence Criner (Pete Danker); Jessica Grayson (Mom); John Thomas (Bill); Monte Hawley (Hamilton); Vernon McCalla (Orville Otis); Ruby Logan (Ruby); Alfred Grant (Morris); Guernsey Morrow (Professor); Herbert Skinner (Attorney); Earle Hall (Headwaiter); The Four Tones (Vocal Quartet)

## What a Guy
(1939)

Unavailable for screening. A lost, or at least misplaced, film. Its absence from *The American Film Institute Catalogue of Feature Films* suggests a short-subject or featurette format.

**CAST:** Ruby Dee; Laurence Criner; Monte Hawley; Mantan Moreland

**City of Chance**
(Fox; 1940)

Actor-become-director Ricardo Cortez also had intended to handle the leading-role duties in this crime melodrama, which Moreland serves with the customary small role.

**CREDITS:** Producer: Sol M. Wurtzel; Director: Ricardo Cortez; Screenplay: John Larkin and Barry Trivers; Photographed by: Lucien N. Andriot; Musical Score: Samuel Kaylin; Running Time: 58 Minutes; Released: January 12, 1940

**CAST:** Lynn Bari (Julie Reynolds); C. Aubrey Smith (Judge); Donald Woods (Steve Walker); Amanda Duff (Lois Carlyle Blane); June Gale (Molly); Richard Lane (Marty Connors); Robert Lowery (Ted Blaine); Alexander D'Arcy (Baron Joseph); George Douglas (Muscles); Harry Shannon (Passline); Eddie Marr (Charlie Nevins); Robert Allen (Fred Walcott); Charlotte Wynters (Helen Walcott); Nora Lane (Dorothy Grainger); Alice Armand (Secretary); Hooper Atchley (Husband); Harry C. Bradley (Husband); Mantan Moreland (Nervous Man)

**Am I Guilty?**
a.k.a. RACKET DOCTOR
(Supreme; 1940)

This black-ensemble crime melodrama boasts virtually the same team of behind-the-cameras *Yiddishe* talents who developed many mass-market horse operas, cops-and-robbers adventures and horror thrillers for the Poverty Row studios. Ralph Cooper plays a physician who finds his healing philosophies

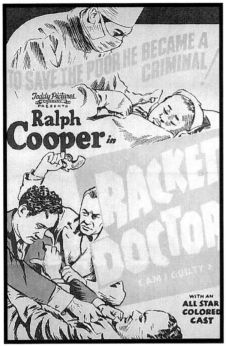

compromised by underworld interests. Marcella Moreland plays a traffic-accident victim who poses a crucial challenge for Cooper. Her work here landed Marcella a modest niche at big-time MGM Pictures, but she preferred to indulge her show-business interests behind the scenes, as a sounding-board for her father's artistry.

**CREDITS:** Producer: A.W. Hackel; Director: Sam Newfield; Story and Screenplay: Sherman L. Lowe, George Wallace Sayre, and Earle Snell; Photographed by: Robert E. Cline; Editor: S. Roy Luby; Sound: Clifford A. Ruberg; Running Time: 71 Minutes; Released: Following Harlem Opening on September 27, 1940

**CAST:** Ralph Cooper (Dr. James Dunbar); Sybil Lewis (Joan Freeman); Sam McDaniel (John D. Jones); Laurence Criner (Trigger Bennett); Marcella Moreland (Marcella); Arthur Ray (Dr. Freeman); Reginald Fenderson (Slick); Monte Hawley (Tracy); Clarence Brooks (Lt. Harris); Jess Lee Brooks (Dr. Fairchild); Ida Coffin (Mrs. Smith); Cleo Desmond (Mrs. Thompson); Alfred Grant (Intern); Matthew Jones (Monk); Dewey "Pigmeat" Markham (Proprietor); Vernon McCalla (Judge)

### Chasing Trouble
(Monogram Pictures; 1940)

Second in the Frankie Darro–Mantan Moreland series, this one exploits the usual amateur-sleuth angle, with some unusually sharp banter between teammates. See *Forgotten Horrors 2: Beyond the Horror Ban.*

**CREDITS:** Associate Producer: Grant Withers; Director: Howard Bretherton; Story and Screenplay: Mary McCarthy; Photographed by: Harry Neumann; Editor: Carl Pierson; Running Time: 64 Minutes; Released: January 30, 1940

**CAST:** Frankie Darro (Frankie O'Brien); Marjorie Reynolds (Susie); Mantan Moreland (Jefferson); Milburn Stone (Callahan); Cheryl Walker (Phyllis Bentley); George Cleveland (Lester); Alex Callam (Morgan); Tristram Coffin

(Phillips); I. Stanford Jolley (Molotoff); Lillian Elliott (Mrs. O'Brien); Willy Castello (Kurt); Donald Kerr (Cassidy); Maxine Leslie (Blonde); DeForest Covan (Jackson)

## The Man Who Wouldn't Talk
(Fox; 1940)

Here is an instance of further unbilled token-casting for Moreland, appearing almost incidentally in the story of a hapless schlub (Lloyd Nolan) who attempts to change his identity to cover up his involvement in a homicide.

**CREDITS:** Producer: Sol M. Wurtzel; Director: David Burton; Stage Play and Screenplay: Holworth Hall, Robert Middlemass, Robert Ellis, Edward Ettinger, Helen Logan, and Lester Ziffren; Photographed by: Virgil Miller; Musical Score: Samuel Kaylin; Editor: Alex Troffey; Art Directors: Richard Day and George Dudley; Running Time: 72 Minutes; Released: February 2, 1940

**CAST:** Lloyd Nolan (Joe Monday); Jean Rogers (Alice Stetson); Richard Clarke (Steve Phillips); Onslow Stevens (Frederick Keller); Eric Blore (Horace Parker); Joan Valerie (Miss Norton); Mae Marsh (Mrs. Stetson); Paul Stanton (Cluett); Douglas Wood (Walker); Irving Bacon (Paul Gillis); Lester Sharpe (Henri Picot); Harlan Briggs (Foreman); Elisabeth Risdon (Juror); Renie Riano (Lilly Wigham); Ernie Alexander (Soldier); Stanley Andrews (Colonel); Mantan Moreland (Robbins)

## Millionaire Playboy
(RKO–Radio; 1940)

Eccentric comedian Joe Penner stars as a pathologically bashful fellow whose wealthy father (Arthur Q. Bryan, Elmer Fudd himself) attempts to cure him of his aversion to women. Moreland appears in modest support.

**CREDITS:** Executive Producer: Lee Marcus; Producer: Robert Sisk; Director: Leslie Goodwins; Story and Screenplay: Bert Granet and Charles E. Roberts; Musical Score: Paul Sawtell; Photographed by: Jack MacKenzie; Editor: Desmond Marquette; Art Director: Van Nest Polglase; Associate Art Director: Albert S. D'Agostino; Costumer: Renié Conley; Assistant Director: Doran Cox; Sound: Earl A. Wolcott; Running Time: 64 Minutes; Released: March 15, 1940

**CAST:** Joe Penner (Joe Zany); Linda Hayes (Lois Marlowe); Russ Brown (Bob Norman); Fritz Feld (G.G. Gorta); Tom Kennedy (Tom Murphy); Granville Bates (Stafford); Arthur Q. Bryan (J.B. Zany); Pamela Blake [a.k.a. Adele

Pearce] (Eleanor); Diane Hunter (Hattie); Mary Beth Milford (Bertha); Mantan Moreland (Bellhop); Frank Faylen (Man); Kathryn Adams (Betty)

## Star Dust
(Fox; 1940)

Director Walter Lang's Cinderella-gone-Hollywood fantasy is essentially a retread of *A Star Is Born* (filmed in 1937), with a radiant star turn from Linda Darnell—who seems to be retracing her own path into the bigger leagues of show business. Moreland has an unbilled Pullman-steward role.

**CREDITS:** Producers: Kenneth Macgowan and Darryl F. Zanuck; Director: Walter Lang; Story and Screenplay: Kenneth Earl, Robert Ellis, Ivan Kahn, Helen Logan, and Jesse Malo; Photographed by: J. Peverell Marley; Musical Score: David Buttolph, Mack Gordon, and Hoagy Carmichael & Mitchell Parish (song, "Stardust"); Running Time: 86 Minutes; Released: April 5, 1940

**CAST:** Linda Darnell (Carolyn Sayres); John Payne (Ambrose Fillmore); Roland Young (Thomas Brooke); Charlotte Greenwood (Lola Langdon); William Gargan (Dane Wharton); Mary Beth Hughes (June Lawrence); Mary Healy (Mary Andrews); Donald Meek (Sam Wellman); Jessie Ralph (Aunt Martha Parker); Walter Kingsford (Napoleon); George Montgomery (Ronnie); Robert Lowery (Bellboy); Hal K. Dawson (Cargo); Jody Gilbert (Maid); Gary Breckner (Announcer); Paul Hurst (Mac); Irving Bacon (Jefferson); Mantan Moreland (George)

## Viva Cisco Kid
(Fox; 1940)

In which the frontier hero of the title (played by César Romero) swears off his womanizing ways—only to fall in love, or something a whole lot like it, at the sight of Jean Rogers. Moreland has an unbilled role as a cook.

**CREDITS:** Executive Producer: Sol M. Wurtzel; Director: Norman Foster; Characters, Story, and Screenplay: William Sydney Porter [a.k.a. O. Henry], Samuel G. Engel, and Hal Long; Photographed by: Charles G. Clarke; Editor: Norman Colbert; Running Time: 70 Minutes; Released: April 12, 1940

**CAST:** Cesar Romero (The Cisco Kid); Jean Rogers (Joan Allen); Chris-Pin Martin: (Gordito); Minor Watson (Jesse Allen); Stanley Fields (Boss); Nigel De Brulier (Moses); Harold Goodwin (Hank Gunther); Francis Ford (Proprietor); Charles Judels (Pancho); Frank Darien (Agent); Mantan Moreland (Cook)

## Girl in 313
### a.k.a. THE GIRL IN ROOM 313
(Fox; 1940)

Ricardo Cortez, the dashing crime-melodrama star, directs this gem about a police agent (Florence Rice) who infiltrates a gang of jewel thieves—only to become romantically involved with chief racketeer Kent Taylor. Moreland has an incidental role as a porter.

**CREDITS:** Producer: Sol M. Wurtzel; Director: Ricardo Cortez; Story and Screenplay: M. Clay Adams, Hilda Stone, and Barry Trivers; Photographed by: Edward Cronjager; Musical Score: David Buttolph, Cyril J. Mockridge, and Alfred Newman; Running Time: 58 Minutes; Released: May 31, 1940

**CAST:** Florence Rice (Joan Matthews); Kent Taylor (Gregg Dunn); Lionel Atwill (Russell); Kay Aldridge (Sarah Sorrell); Mary Treen (Jenny); Jack Carson (Pat O'Farrell); Elyse Knox (Judith Wilson); Joan Valerie (Francine Edwards); Dorothy Dearing (Emmy Lou Bentley); Dorothy Moore (Happy); Julie Bishop [a.k.a. Jacqueline Wells] (Lorna Hobart); Charles C. Wilson (Vincent Brady); Mantan Moreland (Porter)

## On the Spot
(Monogram; 1940)

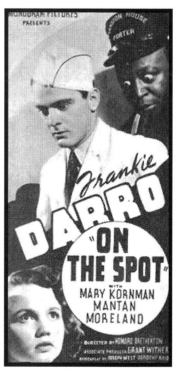

Small-town soda jerk Frankie Darro and his pal Moreland become involved in a crime wave after a doomed gangster tells them of a hidden fortune. See *Forgotten Horrors 2*.

**CREDITS:** Associate Producer: Grant Withers; Director: Howard Bretherton; Story and Screenplay: Dorothy Davenport (a.k.a. Reid) and George Waggner (a.k.a. Joseph West); Photographed by: Harry Neumann; Editor: Russell F. Schoengarth; Sound: Karl Zint; Running Time: 62 Minutes; Released: June 11, 1940

**CAST:** Frankie Darro (Frankie Kelly); Mary Kornman (Ruth Hunter); Mantan Moreland (Jefferson); John St. Polis (Doc Hunter); Robert Warwick (Cyrus Haddon); Maxine Leslie (Gerry Dailey); Lillian Elliott (Mrs. Kelly)

## Maryland
(Fox; 1940)

Henry King directs this neglected classic among horse movies. Fay Bainter, an equestrienne widowed by a riding accident, forbids son John Payne to have anything to do with horses. Walter Brennan steals the show as a devoted trainer. Mantan Moreland might have stolen the show, if only he had been assigned a greater prominence.

**CREDITS:** Producers: Gene Markey and Darryl F. Zanuck; Director: Henry King; Screenplay: Jack Andrews and Ethel Hill; Photographed by: George Barnes; Musical Score: David Buttolph, Arthur Lange, and Alfred Newman; Running Time: 92 Minutes; Released: July 19, 1940

**CAST:** Walter Brennan (William Stewart); Fay Bainter (Charlotte Danfield); Brenda Joyce (Linda); John Payne (Lee Danfield); Charles Ruggles (Dick Piper); Hattie McDaniel (Aunt Carrie); Marjorie Weaver (Georgie Tomlin); Sidney Blackmer (Spencer Danfield); Ben Carter (Shadrach); Ernest Whitman (Dogface); Paul Harvey (Buckman); Spencer Charters (Judge); Erville Alderson (Diggs); Robert Anderson (Lee as a Boy); Stanley Andrews (Dr. John Trimble); Olive Ball (Bit); Patsy Lou Barber (Linda as a Girl); Mantan Moreland (Villager); Clarence Muse (The Rev. Mr. Bitters)

## Laughing at Danger
(Monogram; 1940)

This is a particularly ferocious—though nonetheless essentially breezy and comical—serial-murder entry in the Frankie Darro–Mantan Moreland series. A devil-made-flesh with the heavenly name of Celeste makes life a hell-on-Earth for Frankie Darro and Mantan Moreland in this continuation of the partners' comedy-thriller series. Monogram was drawing such vast popular support for *anything* featuring Moreland that the studio moved the artist's billing up a few notches and made his expressive mug even more prominent than that of Darro on the promotional materials.

*Laughing at Danger* makes no bones about its horrific circumstances: At Celeste's Beauty Shop, a laundry chute yields the grisly discovery of the mortal remains of an operator named Florence (Maxine Leslie). Mary Baker (Joy Hodges), the last person to have visited with the victim, is accused. Page boy Frankie Kelly (Darro) and his pal, Jefferson (Moreland), set out to prove Mary's innocence.

The amateur sleuths learn that Florence had intended to give information on a blackmail racket to a detective named Dan Haggerty (George Houston). Then, the body of Florence's fiancé is discovered in a dumbwaiter. Next, one of Mary's clients (Kay Sutton) turns up dead. A phonograph recording is found of a blackmail message between the latest victim and someone at the beauty parlor. Frankie determines that the boss, Celeste (Veda Ann Borg), has been recording some of her customers' more embarrassing moments  and then using the Dictaphone documents to coerce hush-money payments. A vengeful Celeste and her lawyer (Guy Usher) imprison Frankie and Jeff, but the friends stall their intended execution long enough for the cops to come barging in.

The danger here is nothing at which to laugh, of course—which is what makes the Darro–Moreland pictures so funny *and* so hair-raising. Veda Ann Borg is fine as the schemer-turned-killer, and her final show of malice (at first, merely intending to skip town, then deciding upon blood vengeance) makes for a delectably cold twist.

**CREDITS:** Producer: Lindsley Parsons; Director: Howard Bretherton; Screenplay: John W. Krafft and George Waggner (a.k.a. Joseph West); Photographed by: Fred Jackman, Jr.; Editor: Jack Ogilvie; Sound: William R. Fox; Running Time: 63 Minutes; Released: August 12, 1940

**CAST:** Frankie Darro (Frankie Kelly); Joy Hodges (Mary Baker); George Houston (Dan Haggerty); Mantan Moreland (Jefferson); Kay Sutton (Inez Morton); Guy Usher (Alvin Craig); Lillian Elliott (Mrs. Kelly); Veda Ann Borg (Celeste); Betty Compson (Mrs. Van Horn); Rolfe Sedan (Pierre).

### Pier 13
(Fox; 1940)

This lively if routine crime melodrama finds lawman Lloyd Nolan pursuing a crook (Douglas Fowley) in the name of business and a short-order waitress (Lynn Bari) in the name of extracurricular romance. The waitress' sister (Joan Valerie) proves to be involved with Nolan's criminal quarry. Of course, Moreland has the customary background role.

**CREDITS:** Producer: Sol M. Wurtzel; Director: Eugene Forde; Story and Screenplay: Clark Andrews, Harry Connors, Philip Klein, and Stanley Rauh; Musical Score: Cyril J. Mockridge; Orchestrations: Walter Scharf and Herbert W. Spencer; Photographed by: Virgil Miller; Editor: Fred Allen; Running Time: 67 Minutes; Released: August 23, 1940

**CAST:** Lynn Bari (Sally Kelly); Lloyd Nolan (Danny Dolan); Joan Valerie (Helen Kelly); Douglas Fowley (Johnnie Hale); Chick Chandler (Nickie); Oscar O'Shea (Skipper Kelly); Adrian Morris [a.k.a. Michael Morris] (Al Higgins); Louis Jean Heydt (Bill Hamilton); Frank Orth (Deadpan Charlie); Stanley Blystone (Policeman); Charles D. Brown (Capt. Blake); Maurice Cass (Howard); Frank Darien (Old Man); Hal K. Dawson (Ticket Man); Edward Earle (Peters); Mantan Moreland (Sam)

**Up In The Air**
(Monogram; 1940)

The most memorable entry of the Darro–Moreland series takes place in a big-city radio station where a murderer lurks. Mantan Moreland and Frankie Darro served their comedy-team thrillers as working stiffs who aspire to more glamorous careers. The running irony of the pictures is that these ill-respected citizens are perfectly capable of rising to whatever desperate occasion should arise. In the shining instance of *Up in the Air*, the guys' reality is to labor as a porter and a messenger-boy at a Hollywood broadcasting studio, where they would relish a crack at becoming entertainers.

After they land in trouble for helping another toiler, Anne Mason (Marjorie Reynolds), seek an audition as a singer, Frankie Ryan (Darro) and Jeff (Moreland) find themselves pressed into a more heroic state after an ill-tempered vocalist, Rita Wilson (Lorna Gray), is murdered during a rehearsal. The likeliest suspect is Tex Barton (Gordon James), a pathetic nobody who fancies himself a glamorous cowboy singer but lets show a darker nature in an unguarded moment. Producer Farrell (Tristram Coffin) wants Frankie to keep mum about an argument between Farrell and Miss Wilson; Frankie has Farrell promise to give Anne an audition. Frankie discovers the hiding place of the murder gun—which is traced to Tex, and to an unsolved case in Wyoming. Tex turns up dead.

Following through on evidence found in Tex's quarters, the police arrest Anne, believing her tied to the Wyoming case. It develops that the mystery woman was in fact Rita—who had cuckolded her husband, Tex, for a radio-station boss. An unobtrusive character, radio emcee Van Martin (Alex Callam), confesses to the murders while holding the assembled station brass at gunpoint. Jeff suddenly intrudes, throwing open a door and toppling Martin for an easy capture.

Darro and Moreland get to handle the heroics in high style—with Darro as the impulsive fools-rush-in type and Moreland as the hesitant voice of reason who cannot help becoming involved. While scouring a crime scene, Darro teases Moreland about being afraid of ghosts—a curious confrontation, rather than an exploitation, of stereotype. "It ain't the ghost," Moreland replies. "It's the person that *made* her a ghost—that's what's botherin' me!" The actors also are allowed some pure-comedy showcases apart from the mystery, in scenes where they try to prove what a hit they could be on radio. Darro's brief appearance in blackface might seem offensive today, but in 1940 the *shtick* was still a norm of the waning Vaudeville tradition: Like Al Jolson, Emmett Miller and Bing Crosby before him, Darro is not lampooning African-American sensibilities, but rather trying (a bit too strenuously) to *become black*, while playfully acknowledging a fraction of the debt that white America owes to black America. As the men prepare for a rehearsal, Moreland asks, indignantly: "You don't expect me to speak in no dialect, do you?" When Darro's rapid-fire delivery proves *too* rapid for Moreland's tastes, Mantan halts the routine to tell his overeager partner to slacken the pace. Like the white rock-and-roll acts, from early-day Fleetwood Mac to Eric Clapton, that would attempt almost to *become* the Deep Blues artists they admired, Darro is forcing the process. (Muddy Waters found it necessary to ask Paul Butterfield to slow things down a bit, too, when their paths crossed during the 1960s.) When boss-man Tris Coffin angrily swipes at the black makeup on Darro's face and then glances at Moreland, Mantan snaps: "Don't touch *me*!

*I* don't rub off!" In such subtextual insights into a cross-cultural shadowland, perhaps more so than in its conscious humor, the Darro–Moreland combo is a marvel of quick-wittedness and spontaneous patter. What makes it work is the sense of friendship between players.

Story-wise, *Up in the Air* is a muddle of coincidence and contradiction—standard Monogram fare—that keeps crucial clues well out of the audience's reach. If the unmasking of the killer comes off as less than a satisfactory resolution, then Moreland's inadvertent capture of the culprit compensates plenty well.

Weblog reviews as a class are a mixed bag—more commonly fatuous and ill-informed than substantial and insightful—but this Internet Movie DataBase memo from an enthusiast known as O. Nenslo homes in smartly on Moreland's distinctive style: "…nothing to talk about but Mantan Moreland. The plot is pretty much a series of contrivances [upon which] to hang situations, and the inevitable solution of the 'who killed…?' mystery doesn't seem to be the driving force. It's all about Mantan.

"I have seen him as comedy relief in a dozen movies, and he always steals every scene he is in, but I have never seen him dominate like this. He makes everyone else into his straight man, and constantly subverts and deflates authority figures. Every time someone says 'I've got an idea,' or 'I've been thinking,' [Moreland is] on the spot with his '*Uh-oh*!' There is nothing cowardly (as it often appears in his *Charlie Chan* roles) about his fierce common-sense determination to move away from trouble, not toward it. He sometimes seems like the only one who is not dangerously foolish. Mantan and Frankie Darro work together really well here. And although modern sensibilities may be jarred by Darro's donning of blackface makeup to try to get them a radio job as a comedy duo, they come across as peers and friends, not boss-and-lackey as so often occurs in films of this era.

"The highest point is Mantan's dance scene—inserted into the story for no reason but its sheer entertainment value—in which he is so suave, smooth, cool, cute and downright huggable [that] it's difficult not to exclaim in delight. The movie plugs along gamely in the moments when Mantan is not on-screen, and provides some pretty fair musical numbers, but he is the real shining light in this production."

**CREDITS:** Producer: Lindsley Parsons; Director: Howard Bretherton; Screenwriter: Edmond Kelso; Musical Score: Edward J. Kay and Johnny Lange & Lew Porter (Song, "Doin' the Conga"); Photographed by: Fred Jackman, Jr.; Editor: Jack Ogilvie; Production Manager: Charles J. Bigelow; Assistant Director: Albert Greenwood; Running Time: 64 Minutes; Released: September 9, 1940

**CAST:** Frankie Darro (Frankie Ryan); Marjorie Reynolds (Anne Mason); Mantan Moreland (Jeff Jefferson); Gordon Jones (Tex Barton); Lorna Gray (Rita Wilson); Tristram Coffin (Bob Farrell); Clyde Dilson (Lt. Marty Phillips); Dick Elliott (B.J. Hastings); John Holland (Sam Quigley); Carleton Young (Stevens); Alex Callam (Van Martin); Maxine Leslie (Stella); Ralph Peters (Detective Delaney); Jack Mather (Comic); Dennis Moore (Pringle); Phil Kramer (Gagman)

## Drums of the Desert
(Monogram; 1940)

A Foreign Legion melodrama, with Moreland contributing generous backup service. The yarn is essentially a romantic triangle among B-movie A-listers Ralph Byrd, Lorna Gray and Peter George Lynn. The adventurous tone darkens with the arrival of William Castello as a vengeful Arab. Eddie "Rochester" Anderson, slumming briefly in the minor leagues, delivers a cameo.

**CREDITS:** Producer: Paul Malvern; Director: George Waggner; Story and Screenplay: Dorothy Davenport (a.k.a. Dorothy Reid), John T. Neville, and George Waggner (a.k.a. Joseph West); Photographed by: Fred Jackman, Jr.; Musical Score: Edward J. Kay; Editor: Jack Ogilvie; Décor: Dave Milton; Sound: William R. Fox; Technical Director: Charles Clague; Military Consultant: Charles Townsend; Running Time: 64 Minutes; Released: October 7, 1940

**CAST:** Ralph Byrd (Paul Dumont); Lorna Gray (Helene Laroche); George Peter Lynn (Jean); William Castello (Addullah); Mantan Moreland (Sgt. Williams); Jean Del Val (Col. Fouchet); Ann Codée (Mme. Fouchet); Boyd Irwin (Capt. Andre); Neyle Morrow [a.k.a. Marx] (Ben Ali); Alberto Morin (Hassan); Jack Chefe (Steward); Bud Harrison (Bobo); Eddie "Rochester" Anderson (Sergeant); DeForest Covan (Bit); Rolfe Sedan (Man); John Stark (Bartosh)

**While Thousands Cheer**
a.k.a. CROOKED MONEY; GRIDIRON GRAFT
(Gold Seal/Million Dollar Productions; 1940)

Mantan Moreland has the featured role of trainer to a football champion, played by athlete Kenny Washington, in this black-ensemble crime melodrama involving a gambling-and-blackmail racket. The yarn is very much in the vein of the Joe Louis starrer, *Spirit of Youth* (see above)—almost a retread, in fact. Washington, a Class-of-1940 All-American from U.C.L.A., became one of the first black players to compete in the National Football League following World War II. Washington played most prominently with the Los Angeles Rams.

**CREDITS:** Executive Producer: Harry M. Popkin; Producer: Clifford Sanforth; Associate Producer: Sara Francis; Director: Leo C. Popkin; Story and Screenplay: Joseph O'Donnell; Photographed by: Marcel Le Picard, Herman

Schoff, and Clark Ramsey; Editor: Martin G. Cohn; Production Manager: George M. Merrick; Assistant Director: Gordon Griffith; Sound; Clifford A. Ruberg; Running Time: 64 Minutes; Released: Following Los Angeles Opening on November 14, 1940

**CAST:** Kenny Washington (Kenny Harrington); Mantan Moreland (Nash); Al Duvall (Downey); Jeni Le Gon (Myra); Reginald Fenderson (Phil Harrington); Laurence Criner (Green); Monte Hawley (Johnson); Florence "Suli May" O'Brien [a.k.a. Suli May] (Daisy); Ida Belle Kauffin (Rose); Gladys Snyder (Rose); Edward Thompson (Harding); Tony Doran (Athlete); Joan Douglas (Co-ed); Agnes Floyd (Co-ed); Joel Fluellen (Waiter); Bobby Johnson (Man); Rosalie Lincoln (Co-ed); Guernsey Morrow (Waiter); and Lester Wilkins

## You're Out of Luck
(Monogram; 1941)

Murder-in-a-hotel shenanigans, here, with Frankie Darro and Mantan Moreland in customarily fine form as serving-class representatives who—naturally—prove the only souls capable of saving the day. The lowly-but-noble big-city elevator man has seldom been recognized as the driving force he used to be in high-rise community and corporate life. Before automation made *everybody* an elevator operator for better or worse, these dedicated professionals—who were, economically speaking, just a step or two up from Skid Row—took a distinct tribal pride in seeing to it that each passenger, no matter how crowded the car or how impatiently abusive the riders, reached the appropriate floor in due time.

It is safe to say that few real-life elevator men harbored a desire to play detective, and this quirk is precisely what makes the Frankie Darro-Mantan Moreland team in *You're Out of Luck* such a delight. These guys know their way around the inner chambers of a ritzy hotel, and thus do the actors ground their more extravagant deeds in an unerring practical reality.

If Mantan Moreland is the great unacknowledged comedian of Old Hollywood (see *King of the Zombies*, below), then Moreland and Frankie Darro must certainly want consideration as one of the better comedy teams, ill-recognized. Their starring series of desperate mystery-farces for Monogram holds up as a kind of poor man's Abbott & Costello (whose big-screen teaming Moreland and Darro foreshadowed), and the combination of Darro's overzealous boyishness and Moreland's never-at-a-loss wisecracking wisdom is still a wonder to behold. That they formed—and sustained—an integrated comedy-adventure act long before Robert Culp and Bill Cosby (network television's *I Spy*) or Danny Glover and Mel Gibson (the *Lethal Weapon* pictures) makes their work all the more ripe for rediscovery.

Darro was born Frank Johnson in 1917 in Chicago, the son of circus aerialists. Small of frame and as agile as a prairie catamount, he started out playing adventurous roles as a youngster; a good sustained example of his teen-age work occurs in 1935's *The Phantom Empire* (see *Forgotten Horrors: The Definitive Edition*). Darro was still being (aptly) cast as a kid, for all practical purposes, even into adulthood.

Which brings us to *You're Out of Luck*, which Darro serves as a hotel elevator operator and bellman named Frankie O'Reilly. Frankie and Jeff (Moreland), a garageman and mechanic for the same Carlton Arms, chance to witness a mob hit—latest outburst of a crime wave that has found Frankie's brother, police detective Tom O'Reilly (Richard Bond), hard-pressed to nail a mastermind. Tom considers Frankie a nuisance, but the kid tags along anyhow as they trace Dick Whitney (Tris Coffin), a playboy resident of the hotel, to criminal elements. Tom grudgingly accepts help from Jeff and Frankie in trailing Whitney.

Whitney pulls off a shakedown on a gangster named Johnny Burke (Willie Costello) and passes an envelope full of money to Frankie, with orders to deliver it to the murder victim's sister. Whitney calls for a police raid. Tom breaks into a now-deserted nightclub, only to find himself humiliated by a mocking newspaper report.

Frankie has hidden the envelope within the hotel. Later, when ordered to repair a sluggish lift, Jeff and Frankie find Whitney's body atop the elevator car. It develops that Burke is responsible for the slayings, which were provoked by gambling shenanigans. Burke's hoodlums capture Jeff and Frankie and Sonya

(Vicki Lester), a *femme fatale* who had been involved with both Burke and Whitney. Burke herds the captives into a freight elevator, the better to hold off a police siege. Jeff and Frankie save the day by freezing the elevator via an emergency control panel.

The complications run needlessly thick, what with Vicki Lester walking a fine line between helping the cops and bum-steering them as she tries to lay her mitts on a small fortune in illicit loot, while still seeming a dutiful gang moll; Moreland carrying on an affair with the moll's housekeeper; detective Richard Bond tackling the underworld while fending off an abusive press corps; and a cash-laden envelope defying all attempts to keep track of it. Moreland and Darro keep the messy scenario under control with brisk wordplay and whiplash slapstick reactions—and ultimately, a heroism born of their unique knowledge of the inner workings of an elevator.

**CREDITS:** Producer: Lindsley Parsons; Director: Howard Bretherton; Screenplay: Edmond Kelso; Photographed by: Fred Jackman, Jr.; Editor: Jack Ogilvie; Art Director: Charles Clague; Décor: Dave Milton; Assistant Director: Mack V. Wright; Sound: William R. Fox; Musical Director: Edward J. Kay; Running Time: 62 Minutes; Released: January 20, 1941

**CAST:** Frankie Darro (Frankie O'Reilly); Mantan Moreland (Jeff Jefferson); Richard Bond (O'Reilly); William Costello (Johnny Burke); Vickie Lester (Sonya Varney); Janet Shaw (Joyce Dayton); Kay Sutton (Marjorie Overton); Tristram Coffin (Roger Whitman); Ralph Peters (Mulligan); Paul Maxey (Pete); Paul Bryar (Man); Willy Castello (Man); Jack Mather (Man); Gene O'Donnell (Pete); William E. Snyder (Jack)

## Sleepers West
(Fox; 1941)

A typically slick and breezy entry in Fox's *Michael Shayne* mystery series, starring Lloyd Nolan as the glib sleuth. The setting aboard a passenger train assures the casting-to-type of several black artists—Moreland among them, of course—in porter-type roles.

**CREDITS:** Producer: Sol M. Wurtzel; Director: Eugene Forde; Story and Screenplay: Lou Breslow, Frederick Nebel (from His Novel), and Stanley Rauh; Photographed by: J. Peverell Marley; Editor: Fred Allen; Art Directors: Lewis H. Creber and Richard Day; Musical Supervisor: Emil Newman; Running Time: 74 Minutes; Released: March 14, 1941

**CAST:** Lloyd Nolan (Michael Shayne); Lynn Bari (Kay Bentley); Mary Beth Hughes (Helen Carlson); Louis Jean Heydt (Everett Jason); Edward Brophy (George Trautwein); Don Costello (Carl Izzard); Ben Carter (Leander); Donald Douglas (Tom Linscott); Oscar O'Shea (McGowan); Harry Hayden (Lyons); Hamilton MacFadden (Meyers); Ferike Boros (Farmer); Mantan Moreland (Porter); Charles R. Moore (Porter)

### Footlight Fever
(RKO–Radio; 1941)

Show-business intrigues, leavened by broad comedy and a spot of contrived romance. Moreland is under-employed, as usual.

**CREDITS:** Producer: Howard Benedict; Director: Irving Reis; Story and Screenplay: Bert Granet, Ian McLellan Hunter, and Bert Granet, with Paul Girard Smith; Musical Score: Lucien Denni *et al.*; Photographed by: Robert De Grasse; Editor: Theron Warth; Art Director: Van Nest Polglase; Associate Art Director: Carroll Clark; Costumer: Renié Conley; Sound: Hugh McDowell Jr.; Running Time: 70 Minutes; Released: March 21, 1941

**CAST:** Alan Mowbray (Don Avery); Donald MacBride (Geoff Crandall); Elisabeth Risdon (Aunt Hattie Drake); Lee Bonnell (John Carter); Elyse Knox (Eileen Drake); Charles Quigley (Spike); Charles Lane (Link); Georgia Backus (Imogene); Jay Belasco (Costumer); Eddie Borden (Joe); Frank Bruno (Cabbie); Paul E. Burns (Mover); Chester Clute (Holly); Mantan Moreland (Willie Hamsure)

### Ellery Queen's Penthouse Mystery
(Darmour, Inc./Columbia; 1941)

Another lesser vehicle for Moreland, who nonetheless registers a striking impression from the lower strata of the supporting cast. The yarn concerns the disappearance of an international courier bearing a fortune in gemstones.

**CREDITS:** Producer: Larry Darmour; Director: James P. Hogan; Screenwriters: Frederic Dannay (writing as Ellery Queen), Manfred Lee (writing as Ellery Queen), and Eric Taylor; Musical Score: Lee Zahler; Photographed by: James S. Brown, Jr.; Editor: Dwight Caldwell; Running Time: 69 Minutes; Released: March 24, 1941

**CAST:** Ralph Bellamy (Ellery Queen); Margaret Lindsay (Nikki Porter); Charley Grapewin (Inspector Queen); Anna May Wong (Lois Ling); James Burke

(Velie); Eduardo Ciannelli (Count Brett); Frank Albertson (Sanders); Ann Doran (Sheila Cobb); Noel Madison (Gordon Cobb); Charles Lane (Doc Prouty); Russell Hicks (Walsh); Tom Dugan (McGrath); Mantan Moreland (Roy); Theodore von Eltz (Jim Ritter); and Chester Gan and Richard Loo

### Sign of the Wolf
(Monogram; 1941)

And of course Monogram always treated Moreland better in terms of prominence and clever wordsmithery. Mantan proves predominant in this free-handed adaptation of a Jack London tale from 1920, "That Spot." The tale concerns Moreland's attempts to prevent a fine dog (a magnificent Alsatian Shepherd named Shadow) from falling into the wrong hands.

**CREDITS:** Producer: Paul Malvern; Director: Howard Bretherton; Story and Screenplay: Jack London, Elizabeth Hopkins, and Edmond Kelso; Music: Edward J. Kay; Photographed by: Fred Jackman, Jr.; Editor: Jack Ogilvie; Production Manager: Glenn Cook; Animal Trainer: Frank Barnes; Running Time: 69 Minutes; Released: March 25, 1941

**CAST:** Michael Whalen (Rod Freeman); Grace Bradley (Judy Weston); Darryl Hickman (Billy Freeman); Mantan Moreland (Ben); Louise Beavers (Beulah); Wade Crosby (Mort Gunning); Tony Paton (Red Fargo); Joseph E. Bernard (Hank); Edward Brady (Jules); Eddie Kane (Martin); Brandon Hurst (Dr. Morton); and Herman Hack, Nelson McDowell, and Hal Price (Trappers)

### Mr. Washington Goes to Town
(National/Dixie National; 1941)

Ghostly doings in a haunted hotel, with Broadway-to-Hollywood teammates Mantan Moreland and F. (as in Flournoy) E. Miller on hand to respond appropriately. One of the few films to invert serving-class typecasting for

Moreland—even though the inversion is compromised by a just-a-dream denouement. Moreland & Miller, one of the finer comedy teams of black Vaudeville, stuck together in pictures as well, even though Mantan Moreland's fortunes as a solo artist in Hollywood proved greater than those of Flournoy E. Miller. Three Moreland & Miller movies in particular capture the artists' teamwork pretty much as it must have appeared in the black neighborhood nightspots where they perfected their dead-solid-perfect combination of slapstick *shtick* and absurd wordplay. These are *Mr. Washington Goes to Town* and 1942's back-to-back *Lucky Ghost* and *Professor Creeps*, all from the white producer Jed Buell. Buell's *Up Jumped the Devil* is an interim effort, minus Miller.

Buell, who was as much a well-intentioned huckster as he was a picture-maker, publicized *Mr. Washington* to the black newspapers as "the first all-Negro comedy feature ever made." Of course, most of the talents at work behind the cameras were white—and black actors and singers had been making comedy films since the silent era, both among themselves and with integrated ensemble casts.

But neither Buell's extravagant claims nor his amateurish filmmaking skills can diminish the fun of *Mr. Washington Goes to Town*. It all starts in the jailhouse, where a prisoner named Schenectady (Moreland) learns that he has inherited a hotel. Next thing he knows, Schenectady has arrived at the Hotel Ethiopia, where he puts himself to work as an elevator operator and hires his jailbird pal, Wallingford (Miller), as his assistant.

The hotel proves to contain more unnerving surprises than Schenectady can handle: A gorilla shows up, accompanied by a man in formal attire. Headless men prowl the place, and a knife thrower, an invisible man and a magician terrorize Schenectady and Wallingford. A menacing character named Brutus Blake (Maceo B. Sheffield) challenges Schenectady's ownership of the place and begins dismantling the hotel in search of hidden treasure. The situation has grown intolerable when Schenectady suddenly wakes. The entire misadventure has been a dream.

Wallingford wants to visit the hotel once the pals are sprung, but Schenectady nixes the idea: He has already been there, he says, and he finds the place none to his liking.

**Mantan has his hands full in *Mr. Washington Goes to Town*.**

There is no other cop-out quite as infuriating as the just-a-dream resolution, but at least the ending of *Mr. Washington Goes to Town* is a foregone conclusion. Too many such finales—including those of the otherwise superior film noirs *The Strange Affair of Uncle Harry* (Universal; 1945) and *Fear* (Monogram; 1946)—have come about as hasty afterthoughts to placate the censors. *Mr. Washington*'s dream setting places the film more nearly on a par with the phantasmagorical newspaper cartoons and silent films of Winsor McCay (including *Little Nemo in Slumberland* and *Dream of a Rarebit Fiend*). Buell's customarily shabby production values serve to emphasize the otherworldly ambiance without detracting from the work of Miller & Moreland. The pals' funny business renders it immaterial whether there is a story to be found here.

Curiously, there is no reference to anybody named Washington in Dixie National's pressbook or in either of the rather choppy prints screened in preparation for this book. Maybe Washington is supposed to be Schenectady's last name.

**CREDITS:** Producers: Jed Buell and James K. Friedrich; Associate Producer: Maceo B. Sheffield; Directors: Jed Buell and William Beaudine; Story and Screenplay: Lex Neal and Walter Weems; Photographed by: Jack Greenhalgh; Editor: William Faris; Production Designer: Fred Preble; Production Manager: Bert Sternbach; Sound Effects: Treg Brown; Sound Engineer: Hans Weeren;

Musical Director: Harvey Brooks; Running Time: 65 Minutes; Released: Following Los Angeles Preview on April 11, 1941

**CAST:** F.E. Miller (Wallingford); Mantan Moreland (Schenectady); Marguerite Whitten (Lady Queenie); Edward Boyd (Lonesome Ranger); DeForest Covan (Short Headless Man); Nathan Curry (Cop); Cleo Desmond (Old Maid); Slick Garrison (Man in Barber Chair); Clarence Hargrave (Man with Gorilla); Henry Hastings (Uncle Utica); Charlie Hawkins (Goldberg); Monte Hawley (Stiletto); John Lester Johnson (Tall Headless Man); Walter Knox (Man on Crutches); Vernon McCalla (Invisible Man); Clarence Moorehouse (Gorilla); Florence O'Brien (Chambermaid); Arthur Ray (Blackstone); Maceo Bruce Scheffield (Brutus Blake); Zerita Steptean (Mrs. Brutus); Johnnie Taylor (Magician); Sam Warren (Barber); Geraldine Whitfield (Beautiful Girl)

### King of the Zombies
(Sterling/Monogram; 1941)

The centerpiece of Mantan Moreland's movie-biz career—not so much because it is a great motion picture by conventional norms, but because it allows Moreland as free a rein as he ever experienced to commandeer a film's proceedings. Originally announced during early 1941 as a starring picture for Bela Lugosi, this wild fantasia on an anti-Nazi propaganda theme wound up instead as the most elaborate showcase Mantan Moreland ever found during his short but emphatic movie career. Henry Victor inherited the Lugosi role, as a scientist bent on raising the dead for warmongering purposes, and he brought to it a perfectly serviceable competence that has none of the good-humored subtleties or mournful intensity one would have expected from Lugosi. Meanwhile, Lugosi lavished his gifts upon *Invisible Ghost*.

Moreland transformed an incidental comic-relief assignment into the heart and soul of the picture while rendering *King of the Zombies* one of the few most memorable of the Poverty Row spookers. It might be argued that the 39-year-old Moreland also transformed the film into an outright comedy. In any case, the picture cinched Moreland's credentials early on as a uniquely dependable supporting player and led to consistent employment if not bigger opportunities.

Moreland plays Jefferson "Jeff" Jackson, valet to Naval Intelligence Agent Bill Summers (John Archer). They are airborne with pilot James "Mack" McCarthy (Dick Purcell) over the Caribbean in search of a vanished plane when forced to land on a jungle island. The crack-up strands the party in a cemetery, where the men regain their bearings and proceed to a forbidding castle occupied by Dr. Miklos Sangre (Victor). Sangre seems hospitable enough—although he insists that Jeff be lodged with the servants lest they become resentful, and he seems amused that Jeff finds the butler, Momba (Leigh Whipper), downright

**Jefferson Jackson (Moreland) and Bill Summers (John Archer) search for the *King of the Zombies*.**

creepy. Jeff, who has a wisecrack for even the most unnerving occasion, pretends to mistake Momba for a fellow lodge member and then mutters, "Harlem never was like *this*!"

Prowling about, Jeff begins flirting with a pretty servant, Samantha (Marguerite Whitten). Nearby lurks Tahama (Madame Sul-Te-Wan), a cadaverous-looking cook. "I know a *mu*seum that would give a *for*tune just to have her under *glass*," Jeff observes. Samantha tells him of the zombies that stalk the grounds; Jeff is disinclined to believe her until Samantha summons a few of the living-dead creatures. Jeff hightails it for safety. He cannot get Bill or Mack to believe his account, and Sangre holds Jeff up to ridicule.

It develops—and so what else is new?—that Sangre is "cultivating" zombies for the Third Reich. The idea derives from an earnest Real World interest among some of the more superstitious Nazi chieftains to learn whether the dead might be reanimated as a "*todenkorps*" of unquestioning cannon fodder. But of course the Nazis could never have imagined an Allied secret weapon like Mantan Moreland.

Suffice that the screenplay contains such trappings as come with the turf for pulp-magazine horrors and B-as-in-budget Hollywood spookers—the captive military official, the wraithlike wife of the renegade scientist, the Voodoo ritual, the inevitable loss of control of the massed zombies—and let it be known

Mantan the Funnyman

that Moreland overwhelms the clichés and subverts all manner of black-comedian stereotypes at every turn. The Louisiana-born actor speaks in a richly Southern dialect, which renders his subversions all the more disarming. He admits to being fearful and makes a run for cover when discretion so dictates, but instead of lapsing into the expected scared-silly act, Moreland laughs in the face of danger, demands that the menace be confronted and gives the white guys plenty of jovial back-talk in protesting his second-class citizenship. He also indulges to an unusually great extent in flirtatious banter with the beautiful Marguerite Whitten, bringing his characterization nearer the romantically robust, fully rounded performances that the great Paul Robeson had given in Dudley Murphy's *The Emperor Jones* (1933) and James Whale's *Show Boat* (1936) while moving away from the buffoonish and figuratively impotent portrayals that were the stock-in-trade of Lincoln "Stepin Fetchit" Perry and Willie "Sleep'n' Eat" Best.

Upon learning that he has competition for Miss Whitten's attentions, Moreland seems relieved to learn that his potential rival is dead. Miss Whitten explains that her sweetheart had been killed in an accident involving "a revolving crane." Moreland absorbs this revelation and then comments: "Mmmm-*mmm*! Y'all *sho'* have some fierce *birds* around this country!" He is less pleased to learn that the victim has been revived as a zombie. Later on, Victor decides that Moreland belongs among the zombies. Giving in to Victor's hypnotic influence, Moreland joins the ranks of the living dead with, "*Move* over, boys—I'm one of the *gang*, now." Later, when Miss Whitten challenges his zombiehood on grounds that "zombies can't talk," Moreland replies, "Can *I* help it 'cause I'm lo*qua*cious?"

As tempting as it is to call *King of the Zombies* Moreland's movie, plain and simple, even a cursory viewing will point up the brisk pacing, the conversational flow of dialogue and the keen stylistic technique that director Jean Yarbrough brought to the table. A particularly fine visual invention illustrates the speed with which Moreland reacts to his first encounter with the zombies: The camera exaggerates the comedian's takeoff, then dashes around and ahead of him, seemingly through the very foundations of the castle, and catches him arriving in his boss' room.

Edward Kay's original music, too, is broadly distinctive, built upon tribal chant-like rhythms and incorporating a breezy, jazz-tinged *leitmotif* for Moreland in effective contrast to the low-brass martial cues for the zombies.

John Archer, who plays Moreland's boss, seems more the heroic type, although conventional heroism is almost beside the point here. Moreland was already on a roll in cinema, having left a strong impression as early as 1936 with an unbilled part in *The Green Pastures*. By 1939, he was asserting a genuine mastery of screen acting, particularly in the black-ensemble feature *One Dark Night*—which, the title notwithstanding, is not a chiller but a domestic comedy with faint undertones of crime melodrama and science fiction. Moreland had handled more than 30 scene-stealing bit parts and featured appearances by the time he landed in *King of the Zombies*. He became a favorite with the critics at *Variety*, whose various notices raved that "he works with remarkable ease and at all times is natural" and "never fails to garner a laugh, no matter how feeble the line."

**CREDITS:** Producer: Lindsley Parsons; Director: Jean Yarbrough; Screenplay: Edmond Kelso; Musical Score: Edward J. Kay; Photographed by: Mack Stengler; Editor: Richard C. Currier; Art Director: Charles Clague; Production Manager: Mack V. Wright; Settings: Dave Milton; Sound: William R. Fox and Glenn Rominger; Running Time: 67 Minutes; Released: May 14, 1941

**CAST:** Dick Purcell (Mac McCarthy); Joan Woodbury (Barbara Winslow); Mantan Moreland (Jefferson Jackson); Henry Victor (Dr. Mikhail Sangre); John Archer (Bill Summers); Patricia Stacey (Alyce Sangre); Guy Usher (Adm. Arthur Wainwright); Marguerite Whitten (Samantha); Leigh Whipper (Momba); Mme. Sul-Te-Wan (Tahama); Laurence Criner (Dr. Couillie); James Davis (Lazarus); and Josephine Whitten

## Bachelor Daddy
a.k.a. SANDY STEPS OUT
(Universal; 1941)

Something of a foreshadowing of *Home Alone*, with high-spirited moppet Sanda Lee Henville (a.k.a. Baby Sandy) as a near-waif whose mother has been jailed on an unfair accusation. The absurd plot has to do with a rivalry between candy manufacturers. Moreland handles an incidental janitor role. Part of the *Baby Sandy* series.

**CREDITS:** Associate Producer: Burt Kelly; Director: Harold Young; Screenplay: Robert Lees and Frederic I. Rinaldo; Musical Score: Hans J. Salter and Frank Skinner; Additional Music: Charles Henderson and Heinz Roemheld;

Photographed by: Milton R. Krasner; Editor: Paul Landres; Art Director: Jack Otterson; Associate Art Director: Harold H. MacArthur; Décor: Russell A. Gausman; Costumer: Vera West; Assistant Director: Gil Valle; Sound: Bernard B. Brown and Charles Carroll; Running Time: 61 Minutes; Released: June 4, 1941

**CAST:** Baby Sandy (Sandy); Edward Everett Horton (Joseph Smith); Donald Woods (Edward Smith); Raymond Walburn (George Smith); Evelyn Ankers (Beth Chase); Kathryn Adams (Eleanor Pierce); Franklin Pangborn (Williams); Jed Prouty (C.J. Chase); Hardie Albright (Ethelbert); George Meader (Judge McGinnis); Juanita Quigley (Girl); Bert Roach (Louie); Bobby Larson (Boy); Mira McKinney (Landlady); Griff Barnett (Bailiff); Georgie Billings (Kid); Mantan Moreland (Janitor)

## The Gang's All Here
(Sterling/Monogram; 1941)

Tough luck that Mantan Moreland and Frankie Darro never took their buddy-comedy act to a more accomplished filmmaking company, for as the friends' timing became more polished and their camaraderie deepened, the quality of their Monogram Pictures projects grew ever shabbier. *The Gang's All Here* is a truck-hijacking melodrama of considerable intensity and (melo)dramatic potential, but the uneven script defeats much of that purposeful sense. Director Jean Yarbrough appears well aware of Moreland and Darro as the truer soul of the film and concentrates accordingly upon their teamwork. Their ability to nail a lighter-hearted groove amidst the rampant treacheries remains astonishing. Here we have another of those crackerjack Frankie Darro–Mantan Moreland mysteries, a truck-wrecker melodrama that finds the pals saving the day through a combination of dumb luck and courageous resourcefulness. Although the film represents a lapse for the series overall, the stars are right on the money.

Good ol' Pop Wallace (Robert Homans) is in danger of losing his freight company to a campaign of sabotage and murder. Frankie (Darro) and Jeff

(Moreland) are anything but professional drivers, but Pop's desperate situation moves them to apply. Patsy Wallace (Marcia Mae Jones), the boss's opportunistic daughter, intends to use Frankie to provoke her unassertive sweetheart, a greasemonkey named Chick (Jackie Moran), to jealousy.

Patsy's scheming is nothing compared with what Pop has been hiding:

He and his insurance agent, Saunders (Irving Mitchell), have been splitting the payoffs from the wrecks—but Pop is appalled that the incidents have turned deadly. He pleads with Saunders to call off the wreckers.

Meanwhile, Frankie and Jeff hit the road with a payload and run straightaway into saboteurs. They are saved inadvertently when a traffic cop pulls Frankie over for speeding, and the shipment comes through.

Novice trucker George Lee (Keye Luke) seems so eager to learn the trade that he becomes an intolerable snooper around the Wallace depot. George reveals himself as an undercover insurance investigator after Frankie and Jeff are kidnapped and imprisoned by trucking boss Norton (Ed Cassidy) and his mechanic, the brutal Ham Shanks (Laurence Criner). Pop threatens Saunders with exposure unless Frankie and Jeff are freed safely, but the buddies escape—only to find Pop beaten nearly to death. Frankie comprehends that Pop was strong-armed into playing along with the sabotage racket. After an outlandish last-minute hostage situation involving Jeff, Frankie, Patsy, Chick and the crooked insurance agent, the good guys are saved by another speeding citation.

Probably the least of the Darro–Moreland comedy-thrillers, *The Gang's All Here* takes an inappropriately wide turn into sentimentality with the plight of Robert Homans' "Pop" character, and it allows the irritating Marcia Mae Jones a scene-stealing role that she comes ill-equipped to justify. Jackie Moran, better remembered as Huck Finn in 1938's *The Adventures of Tom Sawyer*, serves here chiefly to prompt Miss Jones to a nagging frenzy. Keye Luke's character wavers between needless comedy relief and real heroism, and the nature of his mission is given away rather too abruptly. Jean Yarbrough's direction meanders badly by comparison with his purposeful handling of *King of the Zombies*, and the photography seems hastily composed. Darro and Moreland are delightful, especially in a scene where Frankie tries to teach his reluctant chum the finer points of truck driving.

Darro and Moreland would wrap things up with the fall-of-'41 release of *Let's Go Collegiate*—a decidedly un-murderous situation comedy.

**CREDITS:** Producer: Lindsley Parsons; Director: Jean Yarbrough; Screenplay: Edmond Kelso; Photographed by: Mack Stengler; Editor: Jack Ogilvie; Assistant Director: Glenn Cook; Sound: Glen Glenn; Musical Director: Frank Sanucci; Running Time: 63 Minutes; Released: June 11, 1941

**CAST:** Frankie Darro (Frankie); Marcia Mae Jones (Patsy Wallace); Jackie Moran (Chick Daly); Keye Luke (George Lee); Mantan Moreland (Jeff); Robert Homans (Pop Wallace); Irving Mitchell (R.A. Saunders); Ed Cassidy (Jack Norton); Pat Gleason (Marty); Jack Kenny (Dink); Laurence Criner (Ham Shanks); Jack Ingram (Matt); Skipper Sam (Skipper the Dog); Paul Bryar (Bob)

## Hello, Sucker
(Universal; 1941)

Show-business intrigues, centering upon a defunct-but-defiant Vaudeville company. Moreland has the usual small role.

**CREDITS:** Associate Producer: Ken Goldsmith; Director: Edward F. Cline; Story and Screenplay: Arthur T. Horman, Maurice Leo, and Paul Girard Smith; Musical Score: Frank Skinner; Additional Scoring: Ralph Freed, Charles Henderson, and Hans J. Salter; Photographed by: Charles Van Enger; Editor: Ralph Dixon; Running Time: 62 Minutes; Released: July 11, 1941

**CAST:** Hugh Herbert (Hubert Clippe); Tom Brown (Bob Wade); Peggy Moran (Rosalie Watson); Lewis Howard (Walter); June Storey (Trixie); Walter Catlett (Conway); Robert Emmett Keane (Connors); Mantan Moreland (Elevator Operator); Elaine Morey (Receptionist); Nell O'Day (Model); Dorothy Darrell (Model); and Louise Currie, Eddie Hall

## Accent on Love
(Fox; 1941)

Ray McCarey's Populist polemic finds an heir to immense wealth and privilege leaving it all behind for a life devoted to the romance of poverty. Moreland appears in passing but leaves the usual emphatic impression.

**CREDITS:** Producer: Ralph Dietrich and Walter Morosco; Director: Ray McCarey; Story and Screenplay: John Larkin and Dalton Trumbo; Musical Score: Cyril J. Mockridge; Musical Director: Emil Newman; Orchestrations: Herbert W. Spencer; Photographed by: Charles G. Clarke; Editor: Harry Reynolds; Running Time: 61 Minutes; Released: July 11, 1941

**CAST:** George Montgomery (John Worth Hyndman); Osa Massen (Osa); J. Carrol Naish (Manuel Lombroso); Cobina Wright (Linda Hyndman); Stanley Clements (Patrick Henry Lombroso); Minerva Urecal (Teresa Lombroso); Thurston Hall (T.J. Triton); Mantan Moreland (Prisoner)

## Up Jumped the Devil
(Dixie National/Consolidated National; 1941)

This black-ensemble comedy can only be presumed lost; proof to the contrary is welcome, of course. Mantan Moreland and Shelton Brooks play bickering chums who land jobs with a wealthy household—only to learn that one of the positions requires a maidservant. Which means that Moreland spends much of the picture in drag. Moreland gets back into manly attire by shooting dice with the luckless gents attending a ritzy party. The villain of the piece is a phoney mystic (Maceo Sheffield), who intends to infiltrate the household for the sake of thievery. Nothing particularly horrific about the film, but the title and the soothsayer angle render it of marginal interest here. Oh, yes—Moreland gets back into manly attire by shooting dice with the luckless gents attending a ritzy party. So much for the notion that black stereotypes belong entirely to the Hollywood mainstream.

**CREDITS:** Producer: Jed Buell; Director: William Beaudine (Anonymously); Running Time: 68 Minutes; Released: Beginning in August of 1941 on a region-by-region basis

**CAST:** Mantan Moreland (Washington); Shelton Brooks (Jefferson); Maceo B. Sheffield (Bad News Johnson, alias Swami Reever); and Florence O'Brien, Laurence Criner, Millie Monroe, Suzette Harbin, Aranelle Harris, Earle Morris

**Cracked Nuts**
(Universal; 1941)

One of the weirder comedies from Universal's B-picture department, with Moreland a bit nearer the front lines of the supporting ranks. Small-towner Stuart Erwin wins a small fortune in post-Depression greenbacks, only to run afoul of a con-artist racket involving the purported invention of a humanoid robot. Shemp Howard, Mischa Auer and William Frawley further distinguish the backup ensemble.

**CREDITS:** Producer: Joseph Gershenson (a.k.a. Joseph G. Sanford); Director: Edward F. Cline; Screenplay: W. Scott Darling and Erna Lazarus; Musical Score: Hans J. Salter; Additional Music: Heinz Roemheld and Frank Skinner; Photographed by: Charles Van Enger; Editor: Milton Carruth; Running Time: 61 Minutes; Released: August 1, 1941

**CAST:** Stuart Erwin (Lawrence Trent); Una Merkel (Sharon Knight); Mischa Auer (Boris Kabikoff); William Frawley (James Mitchell); Shemp Howard (Eddie); Astrid Allwyn (Ethel Mitchell); Ernie Stanton (Ivan); Mantan Moreland (Burgess); Hattie Noel (Chloe); Francis Pierlot (Wilfred Smun)

## Dressed To Kill
(Fox; 1941)

More grim-but-comedic thrills from the *Michael Shayne* franchise—and a typically slick and fast-paced entry from Fox's high-gloss B-picture unit. Lloyd Nolan makes a good-natured but intense Shayne, as usual. William Demarest is at the top of his form as a harried boss-cop, and Henry Daniell and Milton Parsons represent the man-you-love-to-hate quotient to near-perfection. Mantan Moreland's presence is a big bonus on a small scale.

**CREDITS:** Producer: Sol M. Wurtzel; Director: Eugene Forde; Characters, Story and Screenplay: Brett Halliday, Richard Burke, Manning O'Connor, and Stanley Rauh; Musical Score: Cyril J. Mockridge; Musical Director: Emil Newman; Photographed by: Glen MacWilliams; Editor: Fred Allen; Running Time: 75 Minutes; Released: August 8, 1941

**CAST:** Lloyd Nolan (Michael Shayne); Mary Beth Hughes (Joanne La Marr); Sheila Ryan (Connie Earle); William Demarest (Inspector Pierson); Ben Carter (Sam); Virginia Brissac (Lynne Evans/Emily); Mantan Moreland (Rusty)

## World Premiere
(Paramount; 1941)

John Barrymore's headlong descent into bloated self-caricature is grimly well documented by this B-unit ensemble farce, which also features the comparably tragic Frances Farmer. Something of an all-star/no-star situation here, with a *Grand Hotel*-type situation created aboard a passenger train. Director Ted Tetzlaff may have been aiming for a higher-minded satirical tone, but he resorts too often to slapstick when all else (often) fails. Mantan Moreland figures as marginally as usual in his big-studio assignments.

**CREDITS:** Producer: Sol C. Siegel; Director: Ted Tetzlaff; Story and Screenplay: Earl Felton and Gordon Kahn; Photographed by: Daniel L. Fapp; Editor: Archie Marshek; Running Time: 71 Minutes: Released: August 15, 1941

**CAST:** John Barrymore (Duncan DeGrasse); Luis Alberni (Scaletti); Don Castle (Joe Bemis); Ricardo Cortez (Mark Saunders); Virginia Dale (Lee Morrison); Frances Farmer (Kitty Carr); Mantan Moreland

### Let's Go Collegiate
(Monogram; 1941)

Least of the Mantan Moreland–Frankie Darro pictures also departs from the crime-thriller gimmick to take a lighter approach overall. Writes Internet Movie DataBase enthusiast O. Nenslo: "Any old-time college movie has one plot: the big game, the big race or the big dance, and the only way to bring it off is to sneak in a ringer from outside the school. This time it is the big race—a rowing race. (The rowing practice all takes place in front of a bizarre and inexplicable rear-projected vista of *oil wells*.)

"Not even Mantan Moreland can pep up these proceedings—it doesn't make you suffer, nor is it anything to write home about. A pretty harmless way to kill an hour or so."

**CREDITS:** Producer: Lindsley Parsons; Director: Jean Yarbrough; Story and Screenplay: Edmond Kelso; Musical Score: Edward J. Kay; Additional Music: Harry Tobias; Photographed by: Mack Stengler; Editor: Jack Ogilvie; Art Director: Charles Clague; Assistant Director: William A. O'Connor; Sound: Glen Glenn; Running Time: 62 Minutes; Released: September 12, 1941

**CAST:** Frankie Darro (Frankie); Marcia Mae Jones (Bess Martin); Jackie Moran (Tad); Keye Luke (Buck Wing); Mantan Moreland (Jeff); Gale Storm (Midge);

Frank Sully (Herk Bevans); Billy Griffith (Professor); Barton Yarborough (Coach); Frank Faylen (Speed); Marguerite Whitten (Malvina); Marvin Jones (Homer); Paul Maxey (Bill); Tristram Coffin (Slugger); and Gene O'Donnell

**It Started with Eve**
(Universal; 1941)

This brisk and urgent romantic comedy stars Deanna Durbin and Charles Laughton, with Robert Montgomery. Moreland's role is fleeting.

**CREDITS:** Producer: Joe Pasternak; Director: Henry Koster; Story and Screenplay: Hanns Kräly, Norman Krasna, and Leo Townsend; Musical Score: Hans J. Salter; Musical Director: Charles Previn; Voice Coach: Andrés Segurola; Photographed by: Rudolph Maté; Editor: Bernard W. Burton; Art Director and Associate: Jack Otterson and Martin Obzina; Running Time: 90 Minutes; Released: September 26, 1941

**CAST:** Deanna Durbin (Anne Terry); Charles Laughton (Jonathan Reynolds); Robert Cummings (Jonathan Reynolds, Jr. ); Guy Kibbee (Bishop Maxwell); Margaret Tallichet (Gloria Pennington); Catherine Doucet (Mrs. Pennington); Walter Catlett (Doctor Harvey); Charles Coleman (Roberts); Leonard Elliott (Rev. Henry Stebbins); Irving Bacon (Raven); Gus Schilling (Raven); Wade Boteler (Editor); Mantan Moreland (Porter)

**Birth of the Blues**
(Paramount; 1941)

Not to be taken seriously as a factual account of the origins of the blues, this one is more of a birth-of-the-white-boy-blues piece. Bing Crosby and Brian Donlevy front a working-class band that seeks to infiltrate the upper-crust society of New Orleans. Crosby, Donlevy, and a high-spirited Mary Martin form a triangle of inexorably shifting dimensions. Crosby (whose more nearly pure jazz-singer credentials date from the 1920s) has some nice one-on-one interplay with the authentic bluesman Louis Armstrong. Mantan Moreland is deployed among the background complement of musicians.

**CREDITS:** Producers: Monta Bell and Buddy G. DeSylva; Director: Victor Schertzinger; Story and Screenplay: Harry Tugend and Walter DeLeon, with Erwin S. Gelsey and Wilkie C. Mahoney; Musical Score and Supervision: Robert Emmett Dolan; Musical Advisor: Arthur Franklin; Additional Music and Lyrics: Walter Scharf; Ernie Burnett, Ford Dabney, Gus Edwards, Charles Harris, John Leipold, Kerry Mills, Ignace Jan Paderewski, Henry E. Pether, Joe

Primrose, Joe Glover, Harry von Tilzer, Lew Brown, Harry DeCosta, Buddy G. DeSylva, W.C. Handy, Ray Henderson, Karl Hoschna, Barclay Grey, Otto A. Harbach, Fred W. Leigh, Cecil Mack, Edward Madden, Johnny Mercer, George A. Norton, Joe Primrose, Andrew Sterling, and Niccolò Paganini; Photographed by: William C. Mellor; Editor: Paul Weatherwax; Running Time: 87 Minutes; Released: November 7, 1941

**CAST:** Bing Crosby (Jeff Lambert); Danny Polo (Clarinet Double for Bing Crosby); Mary Martin (Betty Lou Cobb); Brian Donlevy (Memphis); Pokey Carriere (Cornet Double for Brian Donlevy); Carolyn Lee (Aunt Phoebe Cobb); Eddie "Rochester" Anderson (Louie); J. Carrol Naish (Blackie); Mantan Moreland (Jailbird); Mary Thomas (Child); Bess Wade (Patron); Evelyn West (Patron)

### Marry the Boss's Daughter
(Fox; 1941)

In which a stray dog plays Cupid for an ambitious young accountant and a big shot's daughter. Moreland has an incidental role.

**CREDITS:** Producer: Lou L. Ostrow; Director: Thornton Freeland; Story and Screenplay: Sándor Faragó, Alexander G. Kenedi, and Jack Andrews; Photographed by: Charles G. Clarke; Musical Director: Emil Newman; Editor: Louis R. Loeffler; Running Time: 60 Minutes; Released: November 28, 1941

**CAST:** Brenda Joyce (Fredericka Barrett); Bruce Edwards (Jefferson Cole); George Barbier (J.W. Barrett); Hardie Albright (Putnam Palmer); Ludwig Stössel (Franz Polgar); Bodil Rosing (Mrs. Polgar); Brandon Tynan (Mr. Dawson); Charles Arnt (Blodgett); George Meeker (Snavely); Frank McGlynn, Sr. (Hoffman); Eula Guy (Miss Simpson); Mantan Moreland (Buck)

### Four Shall Die
a.k.a. CONDEMNED MEN
(Million Dollar Productions; 1941)

This little-seen black-ensemble chiller features an up-and-coming Dorothy Dandridge as an imperiled heiress. Moreland plays the boisterous assistant to a detective. Dorothy Dandridge was already poised for major-league stardom—which proved to be long in coming—when she graced this little-seen chiller/comedy about restless spirits and omens of doom. Encouraged by her mother, the stage-and-screen actress Ruby Dandridge, Dorothy had been performing since age four, first in a song-and-dance routine with her sister, Vivian

Dandridge. Dorothy broke through in Hollywood at 24 with a notable bit part in the Marx Brothers' hit, *A Day at the Races* (1937). Her busiest year over the long haul was 1941, which brought her modest parts in *Lady from Louisiana* at Republic; *Sun Valley Serenade* at Fox; *Bahama Passage* at Paramount; and a showy romantic lead in *Four Shall Die*.

*Four Shall Die* is a black-ensemble piece from a studio of predominantly black ownership. The picture finds Miss Dandridge in the role of an heiress, Helen Fielding, whose crooked former sweetheart, Covey (Jack Carr), plots to regain her affections and her fortune. A spiritualistic medium (Vernon McCalla) summons a disembodied voice foretelling doom.

Upon the apparent fulfillment of the prophecy, Helen's new boyfriend (Johnny Thomas) falls under suspicion. No sooner have detective Pierre Toussaint (Pete Webster) and his boisterous helper, Beefus (Mantan Moreland), arrived, however, than another slaying is reported. One beneficiary prepares to leave the country on the medium's advice, but Toussaint establishes that the supposed victims are alive and well—and awaiting the outcome of a scam to terrorize the heirs.

Its sheer scarcity is reason enough to take an interest in *Four Shall Die*, but the film is neither particularly well made nor original in concept. The credits show an overabundance of producers, suggesting a too-many-cooks situation. Among the players, only Miss Dandridge and Mantan Moreland proved to possess that elusive spark of star quality over the long haul. Moreland had already begun proving his worth at the larger, nearer-the-mainstream studios.

**CREDITS:** Producers: Jed Buell and Clifford Sanforth; Directors: William Beaudine and Leo C. Popkin; Assistant Director; Screeplay; Ed Dewey; Photographed by: Marcel Le Picard; Assistant Directors: George Hippard and Eddie Saeta; Running Time: 72 Minutes; Released: Following New York Opening on December 12, 1941

**CAST:** Niel Webster (Pierre Touissant); Mantan Moreland (Beefus); Laurence Criner (Roger Fielding); Dorothy Dandridge (Helen Fielding); Vernon McCalla (Dr. Webb); Monte Hawley (Dr. Hugh Leonard); Reginald Fenderson (Hickson); Jack Carr (Lew Covey); Jess Lee Brooks (Bill Summers); Edward Thompson (Sgt. Adams); Earle Hall (Jefferson); Harry Levette (Thomas)

### Freckles Comes Home
(Monogram; 1942)

Jean Yarbrough's bucolic study of a small town in economic crisis stops just short of being a heartland heart-warmer, concentrating instead upon a criminal scam to bilk a bunch of rubes out of their life's savings—and dwelling upon a subplot involving a running battle of wits between Mantan Moreland and gruff Laurence Criner.

Hotel handyman Moreland possesses a machine that purportedly locates deposits of gold; he sells this gizmo to visiting chauffeur Criner, whose indignation upon finding it useless leads to any number of confrontations. The actors' teamwork relies extensively upon such stereotypical totems as dice and razors, but they exaggerate the references to an extent that intimates a sly awareness of the absurdities and ironies at play, here.

**CREDITS:** Producer: Lindsley Parsons; Director: Jean Yarbrough; Story and Screenplay: Gene Stratton-Porter and Edmond Kelso; Photographed by: Mack Stengler; Editor: Jack Ogilvie; Running Time: 63 Minutes; Released: January 2, 1942

**CAST:** Johnny Downs (Freckles Winslow); Gale Storm (Jane Potter); Mantan Moreland (Jeff); Irving Bacon (Caleb Weaver); Bradley Page (Nate Quigley); Marvin Stephens (Danny Doyle); Betty Blythe (Mrs. Minerva Potter); Walter Sande (Jack Leach); Max Hoffman Jr. (Hymie); John Ince (Hiram Potter); Laurence Criner (Roxbury B. Brown, III); Irving Mitchell (Mr. Winslow); Gene O'Donnell (Monk); Si Jenks (Lem Perkins); and Earle Hodgins, Jack Mulhall, and Al Thompson

## Andy Hardy's Double Life
(MGM; 1942)

MGM's forcibly wholesome *Hardy Family* series holds up today chiefly as a test of endurance: How much of this syrupy nonsense can *you* tolerate in a sitting? In the present entry, Andy Hardy (Mickey Rooney) finds himself involved with both Ann Rutherford and Esther Williams but proves too much the guilt-ridden sap to relish the two-timing experience. All due respect to the devotées of the franchise, of course. Mantan Moreland's part is too little of a good thing.

**CREDITS:** Director: George B. Seitz; Story and Screenplay: Aurania Rouverol (Characters) and Agnes Christine Johnston; Musical Score: Daniele Amfitheatrof and David Snell; Photographed by: George J. Folsey and John J. Mescall; Editor: Gene Ruggiero; Art Director and Associate: Cedric Gibbons and William Ferrari; Running Time: 92 Minutes; Released: Following New York Opening on January 11, 1942

**CAST:** Lewis Stone (Judge James K. Hardy); Mickey Rooney (Andy Hardy); Cecilia Parker (Marian Hardy); Fay Holden (Emily Hardy); Ann Rutherford (Polly Benedict); Sara Haden (Aunt Milly Forrest); Esther Williams (Sheila Brooks); William Lundigan (Jeff Willis); Robert Pittard (Botsy); Robert Blake (Tooky Stedman); Mantan Moreland (Prentiss)

### Treat 'Em Rough
(Universal; 1942)

The boxing-and-gambling demimonde is the setting for a simplistic tale of family honor and retribution. Moreland's contribution is proportionately larger than many of his other big-studio projects would permit.

**CREDITS:** Associate Producer: Marshall Grant; Director: Ray Taylor; Screenplay: Roy Chanslor; Photographed by: George Robinson; Musical Director: Hans J. Salter; Running Time: 61 Minutes; Released: Following New York Opening on January 17, 1942

**CAST:** Eddie Albert (Bill Kingsford); Peggy Moran (Betty); William Frawley (Hotfoot); Lloyd Corrigan (Gray Kingsford); Truman Bradley (Perkins); Mantan Moreland (Snake-Eyes); Joseph Crehan (Wetherbee); Edward Pawley (Martin)

### Four Jacks and a Jill
(RKO–Radio; 1942)

This poorly written ensemble piece proves to be a star vehicle-by-default for Ray Bolger, whose combination of slapstick agility and song-and-dance mastery accounts for some memorable set pieces. The story, such as it is, involves a struggling band of musicians and their search for a featured vocalist. Mantan Moreland's role is, as usual, underwritten and—but for his vivid presence—expendable in the conventional sense.

**CREDITS:** Executive Producer: J.R. McDonough; Producer: John Twist; Director: Jack Hively; Assistant Director: Dewey Starkey; Story and Screenplay: W. Carey Wonderly, John Twist, and Monte Brice; Photographed by: Russell Metty; Musical Director: Constantin Bakaleinikoff; Dance Director: Aida Broadbent; Musical Score: Harry Revel and Roy Webb; Running Time: 68 Minutes; Released: January 23, 1942

**CAST:** Ray Bolger (Nifty Sullivan); Anne Shirley (Karanina Novak); June Havoc (Opal); Desi Arnaz (Steve Sarto and King Stephan); Jack Durant (Noodle); Eddie Foy, Jr. (Happy McScud); Fritz Feld (Hoople); Henry Daniell (Bobo); Joseph E. Bernard (Jailer); Mantan Moreland (Cicero)

## The Vanishing Virginian
(MGM; 1943)

A heartwarming adaptation of Rebecca Yancy Williams' tales of life in rural Virginia, around the start of the last century. By turns quaint and progressive-minded, the film touches upon such social concerns as Prohibition and women's suffrage but of course reinforces the Old South's patriarchal stance toward its black citizenry. Frank Morgan and Spring Byington are excellent in the pivotal roles. Marcella Moreland's first big-studio assignment finds her unbilled and under-employed, but she proves eminently noticeable. Next up for Marcella: a more prominent part in *Mokey* (which see).

**CREDITS:** Producers: Frank Borzage and Edwin H. Knopf; Director: Frank Borzage; Novel and Adaptation: Rebecca Yancey Williams and Jan Fortune; Musical Score: Earl K. Brent, David Snell, Daniele Amfitheatrof, and Lennie Hayton; Photographed by: Charles Lawton, Jr.; Running Time: 97 Minutes; Released: Following Premiere in Lynchburg, Virginia, on January 23, 1942

**CAST:** Frank Morgan (Robert Yancey); Kathryn Grayson (Rebecca Yancey); Spring Byington (Rosa Yancey); Natalie Thompson (Margaret Yancey); Johnny Mitchell [a.k.a. Douglass Newland] (James Weldon Shirley); Mark Daniels (Jack Holden); Elizabeth Patterson (Grandma Yancey); Juanita Quigley (Caroline Yancey); Scotty Beckett (Joel Yancey); Dickie Jones (Robert Yancey, Jr.); Leigh Whipper (Uncle Josh Preston); Louise Beavers (Aunt Emmeline Preston); Hairston (Mover); Eddie Hall (Deliveryman); Edward Hearn (Juror); Howard C. Hickman (Dr. Edwards); Lois Hodnott (Soloist); Clifford Holland (Soloist); Dolores Hurlic (Sugar Preston); and Marcella Moreland

# Law of the Jungle
(Monogram; 1942)

Jean Yarbrough's back-lot-jungle epic ranks close to Yarbrough's own *King of the Zombies* and Steve Sekely's *Revenge of the Zombies* (which see) in terms of a willingness to make Mantan Moreland the star-by-default. Moreland's portrayal of a Harlem-dweller at large in Africa accounts for a wealth of fish-out-of-water wordplay and slapstick. Moreland approaches the abyss of scared-Negro stereotype, here, proving himself willing to confront such ridiculous imagery in order to invert it to his greater advantage. (Yes, okay, and some other viewers will not read quite so much into the portrayal; no accounting for taste or perception.) Mantan Moreland raises this Nazis-in-the-jungle adventure well above the ordinary. Top-billed Arline Judge is no slouch, either, as a disgraced nightclub singer who has been snookered into helping the enemy. The story, too, allows a tribe of (fictional) native Africans to come to the rescue in a welcome inversion of stereotype.

Nona Brooks (Miss Judge), whose treacherous boss, Simmons (Arthur O'Connell), has made her instrumental in the slaying of a British agent, is wandering aimlessly through the bush-country when she encounters an explorer named Larry Mason (John King) and his helper, Jefferson Jones (Moreland). Simmons has already begun spreading unkind rumors about Nona, but Larry agrees to shelter her on condition she scram the next morning.

Stashed away in Nona's clothing are papers that had belonged to the slain Britisher. The Nazis (Victor Kendall and Feodor Chaliapin) kill Simmons and begin tracking Nona. Larry begins to comprehend Nona's plight, but his bearers are slain by tribesmen in the employ of the Germans. Larry, Jeff and Nona take refuge in a cave littered with human remains, hiding the documents in a skull. The warlike tribespeople capture them, but Jeff saves the day, taking advantage of the kindnesses of a native woman who has developed a crush on him. Jeff and the chief discover that they are lodge brothers. Larry and the chief capture the Nazis.

Jean Yarbrough brings an almost impatient sense of timing to *Law of the Jungle*, dwelling primarily on Moreland's showcase scenes. The director and the show-stopping comedian had worked together to sharper advantage on *King of the Zombies*, but this one makes a nice companion-piece to that well-loved picture. The cave-of-bones sequence is suitably unnerving.

**CREDITS:** Producer: Lindsley Parsons; Director: Jean Yarbrough; Screenplay: George Bricker and Edmond Kelso; Photographed by Mack Stengler; Musical Score: Edward J. Kay; Editor: Jack Ogilvie; Production Manager and Assistant Director: William Strohbach; Sound: William R. Fox and Virgil Smith; Technical Director: Dave Milton; Running Time: 61 minutes; Released: February 6, 1942

**CAST:** Arline Judge (Nona Brooks); John "Dusty" King (Larry Mason); Mantan Moreland (Jefferson Jones); Arthur O'Connell (Simmons); C. Montague Shaw (Sgt. Burke); Guy Kingsford (Whiteside); Laurence Criner (Mojobo); Victor Kendall (Grozman); Feodor Chaliapin, Jr. (Belts); Martin Wilkins (Bongo); Robert Strange (Capt. Anthony Hobson)

## Lucky Ghost
(Dixie National/Consolidated National/Toddy; 1942)

Mantan Moreland and Flournoy E. Miller followed through belatedly upon *Mr. Washington Goes to Town* with this more literally supernaturalized comedy—an improvement over *Washington's* only-a-dream resolution. Producer Jed Buell planned a series of at least five additional titles but then took things only as far as *Professor Creeps*, which was shot and released almost simultaneously with *Lucky Ghost*. Mantan Moreland's burgeoning solo career took prior claim, and he wound up as both a long-term contract player for Monogram and a busy character man at most of the major studios.

Moreland and Flournoy E. Miller are squarely in their Negro Vaudeville element as career loafers Washington and Jefferson, who land in a posh sanitarium run as a gambling palace by the crooked Dr. Brutus Blake (Maceo

B. Sheffield) and his partner, Blackstone (Arthur Ray). Soon, the ghosts of Blake's ancestors convene to lament their having left so grand a place to such a wastrel, and the spirit of Uncle Ezra (Henry Hastings) is sent to throw a good scare into Blake. Ezra arrives just after Washington and Jefferson have won the establishment in a game of dice; the pals run things just as wickedly as Blake had, and the ghosts lay siege to the property while Blake and Blackstone plot to regain control. Ezra confronts Blake while the other spirits send Washington and Jefferson packing.

The slight story benefits from a quick telling—three prints viewed range from 50 to 68 minutes—and from the wisecracking joviality of Moreland and Miller. The gagwriting dredges up such rancid corn as a reference to a nearby town called Goslow; this turns out to be a misread highway sign advising motorists to "Go Slow." Henry Hastings makes a suitably severe lead ghost, and burly Maceo Sheffield is fine as the badman in charge of things. The primitive special effects lend a stage-play sensibility to the crazy doings. A piano-playing skeleton accounts for the closing gag. *Lucky Ghost* has been acknowledged by Sherman Hemsley as an inspiration for the oddball comedy *Ghost Fever* (1987), which features Luis Avalos and Hemsley as cops who encounter an absurd haunting. But of course that jinxed picture had its more immediate origins as a stalled attempt to ride the coattails of 1984's *Ghostbusters*.

**CREDITS:** Producer: Jed Buell; Associate Producer: Maceo B. Sheffield; Director: William Beaudine (a.k.a. William X. Crowley); Story and Scenario: Lex Neal and Vernon Smith; Photographed by: Robert Cline; Music: June Hershey, Lorenza Flennoy, and Don Swander; Editor: Robert O. Crandall; Art Director: Eugene C. Stone; Production Manager: Peter Jones; Assistant Director: Edwin Monfort; Running Time: 68 Minutes; Released: February 10, 1942

**CAST:** Mantan Moreland (Washington Delaware Jones); F.E. Miller (Wallingford Jefferson); Florence O'Brien (Hostess); Maceo Bruce Scheffield (Brutus Blake); Arthur Ray (Blackstone); Jess Lee Brooks (Daniel); Monte Hawley (Man); Henry Hastings (Ghost of Ezra Ulysses Dewey); Florence Field (Ghost of Mrs. Dewey); John Lester Johnson (First Ghost); Edward Thompson (Second Ghost); Nappie White (Chauffeur); Reginald Fenderson (Croupier); Jessie Cryer (Dawson); Harold Garrison (Brown); Lucille Battles (Waitress with Turkey); Lester Christmas (Third Ghost); Ida Coffin (Hat Check Girl); Louise Franklin (Waitress); Aranelle Harris (Waitress); Millie Monroe (Waitress).

## Professor Creeps
(Dixie National & Toddy Pictures; 1942)

Cartoonish horror-movie thrills abound in this black-ensemble romp from director William Beaudine, serving double-duty (under a pen-name, William X. Crowley) as a contributing screenwriter. Private detectives Mantan Moreland and F.E. Miller find themselves dealing with mad scientist Arthur Ray. "Our modern generation knows very little of the old minstrel show, which is a thing of the past, but we must give it credit for being the father of America's stage comedy and the element which promoted Vaudeville," wrote producer Jed Buell in the press materials for this Moreland and Miller gem. "The natural wit and fun of the Negro was personified in these minstrel shows, as the Negro is a natural-born comedian and entertainer... For more than a century...the humor of the Negro...was recognized as the essence of show business...We are trying to recapture...the true value of the old minstrel show and to put it into modern dress."

Its honky-fied condescension notwithstanding, Buell's appeal to the critics

**Professor Creeps (Arthur Ray) gives Mantan a hand in *Professor Creeps*.**

bespeaks a heartfelt sympathy with the very style he was exploiting in such pictures as *Mr. Washington Goes to Town*, *Lucky Ghost* and *Professor Creeps*. Although Buell insisted that *Professor Creeps* "was not...designed for Negro [theaters] alone," still it was black America that gave the picture a marketplace resilience in reissues that proceeded into the 1950s.

"Yes, it's a genuine cure for the wartime blues," wrote the Pittsburgh *Courier*'s Herman Hill, a pioneering civil-rights journalist who had taken many black-ensemble pictures to task for what he called "age-old *Amos 'n' Andy* business" and "dialected dialogue." Reporting from the South Central Los Angeles premiere for a mixed black-and-white audience, Hill raved: "Previewed in typical Hollywood fashion Thursday night at sepia town's leading theater...Jed Buell's latest opus starring gawky F.E. Miller and button-eyed, ground-hoggish Mantan Moreland, [the] Mutt & Jeff of the cinema, all but convulsed the crowd with laughter." Hill may have been caught up in the jovial frenzy of the début ceremonies, or perhaps Jed Buell had picked up the tab for the coverage; in any event, the contrast of this story with Hill's more generally militant writing is of interest.

And yes, the "age-old *Amos 'n' Andy* business" is plenty much in evidence here—and it was an established black style before the white-guy talents behind *Amos 'n' Andy* appropriated the shtick—but the film's good-natured generosity with the scares and chuckles is undeniable.

Inept private eyes Washington (Moreland) and Jefferson (Miller) spend most of their time dodging bill collectors and the landlord (recurring tough-guy player Maceo B. Sheffield). The workload at their agency—where a sign proclaims: "Carrier & Stool Pigeons Furnished"—allows plenty of time for snoozing, and during one such interlude Washington dreams about a big case:

Harlem debutante Daffodil Dixon (Florence O'Brien) reports her boyfriend, Alexander (Clarence Hargrave), missing, and the detectives discover that Alexander is hardly the first of her admirers to disappear. At the home of Daffodil's uncle, the mysterious Prof. Whackingham Creeps (Arthur Ray), the partners attempt to reconstruct the circumstances that had led to Alexander's vanishment. Professor Creeps demonstrates his abilities to suspend gravity and change people into beasts. A disembodied voice—Alexander's—informs the sleuths that several of Daffodil's suitors have been transformed and hidden away, along with a Japanese fellow whom the professor had attacked as a matter of wartime principle. Jefferson is zapped into the shape of a gorilla. The professor gets a dose of his own medicine and is changed into a duck. A "real" gorilla, escaped from a circus, joins the fray, and its handlers capture Jefferson by mistake. Washington suddenly wakes up, unable to tolerate more of the absurd dream.

Such unapologetic silliness earned high marks from *Box Office* and *Motion Picture Daily*, which called Moreland and Miller a "sepia Abbott & Costello." Even *The New York Times* weighed in on a favorable note, likening title player Arthur Ray to "a dark-skinned Bela Lugosi" and noting of the Los Angeles premiere, "No Academy Award-winning production has ever received more enthusiasm." *The Hollywood Reporter* wrote: "It is a revelation to observe how Moreland, long regarded among the big three Negro comics in the industry, goes over with his own race." (The "big three" black comedians of the day would also have included Eddie "Rochester" Anderson and Willie Best.) The *Motion Picture Herald* likened *Professor Creeps* to *Hold That Ghost*, Universal's Abbott & Costello hit of 1941, and as though that weren't enough of a stretch, added: "Veteran William Beaudine's direction makes every foot of film count."

Such overzealous notices miss the point—which is merely that an able cast is having a great deal of fun with a silly story—but still it's keen to see a kind word written about good old William Beaudine. Practically the only nay-sayer was a humorless official of the Motion Picture Association's Production Code Administration, who challenged the film's original title.

Seems *Professor Creeps* had been shot as *Goodbye, Mr. Creeps*. MGM had made the uplifting drama *Goodbye, Mr. Chips* in England in 1939, and Production Code honcho Carl E. Milliken raised a red flag about how spoofs of "important titles" must be submitted for the approval of the "important" producer involved. Another PCA personage, Geoffrey Shurlock, replied that *Creeps*' standing as an "all-Negro" picture posed no threat to the eminence of

*Goodbye, Mr. Chips.* So much for the notion of "separate but equal." Even so, Buell rechristened the film *Professor Creeps.* (No telling why the Production Code's Fun Police neglected to red-flag the earlier *Mr. Washington Goes to Town,* whose title is a patent take-off on Frank Capra's oh-so-important *Mr. Deeds Goes to Town,* from 1936.)

To this day, most people hearing the title of *Professor Creeps* for the first time don't know whether to take the word *Creeps* as a noun or a verb, and some sources have recorded the title as *The Professor Creeps.*

**CREDITS:** Executive Producer: Ted Toddy; Producer: Jed Buell; Director: Associate Producers: Dick L'Estrange and Maceo B. Sheffield; Director: William Beaudine; Story and Screenplay: Robert Edmunds and William Beaudine (as William X. Crowley), with Roy Clements, Jed Buell, and Robert Edmunds; Photographed by: Arthur Martinellii; Editor: Dan Milner; Sound: Ben Winkler; Running Time: 63 Minutes; Released: Following Los Angeles Opening on February 28, 1942

**CAST:** Mantan Moreland (Washington); Flournoy E. Miller (Jefferson); Arthur Ray (Prof. Whackingham Creeps); Florence O'Brien (Daffodil Dixon); Marguerite Whitten (Mrs. Green); Shelton Brooks (Jackson)

### The Strange Case of Dr. Rx
(Universal; 1942)

William Nigh's serial-murder thriller is genuinely suspenseful and generously comical—both functions served well by a sense of heroic, bantering camaraderie between detective Patric Knowles and gentleman's gentleman Mantan Moreland. The yarn involves the slayings of various low-lifes who had been acquitted of criminal charges; an elusive avenger known as Dr. Rx appears responsible. Not to give away too much, y'know.

**CREDITS:** Associate Producer: Jack Bernhard; Director: William Nigh; Screenplay: Clarence Upson Young; Photographed by: Elwood Bredell; Editor: Bernard W. Burton; Art Directors: Martin Obzina and Jack Otterson; Décor: Russell A. Gausman; Musical Director: Hans J. Salter; Musical Score: Hans J. Salter and Frank Skinner, with Ralph Freed; Sound: Charles Carroll; Costumer: Vera West; Running Time: 66 Minutes; Released Following New York Opening on March 27, 1942

**CAST:** Patric Knowles (Jerry Church); Lionel Atwill (Dr. Fish); Anne Gwynne (Kit Logan Church); Samuel S. Hinds (Dudley Crispin); Mona Barrie (Eileen Crispin); Shemp Howard (Sweeney); Paul Cavanagh (John Crispin); Edmund

MacDonald (Bill Hurd); Mantan Moreland (Horatio B. Fitz-Washington); John Gallaudet (Ernie Paul); William Gould (Mason); Leyland Hodgson (Thomas); Matty Fain (Tony Zarini); Mary Gordon (Mrs. Scott); Jan Wiley (Lily); Boyd Davis (Police Commissioner); Victor Zimmerman (Kirk); Paul Bryar (Bailiff); Harry Harvey (Manager); Gary Breckner (Announcer); Eddy Chandler (Cop); Ray Corrigan (Gorilla); Jack Kennedy (Policeman); Joe Recht (Newsboy)

## Mokey
(MGM; 1942)

Marcella Moreland is a spirited delight in a modestly positioned backup role, alongside Billy "Buckwheat" Thomas. The film is oversentimentalized and maudlin, predicated upon the grueling miseries of alienation from one's family. *Mokey* is no *Skippy* (1931), and Robert "Bobby" Blake, né Mickey Gubitosi, is no Jackie Cooper. Blake's attempt at one plot-pivot point to pose as a Negro is a *bona fide* cringe-inducer, although his character's tendency to identify with a black surrogate-family bespeaks a progressive attitude.

**CREDITS:** Producer: J. Walter Ruben; Director: Wells Root; Stories and Screenplay: Jennie Harris Oliver, Wells Root, and Jan Fortune; Musical Score: Lennie Hayton, Milton Ager, Guy Massey, and J.P. Webster; Photographed by: Charles Rosher; Editor: Frank Sullivan; Running Time: 88 Minutes; Released: During April of 1942

**CAST:** Dan Dailey (Herbert Delano); Donna Reed (Anthea Delano); Robert Blake (Mokey Delano); Cordell Hickman (Booker T. Cumby); Billy "Buckwheat" Thomas (Brother Cumby); Etta McDaniel (Cindy Molishus); Marcella Moreland (Begonia Cumby); George Lloyd (Pat Esel)

## Tarzan's New York Adventure
(MGM; 1942)

The abduction of their adopted son (Johnny Sheffield) by a circus crew draws jungle-dwellers Tarzan (Johnny Weissmuller) and Jane (Maureen O'Sullivan) to civilization. This closing entry in MGM's *Tarzan* series is (to invoke star player Weissmuller's comment, from a pre-production interview) "a good, lively show." Mantan Moreland serves the film briefly in his customary big-studio role as a representative of the serving class—stealing the scene, as usual.

The assignment amounted to a homecoming, of sorts, for Moreland: MGM hired the Hagenbeck–Wallace Circus to provide a touch of backlot authenticity. Hagenbeck–Wallace had been Moreland's employer during his early years of moving toward Broadway and Hollywood.

**CREDITS:** Producer: Frederick Stephani; Director: Richard Thorpe; Assistant Director: Dolph Zimmer; Based upon Characters Created by: Edgar Rice Burroughs; Story and Screenplay: Myles Connolly, Gordon Kahn, and William R. Lipman; Photographed by: Sidney Wagner; Musical Score: David Snell, with material by Amilcare Ponchielli, Sol Levy, Fud Livingston, and Matty Malneck; Running Time: 71 Minutes; Released: May of 1942

**CAST:** Johnny Weissmuller (Tarzan); Maureen O'Sullivan (Jane); Johnny Sheffield (Boy); Virginia Grey (Connie Beach); Charles Bickford (Buck Rand); Paul Kelly (Jimmie Shields); Chill Wills (Manchester Montford); Cy Kendall (Col. Sergeant); Russell Hicks (Judge Abbotson); Mantan Moreland (Sam)

## Mexican Spitfire Sees a Ghost
(RKO–Radio; 1942)

Marginalized here within an episode of her own series, the magnificent Lupe Veléz more or less sits this one out while Donald MacBride (an underappreciated comedian and master of the short-fused double-take reaction) and Leon Errol carry the proceedings. Mantan Moreland likewise has too little to do.

**CREDITS:** Producer: Cliff Reid; Director: Leslie Goodwins; Screenplay: Charles E. Roberts and Monte Brice; Musical Score: Constantin Bakaleinikoff, Dave Dreyer, Paul Sawtell, and Roy Webb; Photographed by: Russell Metty; Running Time: 70 Minutes; Released: June 26, 1942

**CAST:** Lupe Veléz (Carmelita Lindsay); Leon Errol (Uncle Matt Lindsey/Lord Basil Epping); Charles "Buddy" Rogers (Dennis Lindsay); Elisabeth Risdon (Aunt Della Lindsey); Donald MacBride (Percy Fitzbadden); Minna Gombell (Edith Fitzbadden); Don Barclay (Fingers O'Toole); John Maguire (Luders); Lillian Randolph (Hyacinth); Mantan Moreland (Lightnin')

## Footlight Serenade
(Fox; 1942)

Victor Mature stars as a brash prizefighter who finds himself railroaded into the starring role of a song-and-dance production. Mantan Moreland is among the backstage players.

**CREDITS:** Producer: William LeBaron; Director: Gregory Ratoff; Story and Screenplay: Kenneth Earl, Fidel LaBarba, Robert Ellis, Helen Logan, and Lynn Starling; Musical Director: Charles Henderson; Dance Director: Hermes Pan; Musical Score and Songs: Ralph Rainger, Herb Magidson, Leo Robin, and Allie

Wrubel; Photographed by: Lee Garmes; Editor: Robert L. Simpson; Running Time: 81 Minutes; Released: August 1, 1942

**CAST:** John Payne (Bill Smith); Betty Grable (Pat Lambert); Victor Mature (Tommy Lundy); Jane Wyman (Flo La Verne); James Gleason (Bruce McKay); Phil Silvers (Slap); Cobina Wright (Estelle Evans); June Lang (June); Frank Orth (Mike); Mantan Moreland (Amos); Irving Bacon (Porter)

### A Haunting We Will Go
(Fox; 1942)

Here we have a lesser star vehicle for the team of Stan Laurel & Oliver Hardy, by now in sad decline from an extended heyday of the 1920s and '30s. (Fox made the egregious mistake of denying the partners the ability to supervise their own makeup preparations—a distinguishing touch that had set Mr. Laurel and Mr. Hardy's films for Hal Roach Studios quite apart.)

A criminal mob hires Stan and Ollie to transport a coffin containing a hoodlum-in-hiding. The casket becomes mistaken for a prop belonging to a theatrical magician's act.

The harsher crime-melodrama setting proves ill suited to Laurel & Hardy's clowning, which requires a prevailing air of larger-than-life un-reality in *all* its characters, whether sympathetic or menacing. The film also denies Stan and Ollie their customary state of grace and air of sympathetic-but-edgy benevolence—treating them instead as inept bumblers, bereft of the shabby dignity that had become their hallmark.

Mantan Moreland's role is typically brief and typically amusing. The lasting impression of this assignment made Moreland a favorite guest, during his waning years, at conventions of a Laurel & Hardy appreciation society known as the Sons of the Desert.

**CREDITS:** Producer: Sol M. Wurtzel; Director: Alfred L. Werker; Story and Screenplay: Lou Breslow and Stanley Rauh; Musical Score: David Buttolph and Cyril J. Mockridge; Musical Director: Emil Newman; Photographed by: Glen MacWilliams; Editor: Alfred Day; Running Time: 67 Minutes; Released: August 7, 1942

**CAST:** Stan Laurel (Stan Laurel); Oliver Hardy (Oliver Hardy); the Great Dante [Harry Jansen] (Dante the Magician); Sheila Ryan (Margo); John Shelton (Tommy White); Don Costello (Doc Lake); Elisha Cook Jr. (Frank Lucas); Edward Gargan (Police Lt. Foster); Addison Richards (Malcolm Kilgore); George Lynn (Darby Mason); James Bush (Joe Morgan); Lou Lubin (Dixie Beeler); Robert Emmett Keane (Phillips); Willie Best (Waiter) Mantan Moreland (Porter)

### Phantom Killer
(Monogram; 1942)

Moreland steals the show here as a janitor who seems unaccountably to have conversed with a murder suspect—who is known to be deaf and mute. Moreland vanishes after a rousingly well-played courtroom scene, leaving an impression far more vivid than that of the remainder of the film. What few critics paid earnest attention to this small gem of a remake in its day, missed the point entirely by mentioning the "uniqueness" of its plot. *Phantom Killer* is, all the same, about as "unique" as a close copy can get, given its origins in one of the better independent shockers of the Depression years, Phil Rosen's *The Sphinx* (Monogram; 1933). Not that the hidden-twin motif is all that groundbreaking an idea to begin with, but the yarn is a treat in either version, an audacious variation on the theme. Where the story-and-screenplay credit goes to Albert DeMond in *The Sphinx*, Karl Brown is given as author and scenarist on *Phantom Killer*. What with Monogram's corporate ownership of the yarn, one can only suppose it could afford to have a short memory as to authorship. The studio had planned originally to keep *The Sphinx* as the remake's title; another work-in-progress title was the cryptic *Man and the Devil*. The final christening of *Phantom Killer*, which fits the film well enough, was a discarded working title of the Monogram picture that had become *Invisible Ghost*.

The remake's finest touch is the casting of Mantan Moreland, Old Hollywood's most dependable and yet most under-appreciated comedian, as a witness to the crime that sets things in motion. Luis Alberni had served the original quite nicely in the equivalent role of an immigrant janitor, but Moreland transforms an unnerving encounter with the murderer and a panicky discovery of the victim into a miniature showcase for his own scene-stealing efficiency. Here lies the truer uniqueness of *Phantom Killer*. A good test of that truism is to see how sorely Moreland is missed after *Phantom Killer* has dismissed his character.

A prominent citizen named John G. Harrison (John Hamilton, later to become indelibly identified with the Perry White role on television's *The*

*Adventures of Superman*) is brought up on murder charges. Harrison is well known to be deaf and mute, but his accuser (Moreland) swears that the killer had asked him for a light and inquired about the time. The resulting humiliation in court drives an ambitious prosecutor (Dick Purcell) to quit his job.

Moreland's showcase comes in three stages: He reacts to the shock of discovering a corpse by heading straight for a quart bottle of booze and downing its contents in a guzzle. Then, while poring over a book of mug shots at headquarters, he renders a

desultory scene at once hilarious and poignant: "Well, looka *there*—High-Pockets Johnson. I *wondered* what happened to *him*. Ol' High-Pockets. He wasn't a bad boy, at that. He was *awful* good to his mother." Finally, in the courtroom, he works the witness stand like a nightclub stage:

"Do you ever drink anything?" Moreland is asked under oath.

"Sho'. *Anything*."

"How much whiskey did you drink that night?"

"Not a *drop*."

"Now, think: That was six weeks ago. How can you be so sure?"

"Sure that I didn't drink any *whiskey*?"

"Yes."

"Well, *that* night, I was only drinkin' *gin*."

No sooner is the case against Harrison dismissed, however, than such killings resume. At length, it develops that the impaired big shot sets out to establish an alibi while his speaking-and-hearing twin goes about a secretive family trade of murdering for money and/or vengeance. John Hamilton is scarcely a match for the scowling intensity of Lionel Atwill, his dual-role counterpart in *The Sphinx*, but he pulls off the masquerade with a somber dignity and accounts grimly for the disclosure of the brothers' secret. The sudden appearance of twin Hamiltons, each with murder on his mind, gets the point across without recourse to tricky camera angles or extravagant lighting effects; the matter-of-fact presentation is enough.

Dick Purcell is fine as the determined prosecutor, and the delicious Joan Woodbury provides both a romantic function and a crucial narrative pivot as a newspaper reporter who endangers herself by taking a hand in the unraveling. Warren Hymer is right in his element of tough-talking comedy as a hard-boiled detective who is also a henpecked husband, and old-timer Kenneth Harlan stands out as a ranking plainclothesman. Director William Beaudine juggles gracefully the desperate urgency, the broad comedy and the bantering sweetheart business, moving things along briskly enough to sidestep the patent implausibility of the brothers' malicious scam.

**CREDITS:** Producer: A.W. Hackel; Director: William Beaudine; Screenwriter: Karl Brown; Photographed by: Marcel Le Picard; Editor: Jack Ogilvie; Production Manager: Ben Gutterman; Assistant Director: Richard L'Estrange; Sound: Glen Glenn; Musical Director: Frank Sanucci

**CAST:** Dick Purcell (Edward A. Clark); Joan Woodbury (Barbara Mason); John Hamilton (John G. Harrison); Warren Hymer (Sgt. Pete Corrigan); Mantan Moreland (Nicodemus); J. Farrell MacDonald (Police Captain); Gayne Whitman (John Rogers); Kenneth Harlan (Lt. Jim Brady); George J. Lewis (Kramer); Karl Hackett (Attorney); Harry Depp (Lester P. Cutler); Isabel La Mal [a.k.a. Lamal] (Mabel Corrigan); Robert Carson (Dave Rigby); Frank Ellis (Kelsey)

### Eyes in the Night
(MGM; 1942)

Mantan Moreland's fairly prominent role here is as butler to gruff-but-amiable Edward Arnold, playing a blind detective named Duncan Maclain. The leading character returned in 1945's *The Hidden Eye*.

**CREDITS:** Producer: Jack Chertok; Director: Fred Zinnemann; Novel and Screenplay: Baynard Kendrick (*The Odor of Violets*), Guy Trosper, and Howard Emmett Rogers; Musical Score: Lennie Hayton and Daniele Amfitheatrof; Photographed by: Charles Lawton, Jr., and Robert H. Planck; Editor: Ralph E. Winters; Running Time: 80 Minutes; Released: Following New York Opening on October 16, 1942

**CAST:** Edward Arnold (Duncan Maclain); Ann Harding (Norma Lawry); Donna Reed (Barbara Lawry); Stephen [a.k.a. Horace] McNally (Gabriel Hoffman); Katherine Emery (Cheli Scott); Allen Jenkins (Marty); Stanley Ridges (Hansen); Reginald Denny (Stephen Lawry); Mantan Moreland (Alistair)

## Girl Trouble
(Fox; 1942)

The romantic conflicts at large here concern a suddenly impoverished heiress (Joan Bennett) and a Venezuelan playboy (Don Ameche).

**CREDITS:** Producer: Robert Bassler; Director: Harold D. Schuster; Story and Screenplay: Vicki Baum, Robert Riley Crutcher, Ladislas Fodor, Ladislas Fodor, and Guy Trosper; Musical Score: Alfred Newman; Photographed by: Edward Cronjager; Editor: Robert Fritch; Running Time: 82 Minutes; Released: October 9, 1942

**CAST:** Don Ameche (Pedro Sullivan); Joan Bennett (June Delaney); Billie Burke (Mrs. Rowland); Frank Craven (Ambrose Murdock Flint); Alan Dinehart (Charles Barrett); Helene Reynolds (Helen Martin); Fortunio Bonanova (Simon Cordoba); Ted North (George); Doris Merrick (Susan); Dale Evans (Ruth); Roseanne Murray (Pauline); Janis Carter (Virginia); Vivian Blaine (Barbara); Trudy Marshall (Miss Kennedy); Robert Greig (Fields); Joseph Crehan (Kohn); Arthur Loft (Burgess); Mantan Moreland (Edwards)

## The Palm Beach Story
(Paramount; 1942)

This ill-recognized high point of the screwball-comedy subgenre captures the writer-director Preston Sturges at a peak of cynical absurdism. More effectively so than Sturges' better-known *The Lady Eve* (1941), *The Palm Beach Story* argues a strong case equating erotic lust with acquisitive greed, as codified in a brilliant monologue from Claudette Colbert. Though under-employed here, Mantan Moreland is in fine company.

**CREDITS:** Associate Producer: Paul Jones; Director and Screenwriter: Preston Sturges; Musical Score: Victor Young, with Additional Music by Felix Mendelssohn-Bartholdy and Ray Noble; Photographed by: Victor Milner; Editor: Stuart Gilmore; Running Time: 88 Minutes; Released: Following New York Opening on December 10, 1942

**CAST:** Claudette Colbert (Geraldine Jeffers); Joel McCrea (Tom Jeffers); Mary Astor (Centimillia); Rudy Vallee (John D. Hackensacker III); Sig Arno (Toto); Robert Warwick (Hinch); Arthur Stuart Hull (Osmond); Torben Meyer (Dr. Kluck); Jimmy Conlin (Asweld); Victor Potel (McKeewie); William Demarest, Jack Norton, Robert Greig, Roscoe Ates, Dewey Robinson, Chester Conklin, and Sheldon Jett (Hunters); Robert Dudley (Weiner King); Franklin Pangborn

(Manager); Arthur Hoyt (Conductor); Al Bridge (Conductor); Fred "Snowflake" Toones (George); Charles R. Moore (Porter); Mantan Moreland (Waiter)

### The Great Gildersleeve
(RKO–Radio; 1942)

Harold Peary's character Throckmorton P. Gildersleeve had originated with a radio program called *Fibber McGee and Molly*, then spun off into a *Great Gildersleeve* series in 1942, lapsing simultaneously to the big screen. The four-picture series spans 1942–1944. Moreland has a butler role; his footage has been scissored from a few prints viewed in recent years.

**CREDITS:** Producer: Herman Schlom; Director: Gordon Douglas; Screenplay: Julien Josephson and Jack Townley; Photographed by: Frank Redman; Editor: John Lockert; Running Time: 62 Minutes; Released: Following New York Opening on December 17, 1942

**CAST:** Harold Peary (Throckmorton P. Gildersleeve); Freddie Mercer (LeRoy Forrester); Nancy Gates (Marjorie Forrester); Jane Darwell (Aunt Emma Forrester); Mary Field (Amelia Hooker); Charles Arnt (Judge Horace Hooker); Lillian Randolph (Birdie Scoggins); Thurston Hall (Gov. Jonathon Stafford); Mantan Moreland (Butler)

### Cosmo Jones, Crime Smasher
a.k.a. COSMO JONES IN CRIME SMASHER
(Monogram; 1943)

This semi-coda to the Frankie Darro–Mantan Moreland crimebuster series finds Moreland teamed with Frank Graham, who plays an absent-minded would-be detective. In a coda of sorts to the Frankie Darro–Mantan Moreland jive-thrillers, Monogram Pictures paired the ticket-selling comedian Moreland with CBS-Radio personality Frank Graham for this spinoff of Graham's long-running broadcast series, *Cosmo Jones*. The Moreland magic is intact, and Graham accounts nicely for himself as the absentminded would-be detective, Prof. Cosmo Jones, but the picture fizzled as a springboard for anything further on the big screen.

Not to say that it doesn't work. Walter Gering, creator of the *Cosmo* radio adventures, contributes a nifty story: Cosmo is pestering the local police department for a job when he chances to witness a gangland murder—part of a crime wave that has the law baffled. Given the bum's rush despite a display of good citizenship, the nerdy professor accepts a lift from a friendly but trouble-prone cop, Pat Flanagan (Richard Cromwell), and finds himself on the scene of the foiled kidnapping of heiress Phyllis Blake (Gwen Kenyon). Cosmo meets Eustace (Moreland), a janitor who himself harbors the urge to play sleuth, and they plot with Flanagan to lure the crooks out into the open.

Phyllis' treacherous fiancé (Gil Stanley) later accomplishes her abduction. Cosmo and Eustace are taken captive, and a hoodlum named Biff (Charles Jordan) is about to mutilate Eustace with a scalpel when Flanagan and Police Chief Murphy (grumpy Edgar Kennedy) arrive to save the day. Phyllis is rescued by her father (Herbert Rawlinson) and Cosmo, and Eustace gives Flanagan a clear shot at Biff.

The picture is a rowdy delight, with coincidences and situational clichés piled on so thickly as to obscure everything but the spirited portrayals. Charles Jordan plays it sadistic and scary as the meanest of the meanies. Moreland is a fast-talking, quick-reacting marvel, as usual, and his camaraderie with Frank Graham and Richard Cromwell is a particularly forward-thinking touch. Gale Storm offers a hint of her TV-sitcom stardom to come as Richard Cromwell's insistent sweetheart.

**CREDITS:** Producer: Lindsley Parsons; Director: James Tinling; Story and Screenplay: Walter Gering and Michael L. Simmons; Photographed by: Mack Stengler; Editor: Carl Pierson; Assistant Director: William Strohbach; Sound: Glen Glenn; Musical Director: Edward J. Kay; Running Time: 62 Minutes; Released: January 29, 1943

**CAST:** Frank Graham (Cosmo Jones); Edgar Kennedy (Murphy); Richard Cromwell (Flanagan); Gale Storm (Susan); Gwen Kenyon (Phyllis Blake); Tristram Coffin (Jake); Charles Jordan (Biff); Gil Stanley (Tom); Herbert Rawlinson (Blake); Mantan Moreland (Eustace); Vince Barnett (Gangster); Emmett Vogan (Man); Maxine Leslie (Gang Moll); Mauritz Hugo and Sam Bernard (Gangsters)

That little devil Mantan offers Lucifer (Rex Ingram) a light in *Cabin in the Sky*.

## Cabin in the Sky
(MGM; 1943)

Stage-to-screen adaptation, with Ethel Waters embellishing upon her 1940 Broadway role as a warm-hearted rustic whose ne'er-do-well husband (Eddie "Rochester" Anderson) finds his soul torn between heaven and hell. Mantan Moreland comes closer to the foreground as a snazzy demon.

**CREDITS:** Producer: Arthur Freed; Associate Producer: Albert Lewis; Directors: Vincente Minnelli and Busby Berkeley; Play and Screenplay: Lynn Root, Marc Connelly, and Joseph Schrank; Musical Score: Vernon Duke, with George Bassman, Roger Edens, Ted Fetter, E.Y. Harburg, John La Touche, Duke Ellington, and George E. Stoll; Photographed by: Sidney Wagner; Editor: Harold F. Kress; Art Directors: Cedric Gibbons and Leonid Vasian; Décor: Hugh Hunt and Edwin B. Willis; Costumers: Irene, Howard Shoup, and Gile Steele; Assistant Director: Al Shenberg; Sound: Douglas Shearer and William Steinkamp; Running Time: 98 Minutes; Released: Following New York Opening on March 27, 1943

**CAST:** Ethel Waters (Petunia Jackson); Eddie "Rochester" Anderson (Little Joe); Lena Horne (Georgia Brown); Louis Armstrong (Trumpeter); Rex Ingram (Lucifer, Jr.); Kenneth Spencer (General and the Rev. Mr. Greene); John William "Bubbles" Sublett (Domino Johnson); Oscar Polk (Deacon and Fleetfoot);

Mantan Moreland (First Idea Man); Willie Best (Second Idea Man); Fletcher "Moke" Rivers (Third Idea Man); Leon James Poke (Fourth Idea Man); Ford Washington "Buck" Lee (Messenger Boy); Bill Bailey (Bill); Butterfly McQueen (Lily); Ruby Dandridge (Mrs. Kelso); Nick Stewart (Dude); Ernest Whitman (Jim Henry); Duke Ellington (Himself); Cab Calloway (Himself); the Hall Johnson Choir; Archie Savage (Dancer); and Aranelle Harris, Henry Phace Roberts, Carmencita Romero

### Slightly Dangerous
(MGM; 1943)

Wesley Ruggles' sparkling comedy stars Lana Turner as a small-towner seeking a more glamorous existence—developing multiple personalities without indulging in any alter-ego psychological-baloney foolishness. Robert Young fares impressively as Miss Turner's befuddled pursuer. Mantan Moreland registers memorably despite his chronic state of big-studio under-employment.

**CREDITS:** Producer: Pandro S. Berman; Director: Wesley Ruggles; Story and Screenplay: Ian McLellan Hunter, Aileen Hamilton, Charles Lederer, and George Oppenheimer; Musical Score: Bronislau Kaper, Daniele Amfitheatrof, Eric Zeisl, with works from Tchaikovsky, Wagner, and Vincent Youmans; Orchestrations: Leonid Raab; Photographed by: Harold Rosson; Editor: Frank E. Hull; Running Time: 95 minutes; Released: Following New York Opening on April 1, 1943

**CAST:** Lana Turner (Peggy Evans); Robert Young (Bob Stuart); Walter Brennan (Cornelius Burden); Dame May Whitty (Baba); Eugene Pallette (Durstin); Alan Mowbray (English Gentleman); Florence Bates (Mrs. Amanda Roanoke-Brooke); Howard Freeman (Mr. Quill); Millard Mitchell (Baldwin); Ward Bond (Jimmy); Pamela Blake (Mitzi); Ray Collins (Snodgrass); Mantan Moreland (Waiter)

### He Hired the Boss
(Fox; 1943)

Mild-mannered Stuart Erwin finds himself besieged with draft-board jitters and romantic complications in this wartime-topical (but nonetheless old-fashioned, deriving from a short story of 1909) comedy, which also involves a black-market import scam and an unexpected discovery of mineral wealth. Moreland's appearance is barely there, but he registers strikingly—as usual.

**CREDITS:** Producers: Sol M. Wurtzel and William Goetz; Director: Thomas Z. Loring; Story and Screenplay: Irving Cummings, Jr., Peter B. Kyne, and Ben Markson; Photographed by: Glen MacWilliams; Editor: Louis R. Loeffler; Running Time: 73 Minutes; Released: April 2, 1943

**CAST:** Stuart Erwin (Hubert Wilkins); Evelyn Venable (Emily Conway); Thurston Hall (Bates); Vivian Blaine (Sally Conway); William T. Orr (Don Bates); Benny Bartlett (Jimmy); James Bush (Clark); Chick Chandler (Fuller); Hugh Beaumont (Jordan); Eddie Acuff (Driver); Mantan Moreland (Shoeshine Man)

### It Comes Up Love
(Universal; 1943)

Culture-clash comedy along the lines of 1927's *The Jazz Singer*, with well-brought-up Gloria Jean forsaking classical music in order to get with the swing-band program. Moreland appears as a janitor.

**CREDITS:** Associate Producer: Ken Goldsmith; Director: Charles Lamont; Story and Screenplay: Dorothy Bennett, Jay Dratler, Charles Kenyon, and Aleen Leslie; Musical Score: Ernesto Lecuona and Frank Skinner, with Irving Actman, Ralph Freed, and Frank Loesser; Musical Director: Charles Previn; Photographed by: George Robinson; Editor: Paul Landres; Running Time: 64 Minutes; Released: April 9, 1943

**CAST:** Gloria Jean (Victoria Peabody); Ian Hunter (Tom Peabody); Donald O'Connor (Ricky Ives); Frieda Inescort (Portia Winthrop); Louise Allbritton (Edie Ives); Mary Lou Harrington (Constance Peabody); Leon Belasco (Orchestra Leader); Mantan Moreland (Janitor)

### Sarong Girl
(Monogram; 1943)

Moreland plays an assistant-sidekick to leading man Tim Ryan in this show-business/burlesque vehicle for the voluptuous Ann Corio.

**CREDITS:** Producer: Philip N. Krasne; Associate Producer: James S. Burkett; Director: Arthur Dreifuss; Screenwriters: Arthur Hoerl, Charles R. Marion, and

Tim Ryan; Musical Score: Gray Benjamin and Lou Herscher; Musical Director: Edward J. Kay; Photographed by: Mack Stengler; Editor: Carl Pierson; Running Time: 63 Minutes; Released: May 28, 1943

**CAST:** Ann Corio (Dixie Barlow); Tim Ryan (Tim Raynor); Irene Ryan (Irene Raynor); Mantan Moreland (Maxwell); William Henry (Jeff Baxter); Damian O'Flynn (Gil Gailord); Johnnie Davis (Scat Davis); Gwen Kenyon (Barbara)

## Hit the Ice
(Universal; 1943)

One of the more effective Abbott & Costello entries, involving a purportedly ailing gangster who stakes out a hospital as a means of casing an intended crime scene. Bud Abbott and Lou Costello play photographers who run afoul of the scam. Mantan Moreland has a scene-stealing bit role.

**CREDITS:** Executive Producer: Milton Feld; Producer: Alex Gottlieb; Directors: Charles Lamont and Erle C. Kenton; Story and Screenplay: True Boardman, Robert Lees, Frederic I. Rinaldo, and John Grant, with Allen Boretz; Musical Score: Harry Revel, Paul Francis Webster, Paul Sawtell, and Sergei Rachmaninov; Photographed by: Charles Van Enger; Editor: Frank Gross; Running Time: 82 Minutes; Released: June 2, 1943

**CAST:** Bud Abbott (Flash Fulton); Lou Costello (Tubby McCoy); Ginny Simms (Marcia Manning); Patric Knowles (Dr. Bill Elliot/Burns); Elyse Knox (Peggy Osborne); Joe Sawyer (Buster); Marc Lawrence (Phil); Sheldon Leonard (Silky Fellowsby); Johnny Long (Himself); Nick Thompson (Husband); Bobby Barber (Candy Butcher); Hank Bell (Coachman); Wade Boteler (Conductor); Mantan Moreland (Porter)

## We've Never Been Licked
(Universal; 1943)

An over-the-top war-propaganda epic, rich with Deep Southern jingoism and foreign-enemy stereotyping. Moreland has more or less a featured role, for a change. Robert Mitchum, even at so early a stage of his career, is immediately recognizable.

**CREDITS:** Producer: Walter Wanger; Directors: John Rawlins and Vernon Keays (Aerial Footage); Story and Screenplay: Nick Grinde, and Norman Reilly Raine (from his "The Fighting Sons of Texas A&M"); Musical Score: Harry Revel, Paul Francis Webster and Frank Skinner; Musical Director: Charles

Previn; Vocal Arrangements: Ken Darby; Photographed by: Milton R. Krasner; Special Photographic Effects: John P. Fulton; Editor: Philip Cahn; Running Time: 104 Minutes; Released: July 30, 1943

**CAST:** Richard Quine (Brad Craig); Anne Gwynne (Nina Lambert); Noah Beery, Jr. (Cyanide Jenkins); Martha O'Driscoll (Deede Dunham); William Frawley (Traveling Salesman); Edgar Barrier (Nishikawa); Robert Mitchum (Panhandle Mitchell); Bill Stern (Himself); Mantan Moreland (Willie)

## Melody Parade
(Monogram; 1943)

The Monogram pedigree brings Moreland more strikingly near the fore in this show-business musical, which approximates the Darro–Moreland formula in having Eddie Quillan play a nightclub flunky who pretends to be a talent agent.

**CREDITS:** Producer: Lindsley Parsons; Director: Arthur Dreifuss; Screenplay: Charles R. Marion and Tim Ryan; Musical Score: Armida, Eddie Cherkose, and Edward J. Kay; Photographed by: Mack Stengler; Editor: Richard C. Currier; Running Time: 76 Minutes; Released: Following New York Opening on August 13, 1943

**CAST:** Mary Beth Hughes (Anne O'Rourke); Eddie Quillan (Jimmy Tracy); Tim Ryan (Happy Harrington); Irene Ryan (Gloria Brewster); Mantan Moreland (Skidmore); Jerry Cooper (Jerry Cooper); Armida (Armida)

## Revenge of the Zombies
(Monogram; 1943)

Subordinate to *King of the Zombies* (see above) as a showcase for Mantan Moreland, the film nonetheless allows the comedian a splendid arena for improvisational patter while affording him the chance to upstage two of Old Hollywood's finer Grand Manner actors: John Carradine (as a Nazi scientist) and Bob Steele (as an undercover law officer). The operative conceit here is that the zombies-for-Hitler campaign of *King of the Zombies* has migrated from the Caribbean onto hallowed American soil. More grimly dreamlike than its predecessor, and clearly motivated by the anger of director Steve Sekely—himself a fugitive from the Third Reich. A far-fetched allegory, of course, but zombies sell tickets, and how better to convey a measure of political anger than with a veneer of imaginative sensationalism? The wartime propaganda films of other nations, whether Allied or Axis-fied, tend to emphasize the noble bravery of the native-born fighting man and foster solidarity among the populace. The American approach, conversely, is to ridicule and/or exaggerate (the fashionable word today would be *demonize*) the evils of the enemy. The Disney machine gave a literal razzing to the Third Reich in a Donald Duck cartoon, "Der Fuehrer's Face," and the Three Stooges—profoundly *Yiddishe* intellects, masquerading as buffoons—portrayed the leading lights of the Third Reich as the ultimate in stoogery.

Monogram took just as extreme an avenue of attack: The studio's Axis-buster films are distinctively horrific in their slow-burn way, more a simmer than a rolling boil. *Revenge of the Zombies*, going somewhat beyond a retread of Monogram's *King of the Zombies* (see *Forgotten Horrors 2*), plants a Nazi scientist (John Carradine) in an isolated Louisiana bayou-country outpost, where he intends to perfect the creation of living-dead servants for the sake of giving Germany "an army that will not need to be fed—that cannot be stopped by bullets."

This elaboration upon *King of the Zombies*, whose tale unfolds in the West Indies, not only suggests the tainting of hallowed American soil by perverse Nazi science but also finds Carradine experimenting upon his own wife (the struggling but still game Veda Ann Borg) in the service of the Reich. Call it *Weiss Zombie*.

John Carradine portrays as cold-hearted a *Seig-Heiler* as ever crossed the screen, a surly menace so dedicated to world domination that he would sacrifice one of the most magnificently beautiful women in Hollywood to the cause. It helps to remember that director Steve Sekely (born Istvan Szekely in Budapest) was a recent fugitive from the Third Reich; his leisurely pacing here suggests a brooding anger that lends metaphorical weight to the supernatural premise. Plain shock value would not serve.

The crucial twist—which has made *Revenge of the Zombies* a surprising favorite in the more culturally well-attuned sectors of the feminist movement—is that Veda Ann Borg resists the hoodoo brainwashing: Though quite dead despite an unnatural mobility, the abused wife retains enough defiance to plot Carradine's downfall. To his further inconvenience, Carradine finds himself playing host to his unwelcome brother-in-law (Mauritz Hugo), a family friend

(Robert Lowery), and their chauffeur (Mantan Moreland, Old Hollywood's most energetic comedian). The doctor seems to have an ally in a visiting Nazi agent (played by Bob Steele, the Western star and all-'round character man), who briefly pretends to be a Southern sheriff and finally proves to be an FBI investigator. Steele make a convincing enough show of loyalty to the Axis, but once he changes into frontiersman attire and announces, "I'd better start by givin' this Heinie the once-over," the audience can pretty well conclude that he's no genuine goose-stepper.

Mantan Moreland, that venerable Chitlin' Circuit entertainer, leaves the film's most lasting impression—despite his having less crucial a role than in 1941's *King of the Zombies*. A Moreland performance in *any* movie is an all-but-pure distillation of mid-century black show business, but Monogram allowed him the freest rein: The little studio's production values are a cut above those of the black independent studios where Moreland often worked, and so the cameras and microphones capture more of his exuberance and his nuanced delivery of ad-libbed remarks. At the bigger studios, Moreland received less prominent billing and was too often encouraged to soft-pedal his gift of gab. In *Revenge of the Zombies*, he marks time with an improvised soft-shoe routine, woos one of Carradine's servants (Sybil Lewis) with irrepressible jive talk, and fires off some inspired patter. Upon hearing a disembodied voice moaning, "Where am I?" Moreland answers, "I don't know where *you*['re] at, but 30 seconds from now, I'm gonna be 'leven miles *away* from here!" Elsewhere, he reports the discovery of a murder victim who has been "shot long, deep, wide and con*sec*utive!"

Moreland has been unfairly dismissed as an Uncle Tom within some fashionable sectors of the black intellectual bourgeoisie. Nowhere do his characters resort to the stereotype of the terrified or cringing servant. And the servant roles he plays, in keeping with the economic and social realities of the period, are hardly deferential. His recurring role of Birmingham Brown, in the Monogram *Charlie Chan* series, is more a fellow sleuth than a hired hand. Nor does Moreland indulge in unreasoning superstition: He exhibits, rather, the pragmatic wisdom to believe what his eyes and ears tell him. Like anyone else with the good gumption to duck out on a threatening situation, Moreland's characters are more indignant than scared in the face of trouble, and resourceful enough to fight or make a run for it as circumstances demand. Moreland is a national treasure, as distinctively fine a comic artist as Bob Hope, Charles Chaplin and W.C. Fields, and it is high time to look past the color bar that has long compromised a popular appreciation of the man.

**CREDITS:** Producer: Lindsley Parsons; Director: Steve Sekely; Screenplay: Edmond Kelso and Van Norcross; Musical Director: Edward J. Kay; Photographed by: Mack Stengler; Editor: Richard C. Currier; Art Director: Dave

Milton; Production Manager and Assistant Director: Richard L'Estrange; Sound: Glen Glenn; Dialogue Director: Jack Linder; Running Time: 61 Minutes; Released: Following New York Opening on August 26, 1943

**CAST:** John Carradine (Dr. Max Heinrich von Altermann); Gale Storm (Jennifer Rand); Robert Lowery (Larry Adams); Bob Steele (Agent); Mantan Moreland (Jeff); Veda Ann Borg (Lila von Altermann); Barry Macollum (Dr. Harvey Keating); Mauritz Hugo (Scott Warrington); Mme. Sul-Te-Wan (Mammy Beulah); James Baskett (Lazarus); Sybil Lewis (Rosella); Robert Cherry (Pete); Franklyn Farnum (Zombie)

### My Kingdom for a Cook
(Columbia; 1943)

In which Southern gentleman Charles Coburn portrays a cantankerous Englishman who pulls a man-who-came-to-dinner scam on a family of small-town New Englanders. Moreland plays a Pullman porter.

**CREDITS:** Producer: P.J. Wolfson; Director: Richard Wallace; Story and Screenplay: Harold Goldman, Lily Hatvany, Jack Henley, Joseph Hoffman, and Andrew Solt; Musical Score: John Leipold; Musical Director: Morris W. Stoloff; Photographed by: Franz F. Planer; Editor: Otto Meyer; Art Directors: Lionel Banks and Edward C. Jewell; Décor: Frank Tuttle; Assistant Director: William Mull; Sound: Edward Bernds; Running Time: 81 Minutes; Released: August 21, 1943

**CAST:** Charles Coburn (Rudyard Morley); Marguerite Chapman (Pamela Morley); Bill Carter (Mike Scott); Isobel Elsom (Lucille Scott); Edward Gargan (Duke); Mary Wickes (Agnes Willoughby); Almira Sessions (Hattie); Eddy Waller (Sam Thornton); Ralph Peters (Pretty Boy Peterson); Ivan F. Simpson (Professor Harlow); Mantan Moreland (Porter)

### Hi' Ya, Sailor
(Universal; 1943)

A music-making sailor (Donald Woods) finds himself scammed by a song-publishing racket in this slight racket-buster spoof. Moreland stands out from a background vantage.

**CREDITS:** Producer and Director: Jean Yarbrough; Story and Screenplay: Fanya Lawrence Foss and Stanley Roberts; Musical Score: Everett Carter, Maxine Manners, and Milton Rosen; Musical Director: Hans J. Salter; Photographed by: Jerome Ash and Jack MacKenzie; Editor: William Austin; Running Time: 61 Minutes; Released: October 15, 1943

**CAST:** Donald Woods (Bob Jackson); Elyse Knox (Pat Rogers); Eddie Quillan (Corky Mills); Frank Jenks (Deadpan Weaver); Phyllis Brooks (Nanette); Jerome Cowan (Lou Asher); Matt Willis (Bull Rogan); George Beatty (George Beatty); Charles Coleman (Doorman); Leo Diamond (Himself); Ray Eberle (Himself); Mantan Moreland (Sam)

### You're a Lucky Fellow, Mr. Smith
(Universal; 1943)

Heiress Evelyn Ankers must marry a wealthy friend-of-the-family (David Bruce) on a deadline in order to claim an inheritance. Complications find Miss Ankers stranded aboard a passenger train and conspiring to wed soldier Allan Jones instead. The setting obliges Mantan Moreland to play a porter.

**CREDITS:** Executive Producer: Milton Schwarzwald; Associate Producer: Edward C. Lilley; Director: Felix E. Feist; Story and Screenplay: Ben Barzman, Oscar Brodney, Louis Lantz, and Lawrence Riley; Musical Score: Frank Skinner, Sonny Burke, Inez James, Buddy Pepper, Hugh Prince, Don Raye, and Ralph Freed; Musical Director: Charles Previn; Photographed by: Paul Ivano; Editor: Ray Snyder; Running Time: 64 Minutes; Released: October 22, 1943

**CAST:** Allan Jones (Tony); Evelyn Ankers (Lynn Smith); Billie Burke (Aunt Harriet); David Bruce (Harvey); Patsy O'Connor (Peggy); Stanley Clements (Squirt); Luis Alberni (Goreni); Francis Pierlot (Doc Webster); Harry Hayden (Judge); Mantan Moreland (Porter); Ken Darby (Himself)

### She's for Me
(Universal; 1943)

B-unit screwballer-with-music finds playboy George Dolenz closing in on heiress Lois Collier, despite the stern guidance of lawyer David Bruce. Moreland occupies that familiar backup role. Action-movie star Ray "Crash" Corrigan puts in a sly reference to his subordinate career as a gorilla impersonator.

**CREDITS:** Associate Producer: Frank Gross; Director: Reginald Le Borg; Story and Screenplay: Henry Blankfort; Musical Score: Pedro Berrios, Pazo Chan, Roberto Martins, Freddie Stewart, Lottie Wells, Maurice Wells, and Harry M. Woods; Musical Director: Charles Previn; Photographed by: Paul Ivano; Editor: Paul Landres; Running Time: 60 Minutes; Released: December 10, 1943

**CAST:** Grace McDonald (Jan Lawton); David Bruce (Michael Reed); Lois Collier (Eileen Crane); George Dolenz (Phil Norwin); Charles Dingle (Crane); Helen Brown (Miss Carpenter); Mantan Moreland (Sam)

## Swing Fever
(MGM; 1944)

Wartime bread-and-circuses escapism to the Nth degree, with MGM's high-standard production values obscuring the incoherence basic to such shallow entertainment. Bandleader Kay Kyser stars in a muddled tale involving heavyweight boxing, big-band swing, hypnosis, cheesecake and morale boosterism for the Boys in Uniform Overseas. Moreland, who could act circles around most of the more prominent players, is as under-employed as usual.

**CREDITS:** Producer: Irving Starr; Director: Tim Whelan; Story and Screenplay: Matt Brooks, Joseph Hoffman, Nat Perrin, and Warren Wilson; Musical Score: Sammy Fain, Sunny Skylar, and Nacio Herb Brown; Orchestrations: Earl K. Brent; Musical Directors: David Snell and George E. Stoll; Photographed by: Charles Rosher; Editor: Ferris Webster; Running Time: 81 Minutes; Released: Following New York Opening on January 27, 1944

**CAST:** Kay Kyser (Lowell Blackford); Marilyn Maxwell (Ginger Gray); William Gargan (Waltzy Malone); Nat Pendleton (Killer Kennedy); Lena Horne (Herself); Morris Ankrum (Dan Conlon); Maxie Rosenbloom (Rags); Mantan Moreland (Woody)

## Chip off the Old Block
(Universal; 1944)

This early starring effort finds Donald O'Connor radiating star power in anticipation of his larger-scale breakthroughs of the 1950s. One might suggest that so slight and unassuming a film as *Chip off the Old Block* is more genuinely entertaining and less exhausting an experience than the overblown, anachronism-ridden, and forcibly precious *Singin' in the Rain*, for which O'Connor is most vividly remembered. Mantan Moreland, at least as gifted a player as O'Connor, is relegated to the usual porter role. Humph.

**CREDITS:** Executive Producer: Milton Schwarzwald; Associate Producer: Bernard W. Burton; Director: Charles Lamont; Story and Screenplay: Robert Arthur, Eugene Conrad, and Leo Townsend; Musical Director: Charlews Previn; Photographed by: Charles Van Enger; Editor: Charles Maynard; Running Time: 77 Minutes; Released: February 25, 1944

**CAST:** Donald O'Connor (Donald Corrigan); Peggy Ryan (Peggy Flaherty); Ann Blyth (Glory Marlow III); Helen Vinson (Glory Marlow, Jr.); Helen Broderick (Glory Marlow, Sr.); Arthur Treacher (Quentin); Patric Knowles (Corrigan); Mantan Moreland (Porter)

### The Resurrected Charlie Chan Series
(Monogram; 1944–1949)

See page 148

### See Here, Private Hargrove
(MGM; 1944)

Real-life journalist Marion Hargrove's timely account of Army boot-camp life was a hit in print (1942) and came to the screen as almost a foregone conclusion. This mostly light-hearted survey of basic training stars Robert Walker, along with Keenan Wynn, Robert Benchley and Chill Wills. But the wartime comedies of Abbott & Costello are a great deal funnier and take up a great deal less of one's viewing time; *See Here, Private Hargrove* moves less briskly, with less outright humor along the way. Mantan Moreland has a (you guessed it) porter role.

**CREDITS:** Producer: George Haight; Director: Wesley Ruggles; Book and Screenplay: Marion Hargrove and Harry Kurnitz; Musical Score: Ted Grouya, David Snell, Earl K. Brent, Lennie Hayton, Frank Loesser, Gen. Daniel Butterfield, and Edmund L. Gruber; Photographed by: Charles Lawton, Jr.; Editor: Frank E. Hull; Running Time: 101 Minutes; Released: Following New York Opening on March 21, 1944

**CAST:** Robert Walker (Pvt. Marion Hargrove); Donna Reed (Carol Holliday); Keenan Wynn (Mulvehill); Robert Benchley (Holliday); Ray Collins (Brody S. Griffith); Chill Wills (Sgt. Cramp); Bob Crosby (Bob); Marta Linden (Mrs. Holliday); Grant Mitchell (Uncle George); Mantan Moreland (Porter)

### Moon over Las Vegas
(Universal; 1944)

Another porter role for Moreland, in a romantic-entaglement comedy starring Anne Gwynne and David Bruce.

**CREDITS:** Producer and Director: Jean Yarbrough; Story and Screenplay: Clyde Bruckman and George Jeske; Musical Score: Gene Austin, Everett Carter, Jimmie Dodd, Walter Donaldson, Frank Loesser, Jimmy McHugh, and Milton

Rosen; Photographed by: Jerome Ash; Editor: Milton Carruth; Running Time: 69 Minutes; Released: April 24, 1944

**CAST:** Anne Gwynne (Marion Corbett); David Bruce (Richard Corbett); Barbara Jo Allen [a.k.a. Vera Vague] (Auntie); Vivian Austin (Grace Towers); Alan Dinehart (Hat Blake); Lee Patrick (Mrs. Blake); Joe Sawyer (Joe); Milburn Stone (Jim Bradley); Addison Richards (Judge); Mantan Moreland (Porter)

## Pin Up Girl
(Fox; 1944)

Bruce Humberstone's showbiz-in-wartime comedy stars Betty Grable as a hot-stuff U.S.O. entertainer. Moreland plays a redcap.

**CREDITS:** Producer: William LeBaron; Director: H. Bruce Humberstone; Story and Screenplay: Libbie Block, Robert Ellis, Helen Logan, and Earl Baldwin; Musical Score: James V. Monaco; Musical Director: Emil Newman; Photographed by: Ernest Palmer; Editor: Robert L. Simpson; Running Time: 85 minutes; Released: Following New York Opening on May 11, 1944

**CAST:** Betty Grable (Lorry Jones); John Harvey (Tommy Dooley); Martha Raye (Molly McKay); Joe E. Brown (Eddie Hall); Eugene Pallette (Barney Briggs); Dorothea Kent (Kay); Dave Willock (Dud Miller); Frank Condos (Dancer); Charlie Spivak (Himself); Mantan Moreland (Redcap)

## This Is the Life
(Universal; 1944)

Another teenagers-in-love starrer for Donald O'Connor. The source is a stage play from 1938 by Sinclair Lewis and Fay Wray. Better for Moreland to play a porter than to be a porter, to lift a line from Hattie McDaniel.

**CREDITS:** Associate Producer: Bernard W. Burton; Director: Felix E. Feist; Play and Screenplay: Sinclair Lewis, Wanda Tuchock, and Fay Wray; Musical Score: Rudolf Friml, Inez James, Sidney Miller, and Buddy Pepper; Musical Director: Charles Previn; Photographed by: Hal Mohr; Editor: Ray Snyder; Running Time: 85 Minutes; Released: June 2, 1944

**CAST:** Donald O'Connor (Jimmy Plum); Susanna Foster (Angela Rutherford); Peggy Ryan (Sally McGuire); Louise Allbritton (Harriet West Jarrett); Patric Knowles (Major Hilary Jarret); Dorothy Peterson (Aunt Betsy); Jonathan Hale (Doctor Plum); Eddie Quillan (Gus); Frank Jenks (Eddie); Frank Puglia (Music

Teacher); Maurice Marsac (Leon); Virginia Brissac (Mrs. Tiggett); Ray Eberle (Himself); Bobby Brooks & His Quartette; Ben Carter (Himself); Joel Allen (Army Sergeant); Johnny Arthur (Ferguson); Brooks Benedict (Headwaiter); Jack Chefe (Waiter); Judy Clark (Dancer); Jean Davis (Girl); Earle S. Dewey (Conductor); Pat Dillon (Fat Boy); Mantan Moreland (Porter)

### South of Dixie
(Universal; 1944)

Tin Pan Alley Dixiana, in which Brooklyn tunesmith David Bruce feigns a Southern-fried pedigree in order to perpetrate a hoax. Authentic Southerner Moreland holds forth from the background.

**CREDITS:** Producer and Director: Jean Yarbrough; Story and Screenplay: Clyde Bruckman and Sam Coslow; Musical Score: Everett Carter, Alex Kramer, Jerry Livingston, Phil Moore, A.J. Neiberg, and Joan Whitney, with selections from Stephen Foster; Musical Director: Sam Freed, Jr.; Photographed by: Jerome Ash; Editor: Paul Landres; Running Time: 61 Minutes; Released: June 23, 1944

**CAST:** Anne Gwynne (Dixie Holister); David Bruce (Danny Lee); Jerome Cowan (Watson); Ella Mae Morse (Barbara Ann); Joe Sawyer (Ernest); Samuel S. Hinds (Col. Morgan); Eddie Acuff (Jay); Marie Harmon (Annabella Hatcher); Oscar O'Shea (Col. Hatcher); Louise Beavers (Chloe); Mantan Moreland (Porter)

### Bowery to Broadway
(Universal; 1944)

Some sharper-than-usual scene-stealing and comedy-showcasing from Moreland (with Ben Carter) in this lively spoof, which finds rival Bowery showmen Jack Oakie and Donald Cook engaging one another in a ritual of chronic one-upsmanship. A more heavily melodramatic midsection slows the pace, but Maria Montez contributes plenty of energy as a fireball who helps with the title's transition from downtown to uptown.

**CREDITS:** Producer: John Grant; Director: Charles Lamont; Story and Screenplay: Arthur T. Horman, Edmund Joseph, and

Bart Lytton; Musical Score: Everett Carter, Walter Kent, and Edward Ward; Photographed by: Charles Van Enger; Editor: Arthur Hilton; Running Time: 94 Minutes; Released: November 3, 1944

**CAST:** Maria Montez (Marina); Jack Oakie (Michael O'Rourke); Susanna Foster (Peggy Fleming); Turhan Bey (Ted Barrie); Ann Blyth (Bessie Jo Kirby); Donald Cook (Dennis Dugan); Louise Allbritton (Lillian Russell); Frank McHugh (Joe Kirby); Rosemary DeCamp (Bessie Kirby); Leo Carrillo (P.J. Fenton); Andy Devine (Fr. Kelley); Evelyn Ankers (Bonnie Latour); Thomas Gomez (Tom Harvey); Richard Lane (Walter Rogers); George Dolenz (George Henshaw); Mantan Moreland (Alabam); Ben Carter (No-Mo')

## Mystery of the River Boat
(Universal; 1944)

This action-adventure serial stars Robert Lowery as a reliably stoic and athletic hero. Lyle Talbot makes an impressive villain. Mantan Moreland contributes some generous comic relief.

**CREDITS:** Associate Producer: Henry MacRae; Directors: Lewis D. Collins and Ray Taylor; Story and Screenplay: Ande Lamb and Maurice Tombragel; Musical Score: Everett Carter, Jimmie Dodd, Milton Rosen, Paul Sawtell, Hans J. Salter, Frank Skinner, and Edward Ward; Photographed by: William A. Sickner; Editors: Norman A. Cerf, Irving Birnbaum, Jack Dolan, Ace Herman, Alvin Todd, and Edgar Zane; a Serial in Thirteen Chapters, Approximately 218 Minutes; Released: Late 1944–Early 1945

**CAST:** Robert Lowery (Steve Langtry); Eddie Quillan (Jug Jenks); Marion Martin (Celeste Eltree); Marjorie Clements (Jenny Perrin); Lyle Talbot (Rudolph Toller); Arthur Hohl (Paul Duval); Francis McDonald (Batiste); Mantan Moreland (Napoleon); Oscar O'Shea (Capt. Ethan Perrin)

## The Naughty Nineties
(Universal; 1945)

One of the better Abbott & Costello showcase pictures, this one also betrays the tensions that would cause periodic estrangements between Bud Abbott and Lou Costello. *The Naughty Nineties* is in effect the artists' first in which their characters do not function wholly as a partnership of more-or-less equals. Abbott plays a showboat entertainer, and Costello plays an all-'round flunky. (Other films that find the boys playing something less than a team include *Little Giant* and *The Time of Their Lives*.)

Mantan Moreland has a marginal role.

**CREDITS:** Executive Producer: Milton Feld; Producers: John Grant and Edmund L. Hartmann; Director: Jean Yarbrough; Screenplay: Edmund L. Hartmann, John Grant, Edmund Joseph, and Hal Fimberg, with Felix Adler Hartmann; Musical Score: Jack Brooks, Edgar Fairchild, Loyd Akridge, Paul Dessau, Albert von Tilzer, H.J. Fuller, Will A. Heelan, Junie McCree, John Stromberg, Chas. B. Ward, and Harry von Tilzer; Musical Director: Edgar Fairchild; Photographed by: George Robinson; Editor: Arthur Hilton; Running Time: 76 Minutes; Released: July 6, 1945

**CAST:** Bud Abbott (Dexter Broadhurst); Lou Costello (Sebastian Dinwiddle); Alan Curtis (Mr. Crawford); Rita Johnson (Bonita Farrow); Henry Travers (Capt. Sam Jackson); Lois Collier (Caroline Jackson); Joe Sawyer (Bailey); Joe Kirk (Croupier); Jack Barbee, Jack Frost, Chick Madden & The Rainbow Four (Themselves); Bill Alcorn (Dancer); Audley Anderson (Card Player); Suzanne Lee Bastian (Baby); Gladys Blake (Girl); Milt Bronson (Gambler); Douglas Carter (Croupier); Jack Chefe (Waiter); Jack Coffey (Dancer); Bing Conley (Croupier); Tony Dell (Croupier); William Desmond (Man); Dolores Evers (Aerialist); Tom Fadden (Gambler); Sid Fields (Man); Mantan Moreland (Man)

## Captain Tugboat Annie
(Republic; 1945)

A featured-ensemble role for Moreland distinguishes this embellishment upon Norman Reilly Raine's series of stories for *The Saturday Evening Post*. Jane Darwell stars as the high-spirited barge operator.

**CREDITS:** Producer: James S. Burkett; Director: Phil Rosen; Stories and Screenplay: George Callahan and Norman Reilly Raine; Musical Score: Edward J. Kay; Photographed by: Harry Neumann; Editor: Martin G. Cohn; Running Time: 70 Minutes; Released: November 17, 1945

**CAST:** Jane Darwell (Tugboat Annie); Edgar Kennedy (Bullwinkle); Charles Gordon (Terry Jordan); Mantan Moreland (Pinto); Pamela Blake (Marion Graves); Hardie Albright (Johnny Webb); H.B. Warner (Judge Abbott)

### She Wouldn't Say Yes
(Columbia; 1945)

Rosalind Russell plays a psychiatrist obsessed with developing a remedy for the wartime malady known as shell shock. Or Post-Traumatic Stress Disorder, to bring the terminology up to a trendier speed. And Moreland? A porter.

**CREDITS:** Producer: Virginia Van Upp; Director: Alexander Hall; Story and Screenplay: László Görög, John Jacoby, Wilhelm (a.k.a. William) Thiele, Sarett Tobias, and Virginia Van Upp; Musical Score: Marlin Skiles; Musical Director: Morris W. Stoloff; Photographed by: Joseph Walker; Editor: Viola Lawrence; Running Time: 87 Minutes; Released: November 29, 1945

**CAST:** Rosalind Russell (Susan Lane); Lee Bowman (Michael Kent); Adele Jergens (Allura); Charles Winninger (Dr. Lane); Harry Davenport (Albert); Sara Haden (Laura Pitts); Percy Kilbride (Judge Whittaker); Lewis L. Russell (Col. Brady); Mary Treen (Passenger); Charles Arnt (Conductor); Willie Best (Porter); Arthur Q. Bryan (Man); Mantan Moreland (Porter)

### The Spider
(Fox; 1945)

Private eye Richard Conte must unravel a web of deadly old secrets in this quasi-remake of a 1931 Fox whodunit of the same title. Moreland is more visible than usual, given the big-studio context.

**CREDITS:** Producer: Ben Silvey; Director: Robert D. Webb; Play and Screenplay: Lowell Brentano, Irving Cummings, Jr., W. Scott Darling, Jo Eisinger, and Fulton Oursler; Musical Score: David Buttolph; Musical Director: Emil Newman; Photographed by: Glen MacWilliams; Editor: Norman Colbert; Running Time: 62 Minutes; Released: During December of 1945

**CAST:** Richard Conte (Chris Conlon); Faye Marlowe (Delilah Neilsen); Kurt Kreuger (Ernest); John Harvey (Burns); Martin Kosleck (Mikail Barak); Mantan Moreland (Henry); Walter Sande (Castle); Cara Williams (Wanda Vann)

### Riverboat Rhythm
(RKO–Radio; 1946)

Ben Carter and Mantan Moreland commandeer a team-comedy showcase in this take of a cantankerous showboat captain (Leon Errol) and a boisterous Southern gentleman (Walter Catlett) at odds with the river-town authorities.

**CREDITS:** Executive Producer: Jack J. Gross; Producer: Nat Holt; Director: Leslie Goodwins; Story and Screenplay: Robert Faber and Charles E. Roberts; Musical Score: Alexander Albert Avola; Musical Director: Constantin Bakaleinikoff; Photographed by: Robert De Grasse; Editor: Marvin Coil; Running Time: 65 Minutes; Released: During March of 1946

**CAST:** Leon Errol (Matt Lindsay); Glen Vernon (John Beeler); Walter Catlett (Colonel Jeffrey "Smitty" Witherspoon); Marc Cramer (Lionel Beeler); Jonathan Hale (Colonel Edward Beeler); Joan Newton (Midge Lindsey); Ben Carter (Benjamin); Mantan Moreland (Mantan); Frankie Carle & His Orchestra

### Tall, Tan, and Terrific
(Pollard Productions; 1946)

Notes Internet Movie DataBase commentator Gary Imhoff: "Don't bother with this movie for its script, acting, direction or editing. But do see it for a rare look at Mantan Moreland's stage-comedy routine, Francine Everett's singing and the other stage acts..."

Francine Everett also handles a key role in 1946's *Dirty Gertie from Harlem, U.S.A.*—a thinly veiled plagiarism of Somerset Maugham's *Rain*, and the last feature-film project of Spencer Williams, Jr.

**CREDITS:** Executive Producer: Robert M. Savini; Producer and Director: Bud Pollard; Screenplay: John E. Gordon; Musical Score: Gene Rowland; Photographed by: Jack Etra; Editors: Bud Pollard and Shirley Stone; Sound: Nels Mindlin; Running Time: 40 Minutes; Released: On a region-by-region basis during 1946–1950

**CAST:** Mantan Moreland (Himself); Monte Hawley ("Handsome" Harry Hansom); Francine Everett (Miss Tall, Tan & Terrific); Dots Johnson (Duke); Rudy Toombs (Gómez); Barbara "Butterbeans" Bradford (Photographer); and the All-

Girl Golden Slipper Band, Thelma Cordero, The Gorgeous Astor Debutantes, Lou Swarz, Milton Woods

### Mantan Runs for Mayor
(Toddy; 1946)

Moreland's later demitasse-features for Ted Toddy's low-rent company (and its affiliates) appear not to have re-surfaced in recent times. See also *Mantan Messes Up*, *The Return of Mandy's Husband*, *She's Too Mean for Me*, *The Dreamer*, *Come On, Cowboy!*, and *Ebony Parade*.

**CREDITS:** Producer: Ted Toddy

**CAST:** Mantan Moreland, F.E. Miller, Fred Gordon, Ruth Jones, and John D. Lee, Jr.

### Mantan Messes Up
(Toddy; 1946)

**CREDITS:** Producer: Ted Toddy; Director: Sam Newfield

**CAST:** Mantan Moreland (Mantan); Doryce Bradley (Girl); and Buck & Bubbles [Ford Washington Lee and John William Sublett], The Four Tones, Eddie Green, Monte Hawley, Lena Horne, Bo Jinkins, Nina Mae McKinney, Neva Peoples, The Red Caps

### The Return of Mandy's Husband
(Lucky Star/Toddy; 1947)

A feeble echo of Negro Vaudeville, *The Return of Mandy's Husband* served to reunite the lapsed comedy team of Mantan Moreland and Flournoy E. Miller, who are responsible for such WWII-era essentials of the *Forgotten Horrors* canon as *Lucky Ghost* and *Professor Creeps*. The placement in 1947 is but an educated guess: *The Return of Mandy's Husband* was never copyrighted as a motion picture, but chief backer Ted Toddy placed an unofficial 1947 copyright

notice upon a sheaf of typewritten dialogue pages, and the New York State Board of Censors accepted the film for consideration on May 13 of that year. A search through *Variety* and other trade papers, and scattered black-community publications, has turned up no contemporary reviews or news items.

Moreland (playing himself as a huckster with an outspoken dread of matters supernatural) and Miller (playing himself, despite a fictional character name) establish a company called the Ghost Association, calculated to bilk customers who will pay to communicate with deceased loved ones. Moreland poses as a medium, Prince Alabastar Amsterdam.

Meanwhile, a henpecked husband named Henry Coffee fakes his death as a refuge from his wife, Mandy. Coffee hides in an abandoned barn, where gangsters take him hostage. This would be the very place that Moreland and Miller have chosen for their début séance. Moreland mistakes the hoodlums for ghosts; after their capture by the police, Miller presents Moreland as the hero responsible for routing the crooks. Henry Coffee remains hidden in the loft.

The pageant of absurdities ends abruptly with a session in which Mandy begs Moreland to conjure her husband's spirit. She swears she would never again mistreat him if only he would come back to life. Henry, overhearing, yells out, "*You* wins, honey!"—whereupon the ceiling caves in and he is plunged, as if from the heavens, into the arms of his wife. The Ghost Association's reputation is thus saved, although one can only wonder how the bogus spiritualists could ever follow such an act.

Mantan Moreland was nearing the end of a distinguished Hollywood career, busy but ill acknowledged for its brilliance, as his brand of humor became anathema to the policies of Race Uplift of the ever more influential National Association for the Advancement of Colored People. The N.A.A.C.P.'s damnably well-intentioned objective here was to commit censorship—not so much upon Art, as upon functioning artists. Those who did not conform would be targeted for removal. The tactic calls to mind nothing so much as the Nazi book-burnings and ethnic-cleansing purges of so few years earlier.

Monogram Pictures' *Charlie Chan* series, in which Moreland played a recurring chauffeur-turned-sleuth role of mixed hilarity and heroism, had just two years more to run. Flournoy Miller, who had become more interested in writing by now, had less to lose than Moreland in terms of professional momentum. By 1950, the N.A.A.C.P. had succeeded in a campaign to discourage the mainstream Hollywood studios from indulging such rambunctious displays of ethnicity lest caricature ensue, and Moreland retrenched into network radio—his brilliance undiminished by the dismissive punishments visited upon him by the forces of Political Correctness.

CREDITS: Executive Producer: Ted Toddy; Running Time: 49 Minutes; Released: During 1947–1948 on a state-by-state basis

CAST: Mantan Moreland (Mantan); Flournoy E. Miller (Alex); and John D. Lee, Jr., E. Hensley, McKinley Reeves, Terry Knight

**Ebony Parade**
(Million Dollar/Toddy/Pollard/Lucky Star; 1947)

**CAST:** As Themselves: Count Basie; Cab Calloway; Dorothy Dandridge; Francine Everett; Pat Flowers; Ruby Hill; Mabel Lee; Mantan Moreland; June Richmond; Vanita Smythe

**Best Man Wins**
(Columbia; 1948)

This amiable, free-handed adaptation of Mark Twain's "The Celebrated Jumping Frog of Calaveras County" features Moreland in an incidental role.

**CREDITS:** Producer: Ted Richmond; Director: John Sturges; Story and Screenplay: Edward Huebsch and Mark Twain; Musical Score: Mischa Bakaleinikoff, with Werner R. Heymann, Howard Jackson, John Leipold, Arthur Morton, Joseph Nussbaum, Ben Oakland, George Parrish, Louis Silvers and Marlin Skiles; Photographed by: Vincent J. Farrar; Editor: James Sweeney; Running Time: 75 Minutes; Released: May 6, 1948

**CAST:** Edgar Buchanan (Jim Smiley); Anna Lee (Nancy Smiley); Robert Shayne (Judge Leonidas K. Carter); Gary Gray (Bob Smiley); Hobart Cavanaugh (Amos); Stanley Andrews (Sheriff Dingle); George Lynn (Mr. Crow); Billy Sheffield (Monty Carter); Marietta Canty (Hester); Mantan Moreland (Vendor)

**She's Too Mean for Me**
(Toddy/Million Dollar/Sack Amusements; 1948)

**CREDITS:** Producer: Ted Toddy

**CAST:** Mantan Moreland, F.E. Miller, John D. Lee, Jr.

**Come On, Cowboy!**
(Toddy/Million Dollar/Sack Amusements; 1948)

A lost, or at least mislaid, film, to all appearances. The very title, however, proved helpful in cinching Mantan Moreland's enshrinement in the National Cowboys of Color Hall of Fame.

**CREDITS:** Producer: Ted Toddy

**CAST:** Mantan Moreland, John D. Lee, Jr., F.E. Miller, Mauryne Brent

**The Dreamer**
(Toddy/Sack; 1948)

This one likewise appears to be a lost film, with surviving vestiges in a vividly conceived poster image.

**CREDITS:** Producer: Ted Toddy

**CAST:** Mantan Moreland, Mabel Lee, Pat Rainey, and June Richmond

**Yes, Sir, Mr. Bones!**
(Lippert Pictures/Spartan Productions; 1951)

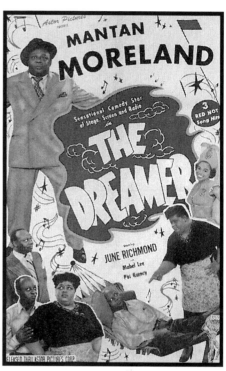

Mantan Moreland's stage partner from 'way back when, Flournoy E. Miller, spent the early 1950s in the curious position of acting as a casting consultant for the network teleseries *Amos 'n' Andy* while denying himself (or being denied) any taste of the stardom thus accrued. Miller did, however, allow himself a role in *Yes, Sir, Mr. Bones!*, a raggedy and minimalistic evocation of old-time minstrelsy. Likely Miller would have cajoled his pal Mantan into an appearance, here—maybe even landed him a role on *Amos 'n' Andy*—if only Moreland had been living in the States at the time. But of course, Moreland was residing in Puerto Rico as a member of the *Duffy's Tavern* radio-comedy troupe.

*Yes Sir, Mr. Bones!* is unrelated to *Amos 'n' Andy* apart from the productions' proximity in a very narrow window of time, and Miller's involvement with both in one capacity or another. Miller's contribution nonetheless qualifies this picture for inclusion in a filmography pertaining to Moreland.

At only 54 minutes in length, the picture is barely even a feature-lengther, and its shabby production values and uneven, pageant-of-skits construction distinguish it as beneath even a Poverty Row standard.

In a book called *The Story of the Blues* (1969), Paul Oliver reproduces two photographs in logical but troubling juxtaposition. One image depicts the blues singer Aleck "Willie" (or "Rice") Miller, a.k.a. Sonny Boy Williamson, in his post-WWII heyday as a radio entertainer—broadcasting on behalf of a milling company's line of baking products and equipped with a custom-outfitted band, complete with a professionally designed logotype embossed onto the head of the bass drum. The other photograph depicts that same Sonny Boy Williamson in his fading years of the 1960s, performing outdoors in homely surroundings with just his harmonica and a drummer, both men attired in rumpled suits of clothing. A logotype of the same sort graces the bass drum, but now it is a crudely hand-painted image. The impression of dignity-under-duress is haunting.

And so it goes with Flournoy Miller in *Yes, Sir, Mr. Bones!* From Broadway and the Harlem Renaissance to a rough-hewn exercise in defiant nostalgia, in scarcely the space of a generation. What a country—and what a strange excuse for a popular culture.

**CREDITS:** Producer, Director and Screenwriter: Ron Ormond; Associate Producer: Jone Carr; Assistant Director: F.O. Collings; Photographed by: Jack Greenhalgh; Music: Walter Greene; Art Director: Frank Paul Sylos; Décor: Red Offenbecker; Special Effects: Ray Mercer; Editor: Hugh Wynn; Running Time: 54 Minutes; Released on a region-by-region basis during 1951

**CAST:** As Themselves: Chick Watts; Cotton Watts; Ches Davis; Flournoy E. Miller; William E. "Billy" Green; Elliott Carpenter; Ellen Sutton; Sally Anglim; Gary L. Jackson; Phil Arnold; Slim Williams; Emmett Miller; Ned Haverly; Brother Bones; Scatman Crothers; Monette Moore; Jimmy O'Brien; Archie Twitchell; Cliff Taylor; Pete Daily & His Chicagoans; Jester Hairston & His Singers; and Boyce & Evans

## Rock 'n' Roll Revue
(Pollard Productions; 1955)

Little to recommend this film as cinema, but plenty in terms of music and comedy—most notably, that of Mantan Moreland. The bare-bones launcher of a loose-knit series, which served more to bring an all-star R&B concert into the hinterlands where such acts were not likely to be touring any time soon.

**CREDITS:** Producer and Director: Joseph Kohn; Running Time: Ranges from 40 to 65 Minutes in Various Versions; Released: Sporadically 1955–1958

**CAST:** As Themselves: Ruth Brown; Willie Bryant; Nat "King" Cole; Larry Darnell; Martha Davis; Duke Ellington; Lonel Hampton; Little Buck; Mantan Moreland; Leonard Reed; Nipsey Russell; Big Joe Turner; Dinah Washington

## Rhythm & Blues Revue
(Pollard Productions; 1955)

A companion-piece to *Rock 'n' Roll Revue* (above), and to the titles immediately following.

**CREDITS:** Producer: Ben Frye; Directors: Joseph Kohn and Leonard Reed; Continuity: Ben Frye and Leonard Reed; Photographed by: Don Malkames; Editor: Arthur Rosenblum; Makeup: Fred C. Ryle; Running Time: 71 Minutes; Released: Sporadically during 1955–1958

**CAST:** As Themselves: Willie Bryant; Freddie Robinson; Lionel Hampton; Count Basie; Faye Adams; Bill Bailey; Herb Jeffries; Amos Milburn; Sarah Vaughan; Nipsey Russell; Big Joe Turner; Martha Davis; Little Buck; Nat "King" Cole; Mantan Moreland; Cab Calloway; Ruth Brown

## Rockin' the Blues
(Pollard Productions; 1956)

Another in a loose-knit series of rock 'n' roll/R&B performance documentaries, vaguely camouflaged as narrative cinema. An odd assignment for art director William Cameron Menzies, better known for such memorable feature-film productions as *Gone with the Wind* (1939) and *Invaders from Mars* (1953).

**CREDITS:** Producer: Fritz Pollard; Director: Arthur Rosenblum; Continuity: Irvin C. Miller; Photographed by: Jack Etra; Production Manager: Henry Van Kirk; Running Time: 68 Minutes; Released: Sporadically during 1956–1958

**CAST:** As Themselves: Hal Jackson; Mantan Moreland; Connie Carroll; The Miller Sisters; Linda Hopkins; Reese La Rue; Pearl Woods; F.E. Miller; Marilyn Bennett; Lee Lynn; Elyce Roberts; William "Billy" Washington

**Basin Street Revue**
(Pollard & Frye; 1956)

Music-and-comedy pageant—like its companion-pieces (above), more a filmed concert than a conventional motion picture.

**CREDITS:** Producer: Ben Frye; Directors: Joseph Kohn and Leonard Reed; Continuity and Dialogue: Ben Frye and Leonard Reed; Musical Arrangements: Frank Foster; Photographed by: Don Malkames; Editor: Arthur Rosenblum; Running Time: 40 Minutes; Released: Sporadically during 1956–1958

**CAST:** As Themselves: Willie Bryant; Sarah Vaughan; Lionel Hampton; Paul Williams; Jimmy Brown; Amos Milburn; Faye Adams; Charles "Honi" Coles; Cholly Atkins; Herb Jeffries; Cab Calloway; Count Basie; Nat "King" Cole; Martha Davis; Frank Foster; Mantan Moreland; Nipsey Russell

**Waiting for Godot**
(Broadway's Ethel Barrymore Theatre; 1957)

A discussion of this Moreland-starring production appears in Chapter Sixteen. Wrote Brooks Atkinson in the *New York Times*: "[Producer Michael] Meyerberg is so infatuated with *Waiting for Godot* that he threatens to produce it year after year in different interpretations. Mike, please!"

Also in 1957, Mantan Moreland graced an October 17 telecast of *The Green Pastures*, part of the *Hallmark Hall of Fame* series. The cast here also included Moreland's *Godot* co-star Earle Hyman, along with Eddie "Rochester" Anderson in the leading role of Noah—the same part he had played in the Warners version of 1936.

**CREDITS:** Producer: Michael Meyerberg; Play: Samuel Beckett; Staged by: Herbert Berghof; Scenery: Louis Kennel; Costumer: Stanley Simmons; Production Supervisor: John Paul; Production Assistant: Frank Baldwin; Staged: January 21–26, 1957

**CAST:** Mantan Moreland (Estragon); Earle Hyman (Vladimir); Geoffrey Holder (Lucky); Rex Ingram (Pozzo); Bert Chamberlain (Boy)

## The Patsy
(Paramount; 1964)

Jerry Lewis' attempted satire of show-business intrigues involves a hotel bellman who finds himself tapped for grooming as a star. The handling is too ponderous, the story too derivative (of such earlier Lewis vehicles as *The Errand Boy* and *The Nutty Professor*), to qualify the film as much more than parody. Sheer slapstick momentum, however, validates the effort: The gags are richly conceived and executed. The under-employment of Mantan Moreland is practically a given; in his WWII-era prime, Moreland could have out-slapsticked Lewis at every turn.

**CREDITS:** Producers: Ernest D. Glucksman and Arthur P. Schmidt; Director: Jerry Lewis; Screenplay: Jerry Lewis and Bill Richmond; Photographed by: W. Wallace Kelley; Editor: John Woodcock; Running Time: 101 Minutes; Released: May 1964

**CAST:** Jerry Lewis (Stanley Belt); Ina Balin (Ellen Betz); Everett Sloane (Caryl Fergusson); Phil Harris (Chic Wymore); Keenan Wynn (Harry Silver); Peter Lorre (Morgan Heywood); John Carradine (Bruce Alden); Hans Conried (Prof. Mulerr); Richard Deacon (Sy Devore); Mantan Moreland (Porter)

## Spider Baby, or The Maddest Story Ever Told
a.k.a. Attack of the Liver Eaters; Cannibal Orgy, or the Maddest Story Ever Told; Liver Eaters, The
(Lasky-Monka Productions; 1964)

A diseased family reverts to savagery in Jack Hill's black comedy, which stars Lon Chaney, Jr., as the clan's sympathetic-but-menacing caretaker. Mantan Moreland plays an incidental early victim—welcome new exposure, at such a stage of his compromised career, but ill attuned to the comedian's finer gifts.

**CREDITS:** Producers: Gil Lasky and Paul Monka; Director, Editor, and Screenwriter: Jack Hill; Musical Score: Ronald Stein; Photographed by: Alfred Taylor; Production Designer: Ray Storey; Makeup: Elliott Fayad; Production Manager: Bart Pat-

**Moreland and Chaney in *Spider Baby***

ton; Sound: Lee Strosnider; Production Assistant: Mike McCloskey; Running Time: 81 Minutes; Previewed: 1964–1965; Sporadic Release: 1967–1968

**CAST:** Lon Chaney, Jr. (Bruno); Carol Ohmart (Emily Howe); Quinn K. Redeker (Peter Howe); Beverly Washburn (Elizabeth); Jill Banner (Virginia); Sid Haig (Ralph); Mary Mitchel (Ann); Karl Schanzer (Schlocker); Mantan Moreland (Messenger); Carolyn Cooper (Aunt Clara); Joan Keller (Aunt Martha)

## Enter Laughing
(Acre-Sajo Productions/Columbia; 1967)

"Mantan Moreland was a good-luck player," Carl Reiner said in 1994, reflecting upon his employment of the comedian in *Enter Laughing* and *The Comic*. "Just having him around was a matter of good luck. I'd have liked to've built a movie around him, but I never had just the right story. A *great* comedian, he was."

*Enter Laughing*, with Moreland in a typically modest role, is Reiner's memoir of his stage-struck youth. The original stage version of *Enter Laughing* plays out more gracefully, but the film conveys well the generosity and boisterous humor that have distinguished Reiner's career over the long haul.

**CREDITS:** Producers: Carl Reiner and Joseph Stein; Associate Producer: Kurt Neumann; Director and Screenwriter: Carl Reiner; Screenwriter and Playwright: Joseph Stein; Musical Score: Mack David and Quincy Jones; Photographed by: Joseph F. Biroc and Albert Taffet; Editor: Charles Nelson; Running Time: 112 Minutes; Released: July-August 1967

**CAST:** José Ferrer (Marlowe); Shelley Winters (Emma Kolowitz); Elaine May (Angela Marlowe); Jack Gilford (Foreman); Janet Margolin (Wanda); David Opatoshu (Morris Kolowitz); Michael J. Pollard (Marvin); Don Rickles (Harry Hamburger); Richard Deacon (Pike); Nancy Kovack (Miss B.); Mantan Moreland (Subway Passenger)

## The Comic
a.k.a. Billy Bright
**(Columbia; 1969)**

Carl Reiner's *The Comic* chronicles the brilliant, troubled career and sad decline of a fictional silent-movie comedian (Dick Van Dyke), seemingly a combination of such Real World artists as Charles Chaplin, Stanley Laurel, Harold Lloyd and Harry Langdon—but crueler and more self-destructive. Mantan Moreland has an incidental role.

**CREDITS:** Producers and Screenwriters: Carl Reiner and Aaron Ruben; Director: Carl Reiner; Musical Score: Jack Elliott; Photographed by: W. Wallace Kelley; Editor: Adrienne Fazan; Production Designer: Walter M. Simonds; Décor: Morris Hoffman; Costumer: Guy C. Verhille; Running Time: 94 Minutes; Released: November 1969

**CAST:** Dick Van Dyke (Billy Bright); Michele Lee (Mary Gibson); Mickey Rooney (Cockeye); Cornel Wilde (Frank Powers); Nina Wayne (Sybil); Pert Kelton (Mama); Steve Allen (Himself); Barbara Heller (Ginger); Ed Peck (Edwin G. Englehardt); Jeannine Riley (Lorraine); Gavin MacLeod (Director); Mantan Moreland (Man)

### Watermelon Man
(Columbia; 1970)

"*Look* at my *skin!*" demands Godfrey Cambridge of a reticent Mantan Moreland. Cambridge, as the star player of Melvin Van Peebles' *Watermelon Man*, is familiar to Moreland's character, a lunch-counter attendant. Until this moment, however, Moreland has known Cambridge as a *white man*—and a bigoted white man, at that.

But now, Cambridge has found himself mysteriously transformed into a Negro. Such is the audacious premise at work here—taken to a courageous, sobering and often-hilarious extreme.

Hence the urgency of Cambridge's plea: "*Look* at my *skin!*" Replies Moreland: "I don't *have* to. I can look at my *own.*" Mantan is as unflappable as ever, and still capable of stealing a scene.

The *New York Times* in 1970 found the film "dreadfully unfunny," an "excruciating travesty" that "demands complete surrender and gives absolutely nothing in return except embarrassment." Perhaps that august publication for politically correct white folks was recoiling from Van Peebles' unsettling combination of militant zeal and broad-stroke comedy; the attitude remains bracing today. Of course, Cambridge as a white man looks like nothing so much as a black guy who had sneezed into a barrel of flour; his immersion in character is sufficient to render irrelevant the insufficiency of the makeup job.

During this same general period, Mantan Moreland also appeared on such network

teleseries as *Marriage: Year One*, *Adam-12*, *The Dating Game*, *Love, American Style* and *The Bill Cosby Show*.

**CREDITS:** Producer: John B. Bennett; Director: Melvin Van Peebles; Screenplay: Herman Raucher; Musical Score: Melvin Van Peebles; Photographed by: W. Wallace Kelley and Herman Raucher; Editor: Carl Kress; Art Directors: Malcolm C. Bert and Sydney Z. Litwack; Décor: John Burton; Makeup: Ben Lane; Running Time: 97 Minutes; Released: May of 1970

**CAST:** Godfrey Cambridge (Jeff Gerber); Estelle Parsons (Althea Gerber); Howard Caine (Townsend); D'Urville Martin (Bus Driver); Kay Kimberley (Erica); Mantan Moreland (Counterman); Mae Clarke (Woman); Scott Garrett (Burton Gerber); Kay E. Kuter (Dr. Wainwright); Charles Lampkin (Dr. Catlin); Erin Moran (Janice Gerber); Irving Selbst (Johnson); Emil Sitka (Deliveryman); Paul Williams (Clerk); Ray Ballard (Passenger); Rhodie Cogan (Mrs. Johnson); Robert Dagny (Passenger); Donna Dubrow (Receptionist); Frank Farmer (Andy Brandon); Karl Lukas (Policeman); Hazel Medina (Widow); Ralph Montgomery (Drugstore Manager); Erik L. Nelson (Doorman); Lawrence Parke (Passenger); Vivian Rhodes (Gladys); Almira Sessions (Woman); Matthias Uitz (Cabbie); Melvin Van Peebles (Sign Painter)

## The Biscuit Eater
(Disney; 1972)

This Disneyfied remake of a boy-and-his-dog classic of 1940 features Mantan Moreland in an incidental role.

**CREDITS:** Producer: Bill Anderson; Director: Vincent McEveety; Story and Screenplay: James H. Street and Lawrence Edward Watkin; Musical Score: Robert F. Brunner, Shane Tatum, and Will Schaefer; Orchestrations: Walter Sheets; Photographed by: Richard A. Kelley; Editor: Ray de Leuw; Art Directors: John B. Mansbridge and Al Roelofs; Décor: Hal Gausman and Emile Kuri; Costumers: Chuck Keehne and Emily Sundby; Makeup: La Rue Matheron and Robert J. Schiffer; Assistant Director: Dick Caffey; Sound: Robert O. Cook, Evelyn Kennedy, and Barry Thomas; Dog Wrangler: Henry Cowl; Title Designer: Alan Maley; Running Time: 81 Minutes; Released: May of 1972

**CAST:** Earl Holliman (Harve McNeil); Pat Crowley (Mary Lee McNeil); Lew Ayres (Ames); Godfrey Cambridge (Willie Dorsey); Beah Richards (Charity Tomlin); Clifton James (Eben); Johnny Whitaker (Lonnie McNeil); George Spell (Tomlin); Mantan Moreland (Waiter); Golden Eddie (Evans); Dick Warlock (Stuntman); and Paul Bradley

# The Young Nurses
a.k.a. Nightingale; Young L.A. Nurses
(New World; 1973)

Roger Corman's New World Pictures, which thrived from 1970 into 1983, dealt in low-budget ($200,000–$300,000) exploitation fare, including a "nurse-thriller" sub-genre that Corman seems practically to have created. *The Young Nurses* is an example, though not particularly, *uhm*, exemplary—having more to do with titillation than with melo-dramatic action or the ironic humor basic to the hospital setting.

The story has to do with a drug-trafficking racket. The greater point is that of parading about an array of voluptuous women in tight-fitting uniforms. Mantan Moreland makes a memorable cameo of his final turn on screen.

**CREDITS:** Producer: Julie Corman; Director: Clint Kimbrough; Screenplay: Howard R. Cohen; Musical Score: Gregory Prestopino; Photographed by: Sam Clement and Daniel Lacambre; Editors: Karen Johnson and George Van Noy; Production Designer: Tim Kincaid; Art Director: Barbara Peters; Assistant Director: George Van Noy; Assistant Editor: Hal Harrison; Running Time: 77 Minutes; Released: April 1, 1973

**CAST:** Jeane Manson (Kitty); Ashley Porter (Joanne); Angela Gibbs (Michelle); Zack Taylor (Donahue); Jack La Rue, Jr. (Ben); William Joyce (Fairbanks); Allan Arbus (Krebs); Mary Doyle (Nurse Dockett); Don Keefer (Chemist); Linda Towne (Chris Whiting); Jay Burton (Manager); John Thompson (Chicken); Kimberly Hyde (Peppermint); Nan Martin (Reporter); Sally Kirkland (Woman); Terrill Maguire (Girl); Dick Miller (Cop); Samuel Fuller (Doc Haskell); James Anthony (Nurse); Jeff Young (Anesthetist); Tom Baker (Floyd); Caro Kenyatta (Lester); Mantan Moreland (Old Man)

# Recommended Video Sources —and a Bit of Context

> Taken together, this body of film [the Tyler, Texas, Black Film Collection, i.e., at Southern Methodist University in Dallas] is a priceless record of the styles and manners, aspirations, and attitudes of black America between 1920 and 1950.
> —*Time* magazine's Richard Shickel

The Academy Awards ceremonies of 2002 seemed to mark a turning point for black artistry within the pop-cultural mainstream. *Seemed* is the operative term here, for with a Lifetime Achievement Oscar for Sidney Poitier and best-performance nods to Denzel Washington and Halle Berry, the Motion Picture Academy's annual ritual certainly appeared to sit up and take notice of a society that had all along been a mainstay—at once well recognized and ill utilized—of the entertainment industry.

Most devotées of cinema know perfectly well the black heritage in motion pictures. Most tend to believe that this contribution dates from the Depression-into-wartime years in corporate Hollywood, stemming from such elaborately mounted films as *Cabin in the Sky*, *The Green Pastures*, *Stormy Weather* and *Hallelujah!*

Less sharply attuned souls will swear and be damned that Sidney Poitier or Sammy Davis, Jr. or James Earl Jones must rank as the first black movie star of any consequence; they would be more nearly correct to cite Davis, who owns a certain pride-of-place as an early-day *child* star—but few people know of that phase of his career. Jones, for that matter, is a second-generation movie actor, and his ancestry lies in the black independent filmmaking industry of which much remains unknown to a mainstream populace.

In an overexcited Oscar-acceptance speech on that night of 2002, Halle Berry at least showed some historical savvy, citing the from-then-until-now likes of Dorothy Dandridge, Lena Horne, Diahann Carroll, Jada Pinkett, Angela Bassett, Viveca Fox and "every nameless, faceless woman of color [who] now has a chance because this door tonight has been opened." Berry might well have named many others—but no, her ramble was altogether too long, to start with.

Berry also voiced a hope-against-hope sentiment for parity for black actresses, what with circumstances appearing more nearly equalized now than ever before. Good intentions, bad timing. For women in 21st-century Hollywood are more objectified as a gender irrespective of color.

Women are less likely nowadays to land roles of self-sufficient gumption than they were during that enlightened age of Great Roles for White Women. Roles of mettle and ferocity fell routinely to Greta Garbo, Barbara Stanwyck,

Judy Garland, Bette Davis, Claudette Colbert, Ann Savage, Veda Ann Borg, Joan Crawford, Carole Lombard, Marilyn Monroe, and even Shirley Temple. Not so, of course, for such black-actress A-list talents of Old Hollywood as Fredi Washington, Louise Beavers, Hattie McDaniel, Marguerite Whitten, Jackie "Moms" Mabley, Ruby Dandridge, Nina Mae McKinney, Lena Horne, Eartha Kitt and Victoria Spivey.

The Old World immigrant businessmen who had invented Hollywood professed a sympathy with What America Wanted—a strategic marketing stance. These resourceful merchants and industrialists made opportunities for black talent, certainly, but largely along the lines of reinforcing stereotypical images. Sometimes, the power of an individual talent could overcome the esthetic prejudice—as in Paul Robeson's authoritative passion in the 1936 *Show Boat* (a major-studio production) and 1933's *The Emperor Jones* (a small-studio effort); or Fredi Washington's rage against the machine in 1934's *Imitation of Life*, as a fair-complexioned daughter who would just as soon not be seen in the company of her blacker-than-black mother (Louise Beavers); or the seething, prejudice-busting allure of Lena Horne in 1943's *Stormy Weather* or Eartha Kitt in *New Faces of 1953*. Such showcase portrayals, however, seldom formed the basis of any sustained bodies of work along such lines.

The field of black-ensemble cinema from the independent studios, spanning from the 1910s until around 1950, offers a truer portrait of the artistry that corporate Hollywood has neglected and/or misused, all along. Production values and technical expertise are lacking in such films, as a rule, but the documentary function is well served here—and earnestness carries more weight than amateurism any day.

Such low-budget films enabled black audiences to see black actors in general-purpose roles during a period in history when no big-studio venture would have cast a black player as a banker, a schoolteacher, a lawyer or a middle-class householder.

And yet, of course, internal prejudices prove manifest: The black-ensemble pictures tend to feature lighter-complexioned players in the more sympathetic or heroic roles, for one thing, and many such films employ broad-brush comedy styles as deeply caricatured as anything from a Dominant Culture studio.

Evidence abounds. Pertinent movies-on-video sources include these:

The Tyler, Texas, Black Film Collection has been packaged *in toto* on a big-ticket set of digital-video disks available through Southern Methodist University. The Web address www.smu.edu/blackfilms is a practical starting-point.

Of comparable interest is the *Black Artists of the Silver Screen* collection, from a Web-based catalogue called Hollywood's Attic. Such films also figure in the dot-com catalogue of Life Is a Movie. The addresses are www.hollywoodsattic.com/blackart.asp and www.lifeisamovie.com.

Alpha Video offers the most concise and readily accessible source of Mantan Moreland's more representative films, including crucial work for Monogram

Pictures Corporation. Alpha also handles a hefty inventory of many of the titles covered in Michael H. Price's collaborative *Forgotten Horrors* books. The Web address is www.oldies.com.

# Acknowledgments

A chance connection during 2000–2001 with the low-profile immediate heirs of Mantan Moreland triggered an overdue surge toward completion of this collection of impressions, an attempt to reconcile empirical biography with some innate cultural biases and a rambling memoir.

The essential framework is that of a near-lifelong fondness for the artistry of Moreland, as first channeled into my collaborative *Forgotten Horrors* series of movie-history books, dating from 1975 into the present day; and then, into an article for the début issue (summer 2000) of Midnight Marquee Press' *Mad about Movies* magazine.

The random-search discovery of a Website memorandum posted by a Toledo- and Los Angeles-based businesswoman named Tana Young—a fleeting reference to her grandfather Mantan Moreland—provided the essential leverage. An exchange of e-mail messages followed. Tana's mother, Marcella Moreland Young (Mantan's daughter, of course), joined in presently. Our first visit by telephone took place in September 2001. Mantan's former wife and Marcella's mother, Hazel Henry Moreland, had died only recently.

I am certain that the Youngs scarcely knew what to make of my initial approach, but we struck up a camaraderie that has endured. Marcella's willingness to summon long-dormant memories, shaded in mingled joy and sorrow, has been extraordinarily big-hearted. Her career in show business (as a child actor of some brief prominence and then as an adviser to her father) has proved quite nearly as fascinating as that which Mantan had pursued.

Thanks are in order, as well, to a good many friends, colleagues, kin, newssources and correspondents who have provided encouragement, information and reality-check insights: Dennis Spies; Josh Alan Friedman; T. Sumter Bruton, III; Ronnie Barker; Jim Vance; Eric Idle; Jim Colegrove; John Wooley; Rudy Ray Moore; Kenneth G. Brodnax; Jan Alan Henderson; Dr. G. William Jones and the Southwest Film & Video Archive; Orrin Keepnews; Dr. Richard W. & Hessie Mae Jones; J. Kerry Price; Mark Evan Walker; Gillespie Wilson; the Rev. V.P. Perry; Charles Warford; Mark Martin; Michael Weldon; Edna Turner; Stephen R. Bissette; Robert Shaw; Spike Lee; Bob Ray Sanders; Terry Zwigoff; Wesley Race; Melvin Van Peebles; Kerry Gammill; Kim Deitch; Marty Baumann; Jim & Gloria Austin and the National Cowboys of Color Museum & Hall of Fame; Robert Crumb; R. Bob Cooper; George E. Turner; Ben Sargent; Steve Brigati; Johnny Simons; Aaron Thibeaux "T-Bone" Walker; Big Joe Turner; Larry D. Springer; William F. Chase; Chris Chatfield; and Gary and Susan Svehla.

My wife, Christina Renteria Price, has provided crucial morale-booster support and smart observations all along, encouraging me in particular never to dampen any of the franker arguments—and accepting the long stretches devoted to research and composition as an essential function.

I acknowledge, above all else, a partiality toward Mantan Moreland's abilities and his munificence in dispensing same. Goodness knows, his self-appointed Nemeses have had half-and-more of a century to hammer their shortsighted case with impunity. And his admirers, as a consequence, have gone largely unaware of the greater sweep of Moreland's eventful life.
—Michael H. Price
www.fortworthbusinesspress.com

# Index

## A

Abbott, Bud & Lou Costello 32, 38, 116, 122, 147
*Adam-12* 114
*Adventures of Superman, The* 119
Alberni, Luis 120
*All in the Family* 114
Altman, Robert 18
*Am I Guilty?* 81
Amarillo (Texas) Independent School District 108
Amarillo (Texas) Junior College 25
*Amos 'n' Andy* 16-22, 27, 33, 53, 74, 93, 143
Anderson, Eddie "Rochester" 22, 52, 87, 111, 115, 125-126,
Anderson, Marion 9
Armed Forces Radio Service 122
Armstrong, Louis 115, 136
Ashworth, Robert A. 108
Atkinson, J. Brooks 104-106, 113, 164
Atwell, Winifred 147
Atwill, Lionel 120
Austin, Gene 25

## B

Ball, Lucille 91
*Bamboozled* 46-51, 81, 146
Barker, Ronnie 23
*Barney Google* 76, 116
Barris, Harry 41
*Basin Street Revue* 94
Beard, Matthew "Stymie" 59
Beatty, Clyde 69
Beaudine, William 132
Beckett, Samuel 104-107
Benny, Jack 22, 52, 87, 111, 115
Berghof, Herbert 106
Berle, Milton 33, 62, 147
Berry, Halle 19
Besser, Joe 103
Best, Willie 22, 50, 76, 118
Biggers, Earl Derr 52
*Birth of a Nation, The* 47
Black Filmmakers Hall of Fame 144
*Black Humor from Slavery to Stepin Fetchit* 113
Blake, Robert "Bobby" 81-82
Blanc, Mel 52
*Blondie* 29

Bloom, John 48-49
"Boll Weevil Song" 50
Boone, Pat 33
Booth, Shirley 91, 102
*Bowery to Broadway* 116
Brackenridge, Hugh Henry 113
Bradford, Roark 61, 107, 112, 113, 145
Brendel, El 104
Brigati, Steve 128
Briggs, Joe Bob 48-49
Brodnax, Jesse James (Mantan Moreland) 62, 143
Brodnax, Mandy 63, 68
Brodnax, Marcella 62-63
Brooks, Mel 46
Brown, Anita 43
Brown, Joe E. 76
*Brown vs. Board of Education* 108
Bruce, Lenny 130
Bruton, Sumter 16-22
Buell, Jed 79-80
Bunche, Ralph 9
*Burns & Allen Show, The* 91
Butterfield, Paul 125

## C

CBS Television 18, 28
*Cabin in the Sky* 113, 115
Cadets, the 94-97
Caedmon Records 112, 145
Calhoun, Red 20
Calloway, Cab 36, 98, 109
Calloway, Jerry 141-142
Cantor, Charlie 91
Carradine, John 118
Carter, Ben 84, 85, 93-94, 116, 122, 123, 124
Carter, Nola Mae Price 142-143
Carter, Woodrow 142-143
Chamberlain, Bert 106
Chaplin, Charles 22, 76, 115, 116
Charles, Ray 36
*Charlie Chan* series 22, 32, 43-44, 52, 54, 60, 83, 84, 85, 86, 87, 98, 99, 115, 117, 132, 148-162
*Chasing Trouble* 45
Chase, William F. 61, 117, 120
Chatfield, Chris 44-45
*Chloe (Love Is Calling You)* 69
Christie, Agatha 56

Clapton, Eric 25
Clark, Bobby & Paul McCullough 69
*Classified X* 100
Cliburn, Van 25, 147
Clyde, Andy 32
Coasters, the 21, 97
Coffin, Tristram 125
Cole, Nat "King" 135
Coltrane, John 113
Columbia Pictures 58, 103
Conlin, Jimmy 93
Conroy, Ben 25
Corliss, Richard 47
Correll, Charles & Freeman Gosden 74, 93
Cosby, Bill 53, 72, 100-102, 114
Costello, Billy 116
Cowboys of Color Hall of Fame 80
Crittenden, Gov. Thomas 64
Crosby, Bing 22, 41
Crumb, Robert 114
Cyclone Records 94, 116

**D**

Darro, Frankie 59, 61, 86, 111, 123-125, 127-128
*Dating Game, The* 114
Davidson, Tommy 46
Davis, Miles 113
*Daynce of the Peckerwoods: The Badlands of Texas Music* 147
DeBeck, Billy 76, 116
Deitch, Kim 114-115
*Devil Bat, The* 61
Dickerson, Dudley 104
Diddley, Bo 33, 133
Dietrich, Marlene 91
*Disco Godfather* 129
Disney, Walt 144-145
Dixon, Willie 95
*Do the Right Thing* 49
*Doctor Death: Seeker of Souls* 104
*Dracula* 40
*Drums o'Voodoo* 69
DuBois, W.E.B. 9
*Duffy's Tavern* 88-89, 90-93, 106

**E**

*East of Java* 76
Ellington, Duke 74, 115
*Elsie's Sportin' House* 107, 147
*Emperor Jones, The* 56-57, 118
Esslin, Martin 106

**F**

*Fahrenheit 451* 53
*Famous Monsters* and related magazines 32
Fields, W.C. 22, 38, 76, 115, 116
Fine, Larry 57, 103, 104, 120
Flack, Roberta 71
Fong, Benson 86, 126
Ford, Robert 64
*Forgotten Horrors* 11, 22, 44, 45
*Forrest Gump* 65
Forten, Charlotte 24-25
Foxx, Redd 87, 93, 130
*Frankenstein* 40, 42, 43
Friedman, Josh Alan 9-10, 16-22, 109

**G**

Gardner, Ed 90-93
Garson, Greer 20
*Ghost Breakers, The* 22
*Ghost Dad* 101
Gleason, Jackie 124
Globe-News Publishing Co. and pertinent publications 35, 37, 104, 108
Glover, Savion 46
*Gone with the Wind* 114, 115
Gordon, Bert 91
Grams, Martin, Jr. 92
*Great Roob Revolution, The* 54
Green, Booty 126
Green, Eddie 89, 91
*Green Pastures, The* 61, 112, 113
Gubitosi, Mickey 81-82
Guthrie, Woody 9

**H**

Hall, Prince 126
*Hallmark Hall of Fame* 61
Hagenbeck-Wallace Circus 68-69
Hamilton, John 119
*Harlem on the Prairie* 79-80
Harlem Renaissance and related figures and developments 70-73, 119
*Harlemwood* 109
Hathaway, Donnie 71
Hayes, George "Gabby" 32
Hecht, Ben 113
Hemming, Sally 45
Henry, Will "Chip" 77-78, 141
"Here Come de Judge" 53
Hill, Jack 54
Holder, Geoffrey 106
Holiday, Billie 113

Hooks, Matthew "Bones" 135, 141-142
Hope, Bob 22
Horowitz, Vladimir 137
House Committee on UnAmerican Activities 56
Howard, Jerome "Curly" 103, 104
Howard, Moe 57, 103-104, 121
Howard, Samuel "Shemp" 57, 103, 120-121
Human Genome Project 55
Hunter, Tab 126
Hyman, Earl 105-107

**I**

*Indefinite Talk* 85, 93-94, 121-124, 127-128
Ingram, Rex 106, 113
Ink Spots 147
Interstate Circuit Theatres 94
*Invisible Ghost* 45
"It's Getting Dark on Old Broadway" 73

**J**

Jackson, Chuck 51
James, Jesse 64-66
*Jazz Singer, The* 47
Jefferson, Thomas 45
Jeffries, Herbert 74, 75, 79-80, 138, 167-170
Johnson, Budd 11
Johnson, Pete & Albert Ammons 76
Jones, Hessie Mae 112
Jones, Dr. Richard W. 35, 108-113
Jones, Will "Dub" 97
*Juke Joint* 16-22

**K**

Karloff, Boris 40, 91
Keaton, Buster 22, 76, 115
Keepnews, Orrin 136-137
Kelly, Emmett 69
Kelly, Walt 59
Kennedy, Edgar 116
Kennedy, Tom 104
King, Dr. Martin Luther 19, 28-30
*King of the Zombies* and related films 21, 31, 33, 34, 38-40, 41-45, 53, 59, 61, 94, 96, 115, 117-119, 133
Kirkland, Elithe Hamilton 114
Knotts, Don 89
Koerner, "Spider" John 25
Ku Klux Klan 78

**L**

La Joya Hotel (Amarillo, Texas) 36
Ladd, Alan 91
"Laffin' Song" 94, 116-117
Lamour, Dorothy 22
*Lash of the Penitentes* 138
Laurel, Stanley & Oliver Hardy 38, 76, 115, 116, 147
Ledbetter, Huddie "Leadbelly" 143
Lee, Spike 46-51, 81, 100, 145
Legion of Decency 94
*Lew Leslie's Blackbirds et Seq.* 69-70, 104, 163-166
Lewis, Jerry 62
Lewis, Meade Lux 76
Lincoln, Abraham 9
Lipsitz, George 72
Lloyd, Harold 116
Logan, Ella 41
Lomax, Alan 25
Lomen, Lillian Beatrice Ralston Wilson 65
Lott, Wilmot 36
Louis, Joe 9, 75, 171-172
*Love, American Style* 114
"Lovesick Blues" 133
Lugosi, Bela 40
Lyles, Aubrey 74

**M**

McDaniel, Hattie 47, 59-60, 110, 115
McGee, Elihu "Black Dot" 76
McQueen, Butterfly 114
McSwain, Angus 141-142
"Ma Grinder, The" 26
Mabley, Jackie "Moms" 53, 100-101
*Malcolm X* 48
*Mad about Movies* magazine 11
*Magic Island, The* 43
Man-Tan lotion 67
*Mantan Messes Up* 89
Markham, Dewey "Pigmeat" 9, 53, 109
Marx Bros. 22, 76, 116, 147
Masonic Lodge and Negro Masonry 126
Maynard, Ken 116
*Meanest Man in the World, The* 111
Mercer, Jack 116
Miller, Diane Disney 144-145
Miller, Emmett 25, 55, 133
Miller, Flournoy E. 16, 21, 55, 70, 74-75, 78-79, 85, 93, 121-122, 123, 124
Miller, Olivette 123
*Mr. Washington Goes to Town* 115
Modern Records 94, 97, 102
*Mokey* 81

Monogram Pictures 60-61, 82, 83, 84, 98, 99, 115, 117, 118, 124, 127, 132, 133
Monroe, Louisiana 63-64
*Monster's Ball* 19
Moore, Rudy Ray 56, 128-132
Moore, Tim "Kingfish" 22, 27, 30, 52, 71, 93, 104, 143, 164
Moreland, Frank 63-64, 67
Moreland, Hazel Henry 13-15, 77, 79, 83, 143
Moreland, Prentice "Prince" 94-97
Murphy, Dudley 53
Murphy, Eddie 100
Muse, Dr. Clarence 75, 76, 172
Myerberg, Michael 106
Myles, Roosevelt "Livinggood" 69, 76, 107, 124, 147

**N**

Nat Ballroom (Amarillo, Texas) 35
National Association for the Advancement of Colored People 18, 35, 39, 44, 53, 58, 83, 87, 88, 99, 108, 109-112
*Negro South, The* magazine 68, 69, 70
Nelson, Ozzie 33
*Network* 46
New York *Times* 104-106
Newfield, Sam 79, 81
*Nothing but the Truth* 22

**O**

"Ode to Critics" 113
Oland, Warner 52, 85
*Ol' Man Adam and His Chillun* 112, 113, 145
Oliver, Paul 24
*On the Real Side: A History of African-American Comedy* 113
O'Neill, Eugene 56
Otis, Johnny 72
*Ouanga* 43, 45
*Our Gang* series 59

**P**

Page, Kevin 10
*Penitente Murder Case, The* 138
Penniman, Little Richard 35
Perry, Lincoln "Stepin Fetchit" 43-44, 47, 76, 100, 109, 118
*Phantom Killer* 31, 54, 119-120
"Phoney Croneys" 58, 104
Poitier, Sidney 101
Popeye the Sailor 116

Presley, Elvis 9
Preston, Amarillo Slim 36
Price, Alan 138
Price, E. Hoffmann 138
Price, Horace 138-140
Price, Jimbo 139
Price, John A. 135, 138-139, 141-142
Price, Kerry 142
Price, Michael 138
Price, Pelinah 138-140
Price, Roger 54, 138
Price, Roland 138
Price, Sterling 138
Price, Vincent 91, 138
*Producers, The* 46
Pryor, Richard 128

**Q**

**R**

RCA Victor 137, 147
*Racket Doctor* 81
Rainone, Thomas C. 129
Raitt, Bonnie 25
Razaf, Andy 64
Ray, Dave "Snaker" 25
"Record Ban Blues" 102
Redding, Otis 37
Reed, Alan 91
Reynolds, Ozell "Larry" 77, 140
*Rhythm & Blues Revue* 61, 94
*Riders of the Frontier* 49-50
*Ripley's Believe It or Not* 91
Ritter, Tex 50
Roach, Hal, Jr. 93
Robeson, Paul 9, 41, 53, 56-57, 110, 115, 118
Robinson, Bill "Bojangles" 47, 109
Robinson, Jackie 9
Robinson, Smokey 25
*Rock 'n' Roll Revue* 61, 94
*Rockin' the Blues* 94
Rohmer, Sax 52
Roller, Dr. Dale 26
Roman Catholic Church 94, 126
Rooney, Mickey 91
Rosen, Phil 59, 61
Rosenbloom, Maxie 91, 92
*Rowan & Martin's Laugh-In* 53

**S**

Sack Amusement Enterprises 73-74
St. John, Al "Fuzzy" 32

"St. Louis Blues" 53
*Saturday Review, The* 52
Screen Actors Guild 50, 81
Seabrook, William 42
Seeger, Pete 25
Sen Yung, Victor 86
*Sepia* magazine group 28-30
Sharpe, David 61
Shaw, Robert "Fud" 25-27, 49
Shermet, Hazel 92
Shore, Dinah 91
*Show Boat* 118
*Shuffle Along* 70, 73
Sissle, Noble 74
Skelton, Red 69, 124, 147
Skulnik, Menasha 62
Smith, Augustus 69
Smith, Bessie 53
*Social Error* 61
*Soul of a Monster, The* 76
Southern Methodist University 16
*Sphinx, The* 120
*Spider Baby* 54
*Spirit of Youth* 75
Spirits of Rhythm 41
Springer, Larry D. 25
Steele, Bob 118
*Story of the Blues, The* 24
"Stranded in the Jungle" 95-97, 102
*Strange Case of Dr. Rx, The* 31, 54, 56, 59, 120-121
Sul-Te-Wan, Mme. 119
Sutton, Ralph 135
Swanson, Gloria 91

**T**

*Tarzan's New York Adventure* 116
Taylor, Janet 40, 147
Taylor, Johnnie 13
Temple of Love & Christ 126-127
Temple, Shirley 47
*Terror of Tiny Town, The* 79
Terwilliger, George 43, 45
Tex, Joe 21, 97
*That Ain't My Finger!* 107, 147
"That's the Spirit" 54, 74, 166
Three Stooges 38, 54, 57-58
*Time* magazine 47
Tinsley, Jack 51
Todd, Bruce 141-142
Toler, Sidney 84-85, 114-115
Toones, Fred "Snowflake" 61, 118

Tosches, Nick 55, 134
Turner, Big Joe 36-37
Turner, Edna 28-30
Turner, George E. 45, 89, 172
20th Century-Fox 84-85
*Two-Gun Man from Harlem* 80
"Two Old Birds" 114-115
Tyler, Texas, Black Film Collection 16-22

**U**

Universal Pictures 101
*Up in the Air* 59, 124-125

**V**

Van Peebles, Mario 100
Van Peebles, Melvin 100
*Vanishing Virginian, The* 81
*Variety* 97-98
Victor, Henry 43

**W**

*Waiting for Godot* 104-107
Walker, Aaron "T-Bone" 36, 38-40, 76, 110, 116-117, 125, 143
Waller, Fats 113, 115, 135-137
Warner Bros. 70, 74
Washington, Dinah 101
*Watermelon Man* 100
Waters, Muddy 71-72, 125
Watkins, Mel 113
Wayans, Damon 46
*Weirdo* magazine 114
"What Did It Getcha?" 94, 117
*Where Dead Voices Gather* 55, 134
White, Lee "Lasses" 32, 132, 134
Whitten, Marguerite 83, 118
Whittenburg, S.B. 35-36, 37, 108
*Who's on First?* 122
William Morris Agency 88, 89, 90
Williams, Hank 133
Wilson, Grady L. 35-37, 38, 94, 108, 135
Williams, Spencer, Jr. 16-22, 93
Willis, Chuck 129
Winters, Roland 84, 85
Winters, Shelly 91
Wolf, Howlin' 71-72

**X**

X, Malcolm 19, 48

**Y**

Yarbrough, Dr. H.D. 26-27

Yarbrough, Jean 41, 59, 61, 114
Yates, Herbert J. 133
*Yes, Sir, Mr. Bones!* 93
Young, Chic 29
Young, Gilbert 126
Young, Marcella Moreland and family 11, 13-15, 28, 50, 59, 66, 77-89, 114, 123, 143-147
Young, Tana 11
"Your Feet's Too Big" 136, 147

## Z

*Ziegfeld Follies* 73

If you enjoyed this book,
call or write for a free catalog
Midnight
Marquee Press
9721 Britinay Lane
Baltimore, MD 21234

410-665-1198
www.midmar.com

Made in the USA
Charleston, SC
29 June 2010